**WARREN, Donald R. To enforce education; a history of the founding
years of the United States Office of Education. Wayne State, 1974.
239p il bibl 73-8209. 11.95**
A searching, well-written and documented study going beyond a narrow interpretation of its immediate subject to a comprehensive and
balanced presentation of the 19th-century origins of national concerns
with public schooling in America. Neither an apologia for public
schooling nor one of the now fashionable revisionist denigrations of
schools and schoolmen, the book recounts efforts to provide equal
educational opportunity "from the top." It begins with the labors of
individual legislators in the late 1820s and of such organizations as
the American Lyceum and the National Teachers' Association and
moves on towards the founding of the Office of Education in 1867.
Warren discusses the relation of the Freedman's Bureau, the Department of Agriculture, and of the Land Grant Act to the Office of Education, narrates the legislative history of the Office's bill in Congress,
and relates at length the contributions and shortcomings of the first
four commissioners from Henry Barnard (1867-70) to William T.
Harris (1889-1906). A concluding chapter on "Barnard's Bureau in the
1970's" is a somewhat strained attempt to tie the Bureau's present experience to its past and reads in part like a brief for the National In-

Continued

WARREN

stitute of Education. The volume presents as appendix the texts of the
acts for the departments of education and of agriculture and a list of
all U.S. commissioners of education. It carries extensive footnotes,
well-chosen and printed illustrations, an excellent select bibliography,
and an index. A fine book that belongs in every college library and in
any basic collection on American educational history.

TO
ENFORCE
EDUCATION

TO ENFORCE EDUCATION

A History of the Founding Years of the United States Office of Education

by Donald R. Warren

University of Illinois at Chicago Circle

Wayne State University Press
Detroit, 1974

Published simultaneously in Canada
by the Copp Clark Publishing Company
517 Wellington Street, West
Toronto 2B, Canada.

Library of Congress Cataloging in Publication Data

Warren, Donald R   1933–
  To enforce education.

  Bibliography: p.
  1.   United States.   Office of Education—History.
I.   Title.
LB2807.W33   1974   379.73   73–8209

for Beverly

Thus the study of history as mere sequence wears itself out. It is a make-belief. There are oceans of facts. We seek that thread of coordination derived from the special forms of importance prevalent in the respective epochs. Apart from such interests, intrinsic within each period, there would be no language, no art, no heroism, no devotion. Ideals lie beyond matter-of-fact, and yet provide the colour of its development.

Alfred North Whitehead, Modes of Thought

Contents

9

Contents

Illustrations

Preface

The founding years of the United States Office of Education encompass a period from the 1830s to the 1880s. The critical events occurred during the 1860s. I have focused on this portion of the office's past, rather than reconstruct its entire history, because these early episodes constitute a significant story and further because the remainder of the agency's history sheds little additional light on the variables influencing its development. I am not suggesting a simple causal relation between the office's origins and its operations in the 1970s. Without lapsing into historicism, however, I endorse the expectation that we can better understand the present agency and plan its future through a study of the individuals, ideas, and events that combined to shape its founding years.

Previously published references to the office's history fail us on a number of counts. Typically, they tell the story of a minor federal agency created for the modest task of collecting and disseminating educational statistics, of an initial period of difficulty during which Congress and the president threatened to abolish the office, and of the successful weathering of those storms in a fight for permanence. Beyond simplifying a complex history, such accounts do not help us assess the reform intentions which generated plans for a national education bureau in the early nineteenth century. Indeed, they tend to ignore those intentions and, hence, contribute very little to our understanding of why the reform hopes were thwarted. They also fail to connect attempts to establish the office with concurrent efforts to promote public education. As a consequence, they miss important evidence that nineteenth-century advocates of public education did not want merely more free schools but also systems of schools.

To Enforce Education constitutes a portion of a larger history, that of federal involvement in public educational policy and

13

practice, the cycles of action and reaction which abetted and retarded nineteenth-century school development, the complementary roles of cultural centrism (termed the lure of homogeneity in Chapter One) and urban growth in promoting school bureaucratization, and the impact of Civil War and Reconstruction on education. For the most part, I have assumed this context in order to focus on the start of the first effort to render American public education more efficient and effective, that is, more systematic and dependable, through a federal agency.

A few minor methodological problems should be identified at the outset. Several terms employed throughout the book may strike readers as overly general. I have used "schoolmen" and "school people" to distinguish local, state, and federal educational administrators from "friends of education" and teachers. Of course, some "school people" also were or had been teachers. The term "friends of education" has been employed, as it was in the nineteenth century, to indicate that diverse group of lay people and non-education professionals, clergymen, doctors, businessmen, and elected officials, who joined in supporting public school development. The term "common school movement" has acquired near mythical status. Taken literally, it can be particularly misleading. I have used it not to refer to a single-purposed effort but as a shorthand indication of what was initially, at least, loosely organized, sometimes conflicting attempts to promote public education in the nineteenth century.

The difficulty of deciphering Henry Barnard's letters, while not important ultimately, should at least be noted. Newton Bateman, the Illinois schoolman, once returned a letter he had received from Barnard with the cryptic inscription that he couldn't make it out. Anyone who has attempted to plow through the various collections of Barnard's papers no doubt shares Bateman's frustration. The man's handwriting refuses to be read. In the pages that follow, readers will find, therefore, "translations" of Barnard's letters which may agree in substance but not necessarily in detail with the original documents.

My aim in writing this book has been to reconstruct the office's founding years, not to defend the agency or celebrate its survival over the years. The tone is critical primarily because I have brought to the research and writing my own perspectives on twentieth-century educational policies and conditions. References to these concerns appear throughout the book. The final chapter, however, expressly links the office's founding years to the present. The parallels drawn between then and now do not endorse a simplistic reading of history backwards, although to some extent backwards is how we recover the past. Rather, they represent attempts to avoid disjoining time into unrelated episodes. Whether the development is healthy or pathological, contemporary proposals for enforcing education bear a striking resemblance to plans for a national bureau of education offered over a century ago. *To Enforce Education* recounts and comments upon this apparently circular movement.

Donald R. Warren
1973

Acknowledgments

A number of colleagues and teachers have assisted with this study. The most important, in terms of time and interest, has been Robert L. McCaul of the University of Chicago, without whose pedagogy and counsel the book probably would not have been conceived nor completed. Roald F. Campbell, now at Ohio State University, helped me untangle the complex policy implications of the Office of Education's founding years, and Mark M. Krug, also of the University of Chicago, provided insight and direction to sources on the Civil War and Reconstruction periods. My colleague and friend Charles A. Tesconi, Jr., of the University of Illinois at Chicago Circle, discussed and argued over the project as if it were his own. His influence is evident throughout the book. Others helped by reading and criticizing all or portions of the manuscript: Val Lynch, Van Cleve Morris, Carol Proudfoot, and Beverly Alaniva Warren.

The project would have remained in the research stage even longer than it did had it not been for the intervention of the late Hilmar A. Sieving, education librarian of the University of Chicago, who agreed that the university should purchase from the National Archives a microfilm copy of the entire outgoing correspondence of the commissioners of education. Many other librarians and archivists gave valuable time to assist in the research: the staffs at the National Archives, the Manuscripts Division of the Library of Congress, Fales Library of New York University, Watkinson Library of Trinity College, the Special Collections Library of the University of Tennessee, the Massachusetts Historical Society, Burton Historical Collection of the Detroit Public Library, Regenstein Library of the University of Chicago, Purdue University Libraries, and the University of Illinois at Chicago Circle Library. I am particularly indebted to Wyndham-Gay Bedell of the Office of Education, John J. Whealen, former historian for the office, Alice Songe, education

17

librarian at the Department of Health, Education, and Welfare Reference Library, and Professor Yuri Nakata, documents librarian for the University of Illinois at Chicago Circle Library.

Reproductions of the portraits of Henry Barnard, John Eaton, Nathaniel H. R. Dawson, and William Torrey Harris were furnished by the Office of Education. Permission to include the portrait of Charles Brooks was granted by the Burton Historical Collection of the Detroit Public Library. The Purdue University Libraries provided the photograph of Emerson E. White. The Audio Visual Division of the National Archives furnished the remaining illustrations, including the photographs of Ignatius Donnelly and James A. Garfield.

A portion of Chapter Seven appeared under the title "National Institute of Education: Questions from the Past," in the January, 1973 issue of *Intellect* (vol. 101, pp. 219–24). I am grateful to the editor for permission to revise that material for inclusion here.

Van Cleve Morris, dean of the College of Education, University of Illinois at Chicago Circle, provided funds to assist me in preparing the manuscript for publication. Rose Naputano, Irene Niebauer, Arlene Perlette, and Earline Wright typed the original drafts. Arlene Perlette and Rose Naputano, both able critics, recorded the various revisions and organized the bibliography. Alice Nigoghosian, editor at Wayne State University Press, assisted mightily in transforming typed pages into a book. I am deeply indebted to her for her careful and critical reading of the manuscript. Finally, Armin Beck, Frederick D. Erickson, now of Harvard, Emanuel Hurwitz, Jr., Eliezer Krumbein, Carolyn L. Dolan, Thomas Linton, Julius Menacker, Van Cleve Morris, Charles A. Tesconi, Jr., Ward Weldon, and Edward Wynne, past and present colleagues in the Policy Studies Department of the College of Education, provided encouragement and an environment of inquiry and concern for the quality of American education which made completion of the manuscript seem worthwhile.

Introduction

*I*n recent years a number of critical studies have provided fresh readings of the history of American education that have challenged a former preoccupation with schools and institutional development. A revisionist history of education has emerged to question the accuracy of inspirational accounts of the public school as the "great equalizer of men." This is not the place for a critique of the revisionists' work. However, at the outset, I want to acknowledge the significance of their contributions, particularly those of Michael Katz, to current understanding of the history of American education and to a renewed vitality and rigor among historians of education.

"As it is being re-discovered," Katz suggests, "America's educational past seems more depressing than uplifting. For much of it is an unpleasant record of insensitivity and bias, or a dreary tale of innovations that did not reach their goals." Fired in equal measure by the "appalling" failures of contemporary public education, particularly urban schools, and their examination of school policies and practices in earlier periods, revisionist historians reject the "liberal progressive" notion that public schools have offered equality of educational opportunity.

> If one believes this society is *not* structured to enhance the dignity of man but rather fosters a dehumanizing quest for status, power, and wealth, then the liberal histories fail to explain how we got where . . . we are. . . . If one starts with the assumption that this society is in fact racist, fundamentally materialistic, and institutionally structured to protect vested interests, the past takes on vastly different meanings.[1]

The "different meanings" have turned on its head the romantically edifying account of American educational development.

19

They depict the school as an instrument of social control wielded by the state and by political and economic elites. Far from delivering the promised equal opportunity across racial, social class, and ethnic lines, it has served a system in which the "children of the affluent by and large take the best marks and the best jobs." While a good many historians question such conclusions, the revisionists have succeeded in challenging the validity of merely descriptive narrations of the American educational past. Rightly, in my judgment, they have called attention to the ironic gap between the educational objectives voiced by common school advocates and actual school policies and practices. In the process they have encouraged more provocative, hence refreshing, educational histories.[2]

In the pages that follow, readers will find added documentation for a number of the revisionists' conclusions. Strictly speaking, however, *To Enforce Education* is not a revisionist history. It is, rather, a narrative examination of reform strategies and their supporting rationales, which amounted to attempts to shape schools "from the top down." More to the point, my perspectives on nineteenth-century school reform efforts and a number of my conclusions do not conform to revisionist premises.

The founding years of the United States Office of Education coincided with the initial phase of American public school development, a process shaped, irreparably later critics insisted, by the hopeful republicanism which baptized the country's birth. In part recovered from idealistic vocabularies of former times, in part provoked by the practical imperatives of nation-building, a new language interposed generous views of man with portrayals of his world as amenable to human ordering. Outlines of an American mission emerged, an ethos of equalitarianism shielded from antinomian discord by optimistic assertions that in the United States, if nowhere else, citizens were obliged to care for the welfare and freedoms of their brothers and sisters.

Education, as formulated during the country's beginning years, represented a national, as over against a sectional, concern and a chance for achieving nationhood. Talk about education braved unsettling realities; it endured, not because schools fulfilled the high expectations, but inexplicably because they did not. American education, as both process and institution, has never escaped the reformist role in which it was cast in the republic's first days.

Although imbedded within suggested national educational

goals formulated in this early period, national school agency proposals found a more congenial context in the educational reforms of northern schoolmen during the Jackson and antebellum periods. Like the common school movement itself, that loose collection of individuals, ideas, and organizations immediately responsible for the initial forms and systems of American public education, the plans reflected the awkwardly mixed hopes of reformers for equalizing educational opportunity and their fears that a culturally plural people would dissolve amid fratricidal squabbles. For reasons both lofty and base, widespread support for the plans did not materialize until after the Civil War. On 2 March 1867, the Department of Education, as the agency was originally designated, began an uncertain membership in the federal bureaucracy, enjoined by Congress to "promote the cause of education throughout the country."

Whether guaranteeing equal chances for schooling or steeling the Union against disintegration, mid-nineteenth century schoolmen found themselves imposing educational forms upon a more or less indifferent public in the classic ways reformers have always presumed to light the path to others' betterment. Yet even in its crudest manifestations, where well-intentioned attempts to enforce education digressed into efforts to control schools and in turn people, the common school movement extended the promise of education as the means for social and individual improvement. The chapters which follow examine one aspect of this promise, the effort to build the federal bureaucratic structures deemed necessary for delivering to the Union dependable, schooled citizens and guaranteeing to citizens unencumbered chances to avail themselves of the benefits of at least basic learning and familiarity with the country's dominant values and accepted modes of thought.

For good or for ill, neither goal has been realized during the Office of Education's century-long history. Well-schooled Americans have fallen short of that dependability longed for by phrasemakers searching for a "silent majority" and access to educational opportunity has remained restricted. The agency's original proponents promised at once too much and not enough. This is the essence of the story to be told here. It is a story of irony and also of paradox.

Irony speaks of acting contrary to expressed objectives, of being surprised by unplanned and undesired outcomes, of being victimized by forces and events one intended to control. In short, it is a rather ordinary and human fact of life, a function of finitude. Finding irony in the founding years of the Office of Education—that some of our educational progenitors who said they wanted to promote equal educational opportunity helped establish a federal agency which promoted almost the exact opposite—is not especially startling. To be sure, the discovery adds spice to assessments of the reformers' actions and offers telling commentary on their trust in bureaucracy as a mode of reform. Also, it encourages appreciation for the extent to which the outcomes of their efforts followed from forces over which they lacked control. Finally, this irony from the past provides part of the context in which we can weigh possible federal roles and their likely effects in promoting education in the twentieth century.

I do not think, however, that irony can take us very far in understanding the office's founding years. First, some of it has a rather simple explanation. Those who advocated the creation of a national bureau of education did not agree on the proposed agency's powers and functions. Likewise, opponents of the plans acted in the service of various, sometimes conflicting, expectations. It is not surprising, therefore, that the agency which was eventually established failed to realize fully either the fears of its detractors or the hopes of its supporters. Second, unless we are prepared to pronounce the initial supporters of the office guilty of deliberately cloaking their support for an educational status quo beneath preachments about equality, we learn from irony little more than that the reformers did not control all the variables shaping the agency during its initial period.

Understanding the office's founding years requires a reconstruction of the reformers' intentions as goals and strategies formulated by time-bound people. How did they diagnose their times, and in light of those diagnoses what did they expect a national bureau of education to accomplish? From what we know of the early nineteenth-century school reformers, they were true believers in the social reforming capability of education. However, on the question of how to deliver popular education to the masses, how to organize and control schools, they remained curiously divided and ambivalent. Irony alone is not a sufficient analytical tool for helping us understand why.

Committed to what historian R. Freeman Butts has called "civilization building," school reformers such as Horace Mann and

22

Henry Barnard understood that "cosmopolitan man," whose rise to prominence in the United States was barely visible in the pre-Civil War period, required, in Butts's words, an education suitable to the conditions of his social environment. They feared and welcomed that environment, resigned themselves to its likely ascendance, and planned their schools accordingly. The more astute among them acknowledged that people living in cities, like people living in more isolated and culturally homogeneous settings, became educated through a variety of influences and agents. In the manner of historian Lawrence Cremin a century later, Barnard viewed education broadly, including in his surveys of learning agents not merely schools, but also colleges, child-rearing practices, parental values, churches, and libraries. He and his colleagues tended to disparage the effects of parents and cultural values on children, particularly if the children were poor or from a minority culture, but fundamentally it was the variety of effect, not merely the effects per se, that frightened them. Also, for the reformers, informal education, acquired from work experience and/or simply living amid relatives and community enclaves, lacked dependability. Needed was organized education, systems of schools, that would reliably complement, compensate for, and in time perhaps supplant informal learnings.[3]

The lure of homogeneity proved to be overwhelming. The dream of enforced, that is, guaranteed, equal educational opportunity narrowed to a drive for uniformity in curriculum, teaching methods, and even school architecture and students' desks. The pioneers of American public education, including those who devised plans for a national bureau of education, maintained a quixotic hope for purposive change and believed that education routinized in common schools offered the surest guarantee of social and individual improvement. Feeding and undermining the process was their double-minded fear and fascination with the changes they saw occurring during the Jackson and antebellum years.

Maxine Greene, the philosopher, is correct, I think, in concluding that these early planners of public education did not grasp the paradox in which they were caught by virtue of their school reform agenda. They forgot or ignored the elementary truth that education shapes and liberates and that therefore it can be both welcomed and dreaded. They understood that their times required new educational forms, and that education's "contours," to use Greene's term, must be suited to particular human needs and

23

conditions. They assumed the new contours would have to be enforced on ignorant and narrowly enculturated people but failed to see cultural differences as valuable and ineluctable learning resources. Equally revealing, they did not see that their proposed education revolution threatened established distributions of political and economic power and, hence, that its success required and abetted far-reaching social change. Apparently, they also failed to recognize that education resists being totally programmed, that it extends beyond any of its institutional forms, and that the latter inevitably remain distressingly incomplete and, as Greene has phrased it, "ragged." If they erred it was not simply in failing to realize their goals, which were in the first place ambivalent and in the second beyond their limited capabilities to achieve. Error rather entered at the start, in their simplistic notions about education and society. It may be, as some of the revisionist historians insist, that they were also pernicious and double-dealing and that their talk of equality covered an intention to support established distributions of political and economic power. I have found evidence that partially supports the latter but little that can support the former. It is more accurate to admit that they lacked intellectual rigor and, in the long run, nerve.[4]

School Reform through Centralization: The Lure of Homogeneity

NATIONAL EDUCATION: AMBIVALENT DREAM

*I*t began as a splendid vision. Or so it has seemed ever since. A diverse people, acknowledging their common destiny, their mutual dependence, could create and maintain a society graced by enlightened citizens and intelligent leaders. They could dot their land with schools designed to distribute educational opportunities and hence guarantee the widest possible participation in the promises of citizenship. Through the popular diffusion of learning, George Washington reasoned, leaders would stand reminded that government was served best by the informed confidence of the people and, in time, the people would come to know and value their rights. In 1791, Robert Coram, the 30-year-old antifederalist editor of the *Delaware Gazette*, argued that the means of acquiring knowledge, which he viewed as nothing less than the means of subsistence, should be furnished by society. Education, he added, should be universally, permanently, and uniformly accessible, not "left to the caprice or negligence of parents, to chance, or confined to the children of wealthy citizens. . . ." According to Thomas Jefferson, the tendency of governments to degenerate into tyranny could be prevented if the minds of the people were "illuminated," especially if they learned to recognize "ambition under all its shapes." Fed by hope that a society fashioned after republican principles could render itself tenacious and less tentative, such musings, although only rough assertions of man's assumed potential for reasonable, autonomous decision-making, nurtured less lilting, more pragmatic equations. The nation's need for educated citizens and leaders dictated the necessity of popular instruction. But the requirement posed a practical dilemma: Can enlightenment, the power source of freedom, be programmed? Can education be enforced? Solutions must walk a delicate line since a careless control of schools or an allegiance to a narrow or static view of learning could undermine the goal of liberation.[1]

Leaders of the American experiment have seemed at times within a breath of crossing that line, as when Washington argued for the establishment of a national university:

> Amongst the motives to such an institution, the assimilation of the principles, opinions, and manners of our countrymen by the common education of a portion of our youth from every quarter well deserves attention. The more homogenous our citizens can be made in these particulars the greater will be our prospect of permanent union.

Although capable of servicing less desirable causes, Washington's rationale rested on the intention to overwhelm sectional and class antagonisms with a fresh set of priorities. The national university, by attracting young men from across the country to study together in the nation's capital and then sending them home armed with higher learning and a national consciousness, suggested a strategy for bringing about a unified, self-governing people. An equally high-minded objective led Jefferson to recommend the application of federal funds "to the great purposes of public education, roads, rivers, canals, and other objects of public improvement." "By these operations new channels of communication will be opened between the States, the lines of separation will disappear, their interests will be identified, and their union cemented by new and indissoluble ties." Such claims taxed the restraints of certainty. Sensible men knew better and would prevail, but the start hinted of audacity, that element of nerve necessary for shaping nation-building experiments with untested strategies.[2]

Admittedly, the vision was utilitarian. Generated by men who thought in terms of a natural aristocracy of the mind, it spoke rarely of intrinsic, personal benefits from education, the sheer joy of knowing. Its authors dreamed and argued for the necessity of an educated people to sustain the new republic, and their translations of the dream attended to the practical concerns of organizing and controlling schools in ways that would ensure their effectiveness. A few of the early proponents of American public education delved into the mysteries of how and why people learn. For the most part, however, they limited their suggestions to proposed national and state agencies or institutions to promote popular acceptance of the idea of public instruction and to encourage uniformity of programs and goals among existing schools and colleges. They knew what education was, assumed its value, and believed in its power to shape and heal men's souls and their society. These were articles of faith which freed them for more practical concerns. Hence, the point was not to dwell solely on education's worth, as though that were a question, but to forge mechanisms for delivering education to people and to propagate institutions—schools—in which education could occur.

The early plans for promoting, organizing, and controlling public schools, which began appearing in the late eighteenth century, reflected not only a nationalistic thrust but also the necessity of compromising the ideals of popular enlightenment and guaranteed school opportunity. Jefferson's plan for public schools in Virginia substituted literacy for illumination as the aim of elementary instruction. In reaching for an accommodation with the state's ruling elite, his plan severely limited educational opportunity for poor people. Even so, the legislature found his bill unacceptable. Proposals for a national university, despite Washington's endorsement, similarly failed to capture congressional interest. Opposition derived both from the lack of precedents for such an institution and congressional fears that its establishment would cost a great deal of money. Assorted schemes for a national system of schools, authored by DuPont de Nemours, Samuel Knox, Robert Coram, and others during the late eighteenth and early nineteenth centuries, shared at least one major starting point. Each presumed the necessity of widely disseminated school opportunity in achieving national unity and fostering the growth of republican institutions. Untouched by political considerations, hence cheerfully roseate, several of their plans projected central boards to promote nationwide uniformity of school programs, diminish the deleterious effects of sectionalism and "excessive individuality," and introduce educational improvements.[3]

The period before 1812 found Americans ill-prepared to countenance dramatic concentrations of power in distant governments, whether state or federal. More significantly, proposals for school promotion by state or national agencies ran counter to the dominant pattern of private and locally sponsored education which had emerged by the close of the eighteenth century. Finally, suggestions that control of the preparation of youth for adulthood should or even could be removed from family, church, and local community challenged the dominant patterns of life in pre-industrial, pre-urban America. Felled by lack of public interest and opposition from local elites grown accustomed to controlling school aims and practices, the proposals slipped into obscurity. Remaining were immodest claims for schools' effectiveness in social formation, an education ideology which a later generation of schoolmen, the vanguard of the common school movement, would revive with vengeance. Idealism, at once vaulting and pragmatic, marked the beginning of American school centralization. Initiated as reform-minded intellectual constructs, proposals for centralization contained at least implicitly the idea of a national bureau of education from the outset.

If there was confidence that the people could attain the threshold of practical freedom through education, the dilemma of forging citizens from the raw materials of a diverse, largely illiterate population frightened others. And fear, too, served to strengthen the centralizing process. Benjamin Rush, the Philadelphia physician who signed the Declaration of Independence and involved himself in a number of educational reform efforts in the post Revolutionary War period, saw schools as instruments for transforming youth into "republican machines." "This must be done," Rush argued, "if we expect them to perform their parts properly. . . . The wills of the people . . . must be fitted to each other by means of education before they can be made to produce regularity and unison in government." The great art of correcting mankind, explained Noah Webster in a revealing phrase, "consists in prepossessing the mind with good principles." For him, schools served government not people. They should fasten their reform activities on the latter because, frankly, people, not society's structures, stood in need of edification. In later years, unnerved by social changes he could not fathom, he worried about the propertyless, "the idle, penniless lounger," having an equal voice with that of the "sober, industrious citizen . . . [who] finds that his property and virtue give him no influence or advantage as a member of the government." With untroubled certainty, Daniel Webster regarded public instruction "as a wise and liberal system of police, by which property, and life, and the peace of society are secured. . . . By general instruction, we

seek, as far as possible, to purify the whole moral atmos-
phere. . . ." [4]

The vision was double-minded. Schools, honored as inclusive guarantors of freedom and freedom's future, served also as
instruments of control to be wielded by those "who know what is
right," to borrow another revealing phrase from Noah Webster.
Frances Wright, an early advocate of unionization and women's
rights, argued with characteristic hyperbole in 1819 that the
equalization of opportunity through education necessitated radical
programs. Denouncing the common school as a halfway measure, she
proposed tightly structured systems of residential schools which
would receive all children from the age of two. Away from
distracting home influences, children would learn equality by sharing
the same kind of food, working at common tasks, and studying the
same subjects under teachers of equal skill. A decade later, Robert
Dale Owen, a colleague of "Fanny" Wright in early attempts to form
activist labor organizations during the 1820s, offered an elaborated
version of the plan for guardianship schools, but he uncovered few
takers among working class people. Arguing that "Public Education
ought to be equal, republican, open to all, and the best which can be
devised," Owen criticized contemporary public education institutions as simply day schools which failed to touch the basic sources of
inequality:

> We conceive, then, that State Schools, to be republican,
> efficient and acceptable to all, must receive the children, not for
> six hours a day, but altogether; must feed them, clothe them,
> lodge them, must direct not their studies only, but their
> occupations and amusements; must care for them until their
> education is completed, and then only abandon them to the
> world, as useful, intelligent, virtuous citizens.

At stake, was "whether aristocracy shall be perpetrated or destroyed;
whether the poor man's child shall be educated or not," Owen
insisted, adding that "education is emphatically the business of the
government." He detected in the common school a form of public
philanthropy unlikely to attract children from families of the
"aristocracy" and too unevenly distributed throughout the nation to
guarantee educational opportunities to children of workers. He
proposed, however, to complete the model, not substitute a different

29

one. He approved of the common school movement's centralizing
tendencies but rightly perceived that it was encumbered by timid
support and its own ambivalence. He intended merely to illuminate
the obvious: equalizing chances for education among rich and poor
across the country required a national plan rigorously enforced.
During the 1830s and beyond, the remarkable common school
crusade gained momentum. The critical issue regarding public
education was not whether schools should be imposed upon society
—few doubted the wisdom of that objective—but rather who would
control them and to which ends.[5]

COMMON SCHOOLING: REFORM FROM THE TOP

Much of the confusion and many of the quarrels about
American public education, particularly those directed at its quality
and at policies affecting its equal distribution, have stemmed from
expectations that fail to appreciate its ambiguous origins. Schools
arose, it has been commonly assumed, in response to popular
demands and over the objections of entrenched elites. They represented an institutional manifestation of the democratic quest for
equal educational opportunity. In reality, almost the opposite was
the case. Equal educational opportunity constituted a major goal of
the common school movement, but it was pursued "from the top" by
segments of the elite classes, for both humanitarian and crassly
paternalistic reasons. It was a reform effort generated for the most
part in behalf of, not by, the intended beneficiaries.[6]

As their movement took shape during the 1830 to 1860
period, common schoolmen worried over the unequal distribution of
schooling opportunity and the social consequences of educational
exclusiveness. They advocated the establishment of state and federal
agencies to guarantee the commonality and inclusiveness of public
learning institutions. As a corollary strategy, they labored to
nationalize their movement and professionalize its leaders and
teachers through the creation of regional and national educational
organizations. Federal involvement in public education represented
both a strategy and an objective of school reformers. The notion of a
federal role in promoting schools, particularly the proposed national
bureau of education, won adherents slowly. But it won them, as
increasing numbers of the friends of public education became

30

convinced that only federal intervention could guarantee schools' inclusiveness and efficient operation. One can miss a central thrust of the common school crusade and the type and scope of the reforms its spokesmen anticipated by viewing federal activity as an interloper, an alien presence, in the public school campaign. On the contrary, federal involvement remained consistent with the movement's original and continuing character. The very idea of nationwide schooling presumed and required a federal stake in its realization. But it took awhile for friends of public education to acknowledge the necessity, much less the wisdom, of a federal role in their crusade, and even longer for them to be comfortable with it.

The common school movement emerged in a time of growing disorder and pervasive change. Sparked by unprecedented urban growth, nascent trade unions agitating for improved working conditions, extension of the franchise, and foreign immigration, the view began to spread abroad that the nation was on the verge of coming unstuck. "All the elements of society are in commotion," warned the Reverend Elipha White, a speaker at the 1837 meeting of the American Institute of Instruction. "The civil, moral, and religious institutions of ages are crumbling before the march of intellect and zeal of reform. . . . Moral revolution—moral chaos seems approaching." Shocked by labor restiveness, Alonzo Potter, the Episcopal bishop of Pennsylvania and a leading spokesman for school reform during the Jackson and antebellum periods, blamed workers for the nation's domestic troubles. They have no just grounds for discontent, he complained, adding that "without virtuous principles and habits, no increase of compensation can either enrich or elevate them." Some watched anxiously the "vast tide of immigration, yearly flowing in upon us," others the "mighty increase of popular strength." Diagnoses varied, but the cure, schoolmen agreed, was public education, "not of the head or heart separately— but conjointly;" only this would save the country from "the recurrence of a French Revolution on American soil." [7]

Moral education must be American education: "If you will make Republican men, you must have Republican Education." It followed as a matter of course "that the foreigners who settle on our soil should cease to be Europeans and become Americans. . . . We must become one nation; and it must be our [the schoolmen's] great endeavor to effect this object so desireable and so necessary to our American welfare." Not isolated or uncommon, such observations rested, perhaps unknowingly, on the assumptions that plurality implied disunion and civil conflict suggested disloyalty. An added implication of the schoolmen's prescription was that social change ran the risk of revolution. Schools became for many of them the way to control and direct change. Elipha White's colleagues in the American Institute of Instruction did not object when he promised, "By making men patriots and Christians, loyal and obedient subjects of civil authority and moral government, education effects an entire change, and restores order complete." [8]

Such rhetoric, heard from common school advocates throughout the Jackson and antebellum periods, cloaked not only a distrust of variation from established norms, but also schoolmen's tacit admission that they were not their own men. Their tendency to view change as pathology allied them with those elements in American society discomforted by trade unions, foreigners, and the extended franchise and, according to Frank Carlton's critique of their movement written a half century later, discredited much of their humanitarian zeal. An early twentieth-century economics professor and labor historian, Carlton adhered to a bias of his own, namely that labor organizations, more than school reformers, deserved credit for the development of American public education. The reformers confused symptoms with illness, Carlton insisted; hence, their prescription, peace and order through public instruction, addressed itself primarily to the manifestations of unrest and disharmony rather than their causes.[9]

Reflecting both change-induced anxiety and their hope that education would play a nation-building role, schoolmen and their supporters championed public schools as objects of civic pride and strategies for keeping children of the poor off the streets. Schools would safeguard the nation against an illiterate electorate and engender common values—political, moral, and religious—among an increasingly pluralistic population. Samuel Lewis, in 1837 the new superintendent of Ohio's common schools, made the point directly:

> No nation can be free and remain so, unless the whole people are intelligent and moral, in other words, have a good, sound Christian education; for let it be remembered that we are a Christian people, and the principles of the former must support the latter.

32

Charles Brooks, Massachusetts clergyman and early advocate of a federal education agency. Courtesy of the Burton Historical Collection, Detroit Public Library, Joseph Klima, Jr., photographer.

Not without difficulty, schoolmen wrenched public instruction from the hands of sectarianism, but substituted an equally dogmatic nonsectarian Protestantism enriched now with explicit nationalism. Spread throughout the land, the common school would fulfill the Enlightenment premise that an educated people could govern themselves.[10]

The movement, however, owed as much to nineteenth-century Prussia as it did to eighteenth-century *philosophes*. After a European tour in 1833, Charles Brooks, a Unitarian pastor in Hingham, Massachusetts, and self-appointed school reformer, confessed, "I fell in love with the Prussian [school] system; and it seemed to possess me like a missionary angel." State supervision of schools and state normal schools particularly impressed him, and many of his colleagues shared his enchantment. The efficiency of the Prussian operation, the rationality of its hierarchical structure, the clarity of goals, the tightness of the organization which articulated secondary schools with universities and teachers' seminaries with the Prussian equivalent of common schools—these were the attractions. Henry Barnard, later to serve as the first United States commissioner of education, was drawn to them repeatedly. Horace Mann, undoubt-

33

edly the best known of the antebellum school reformers, and Calvin
Stowe, Harriet Beecher's husband and a leading schoolman in Ohio,
returned with glowing accounts. In the late 1860s, James A. Garfield,
who recently had introduced the department of education bill in the
House of Representatives, satisfied himself with the strength of the
Prussian system. Most of these observers overlooked or failed to
appreciate the implications of the control mentality permeating
Prussian educational goals and the role schools played in main-
taining, even strengthening, the Prussian social class structure.
Rather, the Americans tended to accept what they saw as a model
for guaranteeing equal school opportunity in the United States. As
Barnard explained:

> In Prussia the Minister of Instruction is one of the most
> important ministers of the State. The Department of Instruction
> is organized as carefully as that of War or the Treasury, and is
> intended to act on every district and family in the kingdom. We
> have not one State officer supported at the expense of the State
> to ascertain the condition of our schools and to give his time and
> mind to the improvement of these valuable institutions. No
> serious responsibility in respect to public education rests
> anywhere.
>   The desultory and imperfect reports of several hun-
> dred scattered individuals can never give a complete view of
> the defects of our schools or the best mode of remedying them.
> Hence one man familiar with the subject should traverse the
> whole ground, discover its actual state, compare different
> schools under different influences, ascertain the origin of the
> apathy and neglect so prevalent and the measures which would
> be at once effectual and acceptable. The energies of a single,
> well balanced mind should be employed in collecting and
> combining materials which shall give greater force and
> efficiency to the system.[11]

Central to the common school movement was the intention
to render schooling inescapable, not for some youth only but for all
of them. That objective informed plans for organizing schools into
city, state, and national systems, and for establishing central school
authorities responsible for winning adherents to the cause of public
education, still not a widely popular idea. As a second and
longer-range assignment the new school officials were expected to
equalize and make commonly available school opportunities within

Henry Barnard, commissioner of education, 1867–70. Courtesy of the U.S. Office of Education.

Engraved by H. W. Smith

their jurisdictions. The effort represented an essentially undemocratic thrust capable of generating an unimaginative and grimly uniform public instruction. The homogenization of citizens represented for Ralph Waldo Emerson the school movement's most frightening possibility.

In addition, the rhetoric of enforced common education extended the promise of inclusion in the nation's schools to all segments of the population, and this motif stood as the movement's relieving ideal. Opportunist and zealot, salesman and missionary, Horace Mann emerged as the ideal's tireless advocate in the school movement's early period. In 1837, he left a promising career in politics to become the first secretary of Massachusetts' newly created State Board of Education. In the course of his twelve-year tenure, Mann became the acknowledged leader of the public education campaign, the "father" of the American common school. He wanted education to be pleasurable, to the end that children would desire it. In schools with skilled teachers who also cared for their charges, children of all classes would acquire the knowledge and attitudes they would need to lead useful and moral lives. Children of the poor, particularly, would find in the schools Mann envisioned avenues to improved economic standing and self respect. The point, he insisted,

was not simply to have schools, but to disseminate learning and morality effectively and commonly across the land. To fulfill the promises of a self-governing republic, he argued in his 1842 July Fourth oration in Boston, all the people must be educated and virtuous. The objective could not be left to chance. "Universal mismanagement and calamity" would surely follow unless the states actively pursued a policy of increasing and improving their free school programs. Actually Mann's address was an ode to the nation's stake in education. He saw in 1842 a "great national crisis" growing out of the deepening hostility separating North from South. Perhaps, he suggested, the crisis could be averted if the benefits of education were diffused more evenly throughout the nation. It appeared unnecessary to state explicitly that national problems required national attention. Later, in 1848, Mann left the field of educational battle for John Quincy Adams' seat in Congress. Years afterwards, Mary Mann explained her husband's action as an attempt to secure national recognition of the schoolmen's cause, perhaps even the creation of a bureau of education. To be sure, Mann continued in his belief that "schools will be found to be the way that God has chosen for the reformation of the world." But in 1848, after twelve years at the head of Massachusetts' schools, he was also weary of the "trammels of neutrality" under which he labored and impatient to join the antislavery crusade.[12]

Mann's "return" to politics (in truth, he had never left, as his many quarrels over the objectives, organization, and control of public education with political leaders, clerics, and schoolmasters, for example, in Boston, attests) signaled a not surprising disparity between hope and reality. In some sections of the country and for particular racial, ethnic, and religious groups, exclusion from common schools occurred, and often hardened into standard policy. But the developing school ideology rarely noted exceptions in its commitment to fostering homogeneity through common education. Fired by urban squalor, the plight of children trooping off to factories, often violent clashes between Protestants and immigrant Catholics, widespread illiteracy, and a patriotism perhaps too ripe, schoolmen here and there mounted drives to make good on the promise of inclusion. For admittedly mixed motives, they sought to realize equality of educational opportunity by fastening order, efficiency, and commonality to the schooling process, and scattering its elementary institutional form even to the edge of the frontier. Charles Brooks's bold pronouncements set in sharp relief both the humanitarianism and fear of the future which inhabited the roots of the school reform crusade:

> All children by nature have equal rights to education. A republic, by the very principles of republicanism, is socially, politically, and morally bound to see that *all* the talent born within its territory is developed in its natural order, proper time, and due proportion; thus enabling every mind to make the most of itself. The republican state stands *in loco parentis* to every child, and is therefore bound to use all the means and capabilities sent by Heaven for its highest aggrandizement.[13]

Charles Brooks was an incorrigible reformer. In his lifetime he joined peace movements (although not during the Civil War), temperance campaigns, and the antislavery crusade. However, his most prolonged effort was in behalf of common schools and teacher seminaries. With an interest in public education that predated his 1833 European tour, he received from his Prussian contacts not so much new ideas but rather a working model for school organization. From 1835 to 1837 he lectured throughout Massachusetts on the Prussian system of schools and its lessons for Americans, addressed the state legislature on the subject, and considered himself responsible for the subsequent passage of the law creating the Massachusetts State Board of Education in 1837.

Brooks introduced a plan for national education in 1839 and off and on for the next three decades polished, refined, and publicized it. The scheme projected a nationwide network of local elementary schools, regional colleges and academies, and national universities. Its essential feature was equality, that is, common goals, curricula, and study materials among the various institutions at each level of the system, whether the school or college was located in educationally advanced Massachusetts or in an isolated rural community. If the nation needed educated citizens, Brooks reasoned, it must make sure that all have equal access to opportunities for learning and also that none miss the benefits of schooling. He proposed centralized school supervision as the way to guarantee system-wide commonality, hence equality of educational opportunity. He also proposed mandatory state participation in the plan in order to satisfy his fears that, despite the nation's need, some would exclude themselves or be excluded by others from educational benefits. The nation should not, indeed could not, tolerate that. Naked control of schools and enforced reform, administered by a possibly distant central agency, left Brooks's fellow schoolmen breathless and rendered the plan unacceptable. But the Massachusetts divine knew what he was about—at least intuitively. If schools engendered domestic peace and national unity, a proposition in which he earnestly believed, the proscription of educationally backward localities, races, and classes necessarily followed. On the other hand, the use of schools as agents of control, implied in Brooks's *in loco parentis*, was apparently acceptable.

The rationale supporting the school movement's centralizing tendencies derived from a premise rarely challenged at the time. Illiterate, provincial people could not be expected to value learning. They had to be led, cajoled, if necessary coerced, into accepting their need—and society's—for the spread and increase of public instruction. The 1835 speech of Thaddeus Stevens in the Pennsylvania House of Representatives opposing repeal of the state's first school-aid law illustrated the schoolmen's thinking. Stevens repeated the traditional arguments for the necessity of popular education in a republic but saved his most telling shots for the state legislature itself. The law had proved controversial, and Stevens addressed himself to the problem of leading an ignorant people out of darkness:

> But we are told that this law is unpopular; that the people desire its repeal. Has it not always been so with every new

reform in the conditions of man? Old habits and old prejudices are hard to be removed from the mind. Every new improvement . . . has required the most strenuous, and often perilous exertions of the wise and good.

Demagogues in all of the political parties were catering to the fears of the people at a time when they needed leaders and statesmen, he continued. "[It] is the duty of faithful legislators to create and sustain such laws and institutions as shall teach us our wants, foster our cravings after knowledge, and urge us forward in the march of intellect." The soaring rhetoric left its mark. The law was not repealed, and Stevens won a place in the hearts of schoolmen throughout the country. He later confided, "That was the proudest effort of my life." [14]

Although support for state supervision of schools increased over the next two decades, schoolmen continued to doubt whether the idea had firmly taken root. As late as 1864 the president of the Cincinnati school board was heard complaining to the Ohio General Assembly, "The truth is, and it is just as well to say it in plain terms, that deeply and vitally as it concerns the *State*, the great majority of *people* care very little about education." If common school spokesmen are to be believed, theirs was less a popular movement than an elitist effort insulated against both opposition and public apathy by the reformers' confidence that they knew how to cure the nation's ills. [15]

NATIONALIZING THE MOVEMENT

In December 1829, Congressman Joseph Richardson, a fellow townsman of Charles Brooks and also a Unitarian minister, managed to stir up a minor controversy in Congress by proposing the establishment of a House committee on education. Reminding his colleagues of the founding fathers' vision of a nation guided by intelligent leaders and citizens, Richardson depicted the proposed committee as a means by which Congress could actively promote education throughout the country. He recognized that many House members questioned the constitutionality of his measure but insisted that the general welfare clause in the Constitution gave Congress the necessary power to act on educational questions. Anyway, he

39

reasoned, no congressional action required for national preservation could be unconstitutional. Opponents of the motion, Democrats and Whigs alike, voiced a single objection: educational policy ought to originate from within the states. William Segar Archer, Virginia plantation owner and later a Tyler Whig in the Senate, thought he saw in Richardson's motion an indirect attempt "to settle a long and complex question of power in favor of the general government." Archer's motion to table the measure passed by 156 to 52. The majority included two future presidents, Buchanan of Pennsylvania and Polk of Tennessee.[16]

Eight years later, William Cost Johnson, a congressman from Maryland, launched another abortive effort to involve Congress in the promotion and support of public education. The Surplus Revenue Deposit Act of 1836 distributed federal surplus funds to the states and allowed them to devote portions of the monies received to school purposes, but Johnson wanted more direct action. In December 1837 he moved that a House committee be appointed to inquire into the propriety of reporting a bill to appropriate an increased portion of the public lands specifically for educational purposes in the states and territories. In a speech that continued over several days, Johnson argued for more aggressive federal support of education. The recent struggle for a school law in Pennsylvania was evidence, he warned, of the need for federal action. Invoking the words of an unnamed educator, he observed that "the inappetence of a people for education is in exact ratio of its ignorance." Neither his oratory nor the statistics he cited showing the amount of illiteracy in the country moved his colleagues. Johnson's motion never came to a vote. Congress remained cool to suggestions for federal involvement in the promotion of education, however indirect, until near the end of the antebellum period.[17]

In a move which in time strengthened immeasurably their insular world even as it rendered their fledgling movement more effective, schoolmen began forming regional and national organizations in the late 1820s. The American Lyceum (a national organization of lecture and discussion societies), the Ohio-based Western Literary Institute, and the American Institute of Instruction, all founded around 1830, included among their goals bringing coherence to the common school movement and raising it to national status. Their members were committed to promoting public education and collecting and disseminating information on school operations across the country. Only the American Institute of Instruction, an organization dominated by New England schoolmen and friends of education, survived through the antebellum period. In 1850, battle-weary veterans of the school crusade, for the most part administrators and intellectuals allied with the movement, rallied briefly to form the American Association for the Advancement of Education. They wanted an organization that would bring together school leaders from across the country to share information, strengthen each other's local and state school reform efforts, and deepen their sense of profession and their competence as administrators. A half-decade later the association dissolved. Needed, schoolmen argued at the time, was a more broadly based organization that would attract teachers, administrators, and other supporters of education, and in addition offer practical assistance to those engaged professionally in the schooling process. In 1857, the National Teachers' Association, which still survives as the National Education Association, came into being to serve these objectives.

Out of the unity of American educators, achieved through national organizations, Henry Barnard predicted in 1839, "will ultimately spring some plan for the diffusion of pure and wholesome knowledge, embued with the soul and energy of all true virtue, through the length and breadth of our vast land." In glorious overstatement, he succeeded in capturing the spirit of the schoolmen's organizing effort: the educational bodies viewed themselves as reform agents dedicated to exerting "external pressure" on local communities to establish and improve public schools. Armed with comparative statistics and other descriptive information gathered at national conferences with their colleagues, schoolmen reasoned, they could redeem local critics or at least silence them into pride or embarrassment depending upon their schools' standing. Difficulties arose when it became clear that success would require the friends of education to educate themselves on the value of reliable statistics and to regularize national procedures for collecting, organizing, and reporting data. The recognition set the stage for what historian Carl Bode once termed the "era of talk" in the school reform movement. Preoccupied with efficiency and the definitions of school administrative functions, schoolmen turned their attention to establishing and maintaining channels of communication among themselves. Through the new organizations, an educational profession became identifiable, its goals and priorities ordered, its language standardized. The

41

meetings provided regular occasions for reaffirming commitments, renewing passion, recounting successes, and admitting fresh recruits to the mission.[18]

With this inward turn of the school crusade, the founding years of the U.S. Office of Education began in earnest. Although the idea of a federal school agency had appeared in the early days of the republic, the rationale and supporting constituency for drives for a national bureau of education emerged from schoolmen's meetings during the 1830 to 1860 period. Not surprisingly, the character of the agency created in 1867 reflected strengths and weaknesses traceable to these later influences. Its establishment served to confirm schoolmen's belief in schools as effective shapers of both people and society and represented a culmination of the school movement's centralizing tendencies. It institutionalized quantitative measures of school reform and the largely untested assumption that even quantitative reform, for example, more schools, public instruction programs extending from kindergarten through college, and nation-wide uniformity of educational goals, programs, and policies, fol-lowed from the indirect external pressure of school statistics collected and published nationally. Plans for a national school agency, at first tentatively and somewhat reluctantly discussed among schoolmen in the 1830s, constituted a reform strategy from the outset. By providing accurate descriptions and comparisons of schools and school systems, the proposed agency could generate popular support for public education. No community, schoolmen agreed, would knowingly countenance ignorance in its midst nor refuse to improve schools shown to be inferior to those in neigh-boring towns and states. Primarily, however, the agency would serve the new educational profession by promoting common objectives and administrative procedures among schoolmen, equipping them with nationally collected school statistics with which to evaluate their efforts, and formalizing communications within the profession. Shaped within the context of the common school movement, plans for a national bureau of education were intended to reform public schools by increasing their number and by strengthening the hand of those promoting them.

Initially, nationalization of the school movement did not encompass petitions to the federal government for legislative or executive action. Rather it began with schoolmen attempting to perform nationwide school census-taking functions themselves. One of the earliest projects of this sort was undertaken by the American Lyceum at its first meeting in 1831. The new organization represented an attempt to forge a national structure out of the local lyceums springing up across the country. Within broad limits, the groups offered discussion and lecture programs, characterized as "mutual education" at the time, dedicated generally to the "diffusion of useful information" and the promotion of common schools. As might be expected, the utility of the information and depth of commitment to the common school idea varied from community to community. Organizers of the American Lyceum proposed to reduce such differences by providing local representatives with opportunities for mutual education at national conferences and by consolidating local school reform efforts. A plan for collecting "facts relating to education" on a nationwide scale was quickly approved at the 1831 meeting. Of particular interest were the number of schools, pupils, and teachers in given localities; cost of school programs; teacher training provisions; curriculum; and laws pertaining to education in the states and territories. Local lyceums were requested to collect the desired information which was to be passed on to county lyceums and eventually incorporated in reports by state organizations to the American Lyceum in 1832. In the meantime, efforts were to be made by the organization's national leaders to secure representation from every state at the second annual gathering. Success of the venture depended upon voluntary effort, and this proved to be its downfall. Delegates to the 1832 meeting, reluctantly admitting that county and state lyceums had not been active in promoting the plan, recognized the need for paid agents to collect and disseminate the information sought.[19]

Crudely applied, the suggestion that gathering and disseminating data constituted an effective reform strategy extended the Enlightenment premise that knowledgeable people would act to reform themselves and the structures of their society. Near the end of his presidency, Washington trusted a similar assumption in recommending to Congress the creation of a national agricultural board to collect and disseminate useful information on farming. By this economical and efficient means, he argued, "the increase of improvement" of agriculture would be effected as farmers became cognizant of their deficiencies and of improved farming techniques.[20]

In 1835 the National Trades' Union attempted to field a plan for the voluntary collection of school data similar to that of the

American Lyceum; but because the Trades' locals never warmed to the project, it too had disappointing results. Other educational organizations, such as the American Institute of Instruction soon learned, as the Lyceum had learned, that voluntary groups were not effective instruments for collecting reliable information on school conditions. Schoolmen insisted that without such information they could not adequately describe the country's educational needs, identify communities or states where need was greatest, or make plans for school improvement.

Although historical treatments of the American public school crusade typically overlook the fact, drives for state and national school agencies originated from similar circumstances, attempted to realize similar goals, on different levels, of course, and confronted the same opposition, often from the same opponents. Both campaigns emerged at approximately the same time, during the early years of the common school movement, amid schoolmen's growing recognition that their crusade cut across local and regional attachments. Infused with passion by nationalistic goals and the grail of administrative orderliness, both sought the establishment of government bureaus modeled upon the presumed reform effectiveness of collecting and disseminating school data. Both campaigns encountered opposition not only because they lacked a popular base but also because they posed explicit threats to the prerogatives of local elites in determining the curricula and policies of public learning institutions. For the most part, both efforts shared the same leadership, schoolmen and friends of education with an urban base and/or a national perspective on school reform gained through participation in one of the major educational organizations. Both types of agencies were proposed as reform strategies intended to enforce education by strengthening and formalizing external pressure on communities to establish public schools or improve those already in operation.

Success came first on the state level as state legislatures agreed to establish boards or offices for the supervision of public schools throughout the Jackson and antebellum periods. The victories did not come easily. Schoolmen and politicians alike were uneasy about the costs involved and possible threats to local authorities. Initially, none of the state school officials were empowered to do much more than collect and disseminate information on school conditions and submit annual reports to their legislatures with recommended improvements. Their right to inspect schools was implied, if not stipulated outright. The job was enormous (few states gathered reliable data on schools within their borders), but the strategy was transparent. Towns and districts which saw their schools cast in a relatively unfavorable light in the state official's report presumably would be moved to upgrade them. The early advocates of state supervision assumed that civic pride, boosterism, and the competition among cities for regional dominance and cultural distinction could be counted on to rally support for school improvement in a delinquent community. Although capable of exerting little more than indirect external pressure, the new state school officials expected to achieve the equalization of educational opportunity throughout their states. Their objectives included the creation of more schools and greater uniformity in matters of curriculum, textbooks, and criteria for teacher selection among schools within their jurisdictions. The means to these ends, one should remember, were the regular collection and publication of school data.

In rural areas where social and cultural homogeneity prevailed, people apparently exhibited little anxiety over their schools' exclusiveness, inequality, or inefficiency. The qualification is required because recently initiated research into the effects and conditions of nineteenth-century education in rural America has not yet yielded results that can support broad generalizations. What has been learned so far is not surprising. Rural schools formed part of a system of educating agents that included church and family. Alone, schools were not particularly important, but combined with other parts of the system, they initiated youth into the local culture, equipping them with the skills, attitudes, and learnings they needed to function in it. Controversies over school control and equal educational opportunity rarely arose because neither was problematic. Schools were not controlled democratically, but neither were they shaped exclusively by local elites. In a direct, rather uncomplicated way they reflected the immediate social environment. Actually, in rural America the culture, not its schools, educated the young. If one was interested in serious book learning, he was probably just as well off not going to the community school.

Common school reformers worried over the provincialism thus encouraged, but their designs for state and national educational agencies emerged primarily in response to school problems plaguing

45

urban areas and city leaders' desires for "civilizing" institutions. Emphasizing the singular importance of schools in educating children produced, in addition to centralized school bureaucracies, credential-granting schooling agents alienated from the type of strong cultural base supporting rural schools. Rural communities tended to oppose the effort both because they did not want outsiders interfering with their schools and because they did not see that they needed assistance. Schools as isolated socializing agents were simply not that important to them.

Other opponents, however, quickly perceived the political challenge posed by the schoolmen's campaigns. Although its position varied from state to state, the Democratic party, for example, frequently discovered that it could not support the establishment of state school agencies, however ringed with restrictions. Party spokesmen feared that endorsements of the agencies would threaten the often delicately balanced Democratic coalition of ethnic, religious, labor, and other special interest groups, some of which had never been particularly enamored of the school movement or its leaders. For much the same reason, Democrats tended to oppose even more strenuously efforts to involve the federal government in school promotion. Also, some Jackson men saw school reform as a Whiggish attempt to pacify the masses, which to a limited extent it was. At issue was the level of government at which centralization was to occur and, by extension, whether schools would be inclusive institutions, how much they would cost, and who would pay for them. By 1860 barely 50 percent of the states could boast of officials responsible solely for supervising public schools within their jurisdictions. Localism, control of schools by local elites, thus gave way slowly—in some areas not until after the Civil War, in others not at all. Throughout, controversy centered around the question of who controlled schools, not whether education should be enforced. Also not at issue was *in loco parentis*, the use of schools as control agents.

During the antebellum years, neither became the issue, as schoolmen preoccupied themselves with what Francis Keppel, U.S. commissioner of education from 1962 to 1966, has termed the revolution for quantity education. Adhering in linear fashion to their self-appointed task, they launched plans for public high schools, campaigns for educating females, and studies of school architecture. Exceptions appeared among them, but for the most part these heirs of the Enlightenment bequest were sensible people, first-generation

46

bureaucrats. More than strident conflicts over slavery, economic uncertainties, and unsettling political realignments and clearly more than the imaginal impact of the frontier and western gold, school-men's absorption with duty formed the immediate context of efforts to nationalize their movement and determined their reaction to projected federal roles in school promotion.

A NATIONAL SCHOOL AGENCY: INITIAL PROPOSALS

A variety of plans came forth. In 1840 one group of citizens urged Congress to establish a department of agriculture and education to assist teachers in satisfying the vocational requirements of farm children. Continuing to seek supporters for his system of national education, Charles Brooks hoped at least for a national normal school which would prepare the way for the subsequent creation by Congress of a federal department of public instruction. Robert Dale Owen, during the mid 1840s a congressman from Indiana, vainly attempted to win his colleagues' approval of a plan for the Smithsonian Institution establishing the agency as an educational promotion bureau with a national normal school attached. The plans represented a wide assortment of perspectives on the proper federal role in education, but a common thread running through all of them was reliance upon the reform effectiveness of school data centrally collected and disseminated nationally.[21]

For a number of reasons the American Lyceum failed to act on the suggestion, heard at its 1832 meeting, that it employ a national school agent. The organization never developed a strong national structure and perennially found itself short of funds. More to the point, the proposal elicited mixed responses from Lyceum members. Some opposed it as unwise or improper; others simply professed no interest in the project. During the two decades prior to the Civil War, however, the national school agent idea gradually gained advocates. It became the focal point of discussions at two national gatherings promoted by Lyceum spokesmen in 1839 and 1840. The 1839 meeting, initially proposed by Charles Brooks, examined several ways the federal government could augment the spread of public instruction, including use of the Smithson bequest for establishing a national school agency. Also considered was William Cost Johnson's plan to return to the states federal funds

47

earmarked for educational purposes. Resolutions approving both proposals were forwarded to Congress. Confrontation over Brooks's more radical plan for national education was avoided when the irrepressible schoolman took himself to Europe before the meeting convened.[22]

The 1840 convention was dominated by more cautious reformers, Alexander D. Bache, for one, who was Benjamin Franklin's great grandson. It rejected suggestions for federal involvement in education in favor of the original Lyceum proposal for a privately employed national school agent. Delegates agreed to launch a campaign to collect funds for the prospective agent's salary and even passed the hat among themselves, but 1840 proved not to be a propitious year for ad hoc fund raising. A wild and exhausting presidential campaign occupied the country, only barely released from the hard realities of the 1837 panic.[23]

One reason the agent was never hired, beyond lack of funds and general interest, may have been that the action seemed unnecessary. During the period from 1838 to 1840, several educators, including Brooks, Barnard, and Mann, suggested expanding the 1840 census to include items designed to provide "the statistics of illiteracy, together with information respecting schools, academies, and colleges in the several states." In 1838 and 1839 Barnard traveled to Washington to discuss the proposal with President Van Buren and the secretary of state, whose department at the time was responsible for conducting the decennial census. Barnard took along his own proposed schedules for securing the desired information. An intense young scholar, not yet 30 years old, whose preeminence in the common school movement would be shadowed only by Horace Mann, Barnard convinced the president that such statistics were necessary to "a proper understanding of one of the vital interests of the country" and would be of special utility "to those who were laboring to improve the educational systems of the various states." Barnard's success, insignificant perhaps at the time, represented the first official step toward establishment of a federal school agency.[24]

In 1849 interest in the national school agent proposal resurfaced. The friends of education came together in October of that year "to strengthen and systematize educational advancement in the United States." As president of the convention, Horace Mann opened the session with a fresh affirmation of schools' social reforming power. Spread abroad every state and hamlet, they might yet, he thought, enable the Union to silence the secessionist threats heard even now on the floor of Congress. Nothing less than national unity should be the educators' ultimate objective in developing and improving schools. Needed, Mann concluded, were a permanent national organization of schoolmen and uniformity in the methods of organizing and reporting school data. Both strategies would enable educators to locate regional deficiencies in the quantity and quality of public education and draw intelligent comparisons among the nation's schools. The delegates agreed. In addition to laying plans for the organization of the American Association for the Advancement of Education, they appointed a committee to devise means for collecting reliable school statistics throughout the nation and endorsed a resolution to Congress requesting creation of a bureau of education in the Department of the Interior "to obtain and publish annually statistical information of Public Education in the United States." [25]

The petition aroused little interest in the Capitol. Failing to survive its committee assignments, it never reached the floor of Congress for debate. During the next decade, resolutions from both the American Association for the Advancement of Education and the National Teachers' Association endorsing the census bureau proposal met similar fates. Whether schoolmen could have overcome congressional opposition is doubtful, but they initially expended little energy attempting to do so. At the 1866 meeting of the American Institute of Instruction, when their efforts seemed close to success, someone had the temerity to suggest that the friends of education had in the process proved themselves to be politically impotent and naive.[26]

Henry Barnard presented the initial outline of his famous plan for a central educational agency to the second National Convention of the Friends of Education in 1850. The same year, the American Institute of Instruction received a modified version of the plan detailing a central educational bureau for New England. Neither organization greeted his efforts with enthusiasm. Four years later, fresh from yet another European tour, he unveiled his comprehensive "plan for the 'increase and diffusion of knowledge' of education, and especially of popular education, and measures for its improvement through the Smithsonian Institution or the American Association for the Advancement of Education." [27]

The proposal called upon the institution or the association to employ an "agent for education," and provide him with an office and space for a national educational library and museum in the capital. Far more than a mere collector and disseminator of school statistics, the agent was to be an international expert on the whole field of education, plan annual conferences of friends of education, submit to the sponsoring organization an annual report on the progress of education in each state and, if possible, each country, and edit a national educational journal. Barnard recognized educators' need for reliable, uniformly reported school statistics, but insisted that the mere enumeration of teachers, pupils, and schools provided an inadequate framework for reform. Implying that even friends of education needed their horizons expanded, he suggested that the actual increase and improvement of schools proceeded from an enlarged vision nourished by educational history, comparative statistics coupled with descriptions of school programs, and reports on recent innovations—all collected internationally and disseminated among the American people and their school and political leaders. Doubly assisted, local and state educational officials would not only be confronted with relative deficiencies in their schools but also equipped with ideas and alternative programs, in short, with practical incentives for improvement.

Barnard anticipated these results whether the central agency was privately sponsored by the association or incorporated in the work of the Smithsonian. He preferred the latter because the institution, in his opinion, was the logical agency to be involved in the increase and diffusion of knowledge about education and schools. To his consternation, the Smithsonian's executive secretary, Joseph Henry, rejected the plan; and the association, divided over proposals for nationalizing education, set it aside when funds to employ the agent failed to materialize. The following year, in 1855, Barnard launched the *American Journal of Education*, declaring his intention to realize the plan independently, if not all at once, at least in steps.

Seven years later, Senator James Dixon of Connecticut led an effort to have the educator elected to the Smithsonian's Board of Regents, only to have the nomination opposed by Henry. Barnard's long and bitter reply to Dixon's news traced the origins of his conflict with the institution's executive secretary. In Barnard's view, educational results, direct and indirect, might have accrued to the nation had Henry been willing in 1854 to incorporate the schoolman's plan for a central agency in the work of the Smithsonian:

You say my nomination as Regent of the Smithsonian Institution is opposed by Prof. Henry, and that he favors the appointment of President [Theodore Dwight] Woolsey of Yale College— Now there can be no better man. . . . You may be sure that Dr. Woolsey will embrace something besides bugs, living or dead, and "the dry bones of science" in his more generous views of "knowledge," "the increase and diffusion" of which "among men" it was Smithson's object to promote by his remarkable bequest.

     As for Prof. Henry's opposition to me, it grows out of my early and persistent efforts to get the science and art of Education recognized as worthy of both increase and diffusion through the agency of this bequest . . . we have in this country no national and as far as other countries are concerned no international medium of diffusion. In the prosecution of these efforts I submitted several years ago at the request of Bishop Potter, and several prominent friends of educational improvement a "plan" to Prof. Henry, which he did or promised to lay before the Regents. If that Plan, or something like it could have been adopted in the early organization of the Institution, with an appropriation of a sum not exceeding $3000 . . . a year from the income of the bequest—a sum which would not have embarrassed its operations in the increase and diffusion of knowledge in other directions, we should have had . . . in the city of Washington a system of Public Schools, which instead of being among the poorest, would have been among the best of the country. This would have been one of the immediate but indirect results of the Educational meetings and consequent local efforts [in the Capital]. Such results have followed similar meetings and efforts elsewhere. And this would have been no charge to [the] Institution.[28]

     In addition, Barnard continued, the Smithsonian would have housed an educational library and museum, encompassing "Educational Books, Pamphlets, and Material Aids of Instruction similar to the Educational Department in London, which was the result of the International Conference in 1854." In time, the "Repository would have grown into a great institution of plans and models of schoolhouses and furniture, of apparatus, maps, and other aids of Instruction, of Textbooks and Treatises on the History, Biography, Systems, Institutions, and Methodology of Education," capable of providing practical assistance to city and state officials throughout the country wishing to establish or improve public schools. To no avail, Barnard had offered to deposit his own sizeable library, "probably the largest in the country," with the institution to serve as a nucleus of the proposed educational repository. An officially sanctioned national journal of education would have been launched, Barnard argued, and finally, "without any recognition on the part of Congress of national education," there would have been in the annual report of the Smithsonian, a report of the educational agent,

> giving a summary of the progress of Education in each State, and to some extent, of different countries—and thus the advances which had been made in any one section, city, state or country would have become the property of every other, and been the means of perfecting all state and local systems and institutions, and thus advancing and perfecting the knowledge and virtue of the whole people.

Advancing and perfecting knowledge and virtue—these were the fruits Barnard anticipated. Had his plan been inaugurated in 1854, he suggested, "we should not have the appalling fact of more than a half million of the white adults of this country unable to write their names or read the vote they may cast into the ballot box." Most important, where "there is now no system or an imperfect and inefficient system of public schools, we might have had an efficient system at work in every state."

Barnard's plan reflected his fascination with European education; but a more immediate and obvious influence was the work of indirect external pressure being perfected on a smaller scale by state school officials in the North and Midwest. As the former chief school officer in Connecticut and Rhode Island, he not only knew of this work, he had been one of its pioneers. A third influence was his own ambition. With the appearance of his 1854 plan, the national school agent, long an idea in search of an author, found a claimant. Barnard wanted the job and shaped its description to suit his own scholarly predilections.

Given his experience as a school administrator, Barnard's lack of attention to administrative matters in his plan is revealing. The responsibilities of the central school agent were outlined in burdensome detail; yet Barnard proposed no staff to assist in carrying the enormous work load. With the same cavalier detachment he avoided the mundane question of money. To finance a national school agency privately would have involved the association in repeated fund-raising campaigns, not a likely possibility for an organization barely able to muster its members for annual meetings. In establishing the Smithsonian Institution, Congress had rejected efforts to include direct promotion of public education among its programs. This, in addition to limited funds, made even more remote the chance that the institution could underwrite Barnard's project. Beyond worrisome financial questions lay the complexities of control. Barnard failed to explain how the national agent, either as a private or quasi-public official, could gain the cooperation of state and local school leaders in collecting educational information. Lacking the authority to require their cooperation, the national agent would be forced to rely upon voluntary assistance, the flaw which had undermined the Lyceum's 1831 plan.

Barnard's proposal, although a more comprehensive plan than the projected bureau of educational statistics, rested nevertheless on the presumed reform effectiveness of educational information collected and published nationally. Overcoming opposition to common schooling clearly required action more direct than the dissemination of comparative school data or even the more cerebral exertions of Barnard's proposed national educational agent. Barriers to the increase of common schools could be attributed to local inertia, sloth, and schoolmen's lack of practical suggestions on how to establish and improve schools in their vicinities. Other sources of opposition, however, could also be found:

1. taxpayers who failed to appreciate the costs of schools or the notion that they should finance the education of others' offspring;
2. middle and low income people who doubted the value of public high schools to their children;
3. Roman Catholics who detected a Protestant bias in the common schools;
4. parents who favored private education for its social prestige value or its religious instruction; and
5. citizens dead against the proposition that everyone should be educated or even schooled.

The indirect strategy, reform by example or suggestion, could have at best limited effectiveness amid the contending values of a pluralistic society. This may explain why many school reformers continued to cling to the arcadian hope of a homogeneous union of states. Barnard and other schoolmen, pushing for a modicum of federal involvement in school promotion, acknowledged their plans' weaknesses but elected the way of indirection as the most likely to succeed given the heightening sectional feelings and sharpening polarization over the slavery issue characteristic of the late 1850s. After all, the strategy was meeting gradual success on the state level.

If Barnard entertained any illusions about the acceptability of his plan, he must have been jolted by the cool reception it received from his fellow schoolmen. The problem, mourned Zalmon Richards, first president of the National Teachers' Association, derived from teachers' ambivalence toward "nationalization" of the school crusade, not the flaws inherent in Barnard's proposal. A number of other suggestions for nationalizing school reform appeared in the 1850s, including an attempt by A. D. Bache to revive interest in a national university; but in each case schoolmen's responses were lukewarm. Toward the close of the decade, members of the National Teachers' Association reached consensus on the plan for a national bureau of educational statistics but failed to support the proposal beyond endorsing brief resolutions at annual meetings.[29]

AMBIGUITIES OF ENFORCED EDUCATION

The founding years of the Office of Education would be easier to reconstruct, the story simpler and more dramatic, if this initial period could be depicted as a conflict between forces of centralization (representing undemocratic school control) and the defenders of decentralization (representing democratic control). However, the issue over school control was much more complex. Decentralized control, especially in towns and cities but also in outlying districts, could be highly centralized through the influence of local elites. It did not necessarily generate popular support for public schooling, inclusive and equal educational opportunities, or democratic policy-making procedures. And, of course, it was powerless to equalize education within a state or throughout the nation. In actuality, the conflict over school centralization tended to pit the forces of centralization against each other, the issue being the level of authority (local, state or federal) that would ultimately shape public school programs and policies. Intermingled with the level of

54

authority issue was the question of the role of professional educators in school control and management. Professionalism and bureaucratization, viewed initially as reforms for guaranteeing common, that is, equalized, learning opportunities, occurred at state and local, particularly urban, levels. Later, they would also shape the roles and functions of the U.S. Office of Education. And wherever they took hold, both strengthened the centralizing tendencies in American public education. Ironically, both also proved to be curiously and stubbornly provincial. To be sure, democratic control of schools did not constitute a major objective of the schoolmen advocating state and federal educational offices. They wanted popular support for their movement, not popular control of schools. Their campaigns for state school agencies and suggestions for federal involvement in school promotion represented attempts to render schools more efficient and more effective. Effectiveness, it was believed, required an inclusive student population, not democratic control of schools. The aim was to realize greater homogeneity through common education, not to alienate with patterns of exclusion and inequality.

The objective collided with exclusionary practices generated and reinforced within local communities. In the North, as well as in the South, large segments of the population were either excluded from public schools or if included denied a voice in determining their goals, curricula, and policies. Exclusion thus came in a variety of forms, for example, the blatant anti-Catholic bias of teachers and textbooks which crippled the schools of the Public School Society in New York City during the 1830s and '40s. The list of those with limited access to public schools is impressive by its length if nothing else—newcomers and outsiders, immigrant parents, especially non-Protestants and communicants of pietistic sects, black people, Indians, farm migrants in cities, and working class people generally.

Southern participation in national educational organizations associated with the common school movement was minimal during the Jackson and antebellum years. But southern leaders' rejection of the movement cannot be taken as evidence that they or their constituents held education in low esteem, a point of view many common school advocates found inviting. The laws proscribing education of slaves, which swept through southern legislatures after a series of slave revolts in the early 1830s, showed, if nothing else, respect for the subversive power of learning. More positive evidence of southern interest in education can be found in the increasing numbers of public and quasi-public schools and academies which appeared during the antebellum years, particularly in the cities. Not lack of appreciation for learning but uneven commitment to common schooling opportunities characterized southern education during this period. And the dominant mode of school control remained local or private. Except in North Carolina, state agencies for supervising and promoting public instruction could not be found. Missing, in short, was the drive for quantity education which had eventually taken shape in the North, an effort entangled as both cause and effect with the articulation of common school objectives: national unity, patriotism, and shared values through uniform educational programs. Unmoved by the lure of homogeneity, southerners apparently intended to remain near their own agents of control and hence opposed extending the process of school centralization even to the state level. Finally, but clearly not the least significant, southern leaders during the 1850s, equipped with prescience sharpened by years of defending the "peculiar character" of their people, increasingly perceived the common school as a breeding ground for abolitionists. Later they would also oppose the creation of a federal department of education, viewing it as an extension of the free school system, "that hated New England institution." [30]

The ambiguities of American school centralization become clear as one examines the implications of campaigns for inclusive public schools. Education planned *for* people *not with* them, fashioning people not fashioned by them, encourages exclusiveness of a different order: people whose hearts and heads have been schooled for obedience, kept, in part by their own acquiescence, in their political and economic places. The common education of all, recorded and measured with increasing efficiency in comparative statistics, served, on the one hand, as a means for promoting effective social control. Yet it also stood as a beneficent translation of the original assertion that in a self-governing republic all of the people must be educated. Either alternative assumed the necessity of enforcing education, a goal anticipating the reform of people and society itself as outcomes. In 1860 the idea of a national bureau of education evoked similar ambiguities and hopes. It bears emphasizing, however, that development of the school movement's reform agenda reflected not so much schools' accomplishments during the 1830 to 1860 period—for example, their impact on children and parents or their success in delivering common school opportunity—

as the belief of schoolmen and friends of education in the reforming potential of schools. Accordingly, initial proposals for a national educational office envisioned an agency to assist and encourage an emerging educational profession in realizing its dreams. The plans promised school reform through an upward extension of a still-forming school bureaucracy.

2 Campaigns for a National Bureau of Education: Response to Crisis

WAR AND NATIONAL EDUCATION

Thirteen years later, in 1880, Henry Barnard still insisted that passage of the Department of Education Act resulted primarily from the absence of southern representation in Congress. Despite overwhelming evidence to the contrary, he could never free himself from believing that Democrats in general and southerners in particular loomed as the new agency's most fearsome enemies. His belief represented a minor untruth, a mixture of half-fact romantically befuddled, not unlike other partial explanations current at the time, for example, that white southerners fought to save a gentle civilization or that their northern counterparts rushed into battle to liberate black men from slavery. Barnard's explanation implied a periodization of the American past, not unheard of before or since. For him, secession and Civil War prepared the way for a significant turning point in American public school development. He also succeeded in simplifying the convoluted train of occurrences which resulted, as much by accident as by design, in the creation of the Department of Education in 1867.[1]

For advocates of common schooling, war arrived as a disruption and temporary cure. Although business as usual became impossible, no outbreak of new ideas about educational goals or school organization followed as direct effects from the events of 1861. Nor in the long run was there dramatic recovery and implementation of the original vision that the people must be educated, that literacy and common morality represented an inadequate translation of the hope for enlightened citizens who if nothing else could perceive the subtle shapes of ambition in the workings of government. In respect to these matters, no turning point in

58

American school history occurred in the 1860s. Still, for two—three at the most—heated years following Appomattox, chances for more startling consequences appeared strong, not because of oratory, which flourished, but because national and private pain drove so many citizens and leaders alike to the realization that the country needed healing and that learning spread broadly and indiscriminately might help. In the wake of prolonged conflicts over reconstruction policies, backlashing notions of white supremacy, and uncomplicated inertia, however, public zeal flagged, and appeals for equal schooling opportunities and universal education subsided. In all honesty, large numbers in both the North and the South—workmen, shopkeepers, farmers, recent immigrants, in general those with modest incomes and aspirations, especially the ones rendered poor by the war—were never very zealous anyway. Schools and talk about schools must indeed have seemed far removed from their more immediate worries. Black people, particularly freedmen, represented a notable exception. Their clamor for schools and learning startled the reformers' fondest hopes. For a host of reasons, the opportunities slipped away. The drive for a national bureau of education, beginning for all practical purposes in 1865 and ending two years later with the agency's creation, served as one of the arenas in which promises of school reform were made and subsequently withdrawn.

Even before the start of hostilities, educationist passion, reborn of moral outrage, converged on the South with the novel, if predictable, view that the lack of common schools in that region lay at the source of the nation's domestic conflict. "Ignorance shattered the Union," concluded a speaker at the American Institute of Instruction's 1861 meeting, and only the spread and improvement of popular instruction could re-establish it. Two years later, Connecticut schoolman B. G. Northrop invited his institute audience to believe that "the Rebellion was made possible only by the absence of the Free Schools in the South." Had southern people been educated, he continued, the Articles of Secession would have failed in every state, for the masses would have seen through the plots of their leaders. As it was, the masses conformed to the "widely acknowledged alliance of treason and ignorance." Noting the tradition of free common schools in the North which taught children "to value personal worth and intrinsic merit wherever developed," Samuel Stillman Greene (1865 president of the National Teachers' Association) argued that the lack of such schools in the South had

59

engendered "sectional and selfish jealousies" which in turn had led to war. "Education is the chief unifying process on which we can rely for a permanent peace," he concluded, echoing a sentiment heard throughout the war years among northern schoolmen.[2]

Armed with such justification, northern enthusiasts determined to impose the New England common school on the confederate states. "The old slave states are to be a new missionary ground for the national schoolmaster," announced Charles Brooks, while Samuel Greene, and others who should have known better joined in the proclamation. Southern whites, they argued, stood in need of citizenship schooling designed to reclaim their loyalty. Long before black educator Booker T. Washington appeared on the scene, white northern schoolmen agreed that "thorough education" for black people meant "basic instruction in the 3 R's, moral education, and industrial training." That southern people, unionists and secessionists alike, whites as well as blacks, deserved to be consulted on plans for their education, or even that doing so might be a clever strategy, apparently never occurred to the northerners. Instead, one heard from common schoolmen in the 1860s self-congratulations, using the rhetoric, rationale, and ambiguous appeals for enforcing education devised during their movement's formative years. The enthusiasm was not new either, except in contrast to the quiet fatigue that had moderated claims of schools' social reform capability during the 1850s. Henry Barnard, speaking to the Ohio Teachers Association in 1865, managed to express the movement's fresh sense of mission, while revealing how little secession and war had affected his thinking about schools' objectives:

> There is a duty incumbent upon all of us, in reference to the great national results that have grown out of the war. We are not the same people; our history is not the same as it would have been if we had not gone through the experience of the last four years. It has settled some questions in regard to the nationality of this people; and that great truth must from this time forward be taught not only as a part of history, but must be recognized in the daily life of every citizen of this country; and to be so taught, it must come into the schools and be taught in the same words and in the same spirit in every part of the land.[3]

Buried beneath the leaden idealism and hopelessly overdrawn characterizations of the nation's schools were remnants of

Emerson E. White, Ohio school-
man and leader in the effort to create a
national bureau of education. Courtesy
of the Archives, Purdue University Li-
braries.

hopes on which American public education began: schooling insist-
ently linked to national welfare and the consequent requirement that
no one be omitted from either. Roles played by well-educated
southerners in the secessionist effort, antebellum growth of public
schools in the urban South, the lifeless uniformity, decried at times
even by Henry Barnard, creeping into American common education,
the low-quality schooling available to rural children North and
South—these phenomena, which would have blurred their stark
contrasts of education in the two regions, the schoolmen overlooked.
The essential difference between northern and southern education,
Greene explained more accurately, lay not in the quality of schooling
offered but in its amount and distribution. Hence, "some scheme
must be devised which shall have the sanction and protection of
Government for the universal education of the Southern people,"
particularly, he added, freedmen and poor whites. Emerson E.
White, Ohio's commissioner of common schools, agreed. Addressing
the first meeting of the National Association of School Superintendents in 1866, he cautioned his audience to remember

> a fundamental law running through the entire history of
> educational progress. . . . An ignorant community has no
> inward impulse to educate itself. Just where education is most
> needed, there it is always least appreciated and valued. . . .

> The demand for education is always awakened by external
> influences and agencies.[4]

In the past, not all northern schoolmen had agreed with
White's law of external pressure. Many had fought the imposition of
a state system of supervision upon their schools and even more had
rejected proposed federal roles in school promotion. When reports of
southern resistance to reconstruction began circulating throughout
the North, however, doubters among them lapsed into silence. The
N.T.A. gathered in August 1865, amid northern fury over southern
harassment of Union soldiers, loyal whites, and black people.
Headline accounts of clandestine mob brutality by strangely named
organizations reverberated across the country. Enraged by the
mistreatment of northern teachers who had followed the Union
armies south, many with a missionary's zeal for educating former
slaves, schoolmen found reasons aplenty, solidly moral ones, for not
consulting southerners, particularly whites, on plans for their education. With a mixture of enthusiasm and despair, they turned to the
idea of a national bureau of education as a mechanism for enforcing
the equal distribution of common schooling in the South. Nourished
thus by war fever, outrage, self-righteousness, and long-standing
confidence in education's reforming potential, the modest, thirty-
five-year-old plan for providing states and communities, but more
directly school administrators, with incentives for school improvement in the form of comparative statistics, blossomed into a strategy
for guaranteeing the literacy, loyalty, and morality of black people
and southern whites through enforced common education. Isolated
voices even ventured to add that the proposed federal agency might
also serve to improve the quality of education and equalize schooling
opportunities among Union states and territories.

A National Bureau of Education: Models of Federal School Reform

Three loosely constructed plans for a national education
bureau emerged from schoolmen's wartime deliberations. None was
new or, with the possible exception of Charles Brooks's proposal,
distinctive from the others. Each plan projected a federal agency

intended to thrust school reform into the forefront of reconstruction programs. Differences among them, for the most part implicit and subtle, concerned the mode of enforcement to be employed by the agency.

The plan for a national bureau of educational statistics, endorsed with mild interest in N.T.A. resolutions before and during the war, represented a refinement of the 1831 American Lyceum scheme for the collection and dissemination of school data. Urged on by Samuel Greene, James P. Wickersham, Andrew Jackson Rickoff, and other N.T.A. spokesmen, delegates to the organization's 1865 gathering supported the plan with unprecedented enthusiasm. Chided by Rickoff for their unhealthy detachment from politics, schoolmen organized state committees to lobby for their plan. Six months hence, in February 1866, the National Association of School Superintendents, an outgrowth of the N.T.A., met in Washington to elicit active congressional support for the proposed agency. To this gathering, Emerson White addressed his persuasive rationale for a federal school agency, culminating a decade of discussions within the N.T.A.

In White's view, three educational policy options confronted the federal government in the aftermath of the war. It could (1) establish a national system of education; (2) require states to maintain systems of public schools; or, (3) "by conditioned appropriations and by a system of general inspection and encouragement through the agency of a National Bureau of Education, induce each State to maintain an efficient school system." Fearing the dampening of state initiative and the removal of school control from municipal and state authorities, he rejected the first two alternatives. Only to ensure schooling for freedmen, whom "government must protect and educate," should federal intervention be encouraged. For White, the third alternative remained safely within American political and educational traditions. The proposed bureau, "without its being invested with any official control of the school authorities in the several states," could, in his words, "revolutionize" American public instruction. Change would result primarily from the agency's securing more uniformity and accuracy in collecting and disseminating school statistics. In addition, the bureau would be entrusted with responsibility for determining the comparative value of state and local school systems; diffusing knowledge of school laws and types of school organization found in the states; publishing reports on educational experiments; aiding communities in establishing schools; and publicizing "correct ideas about the value of education." The work of the bureau in the South, thought White, would provide the necessary complement to land reform efforts being pushed in Congress. New property holders, if educated, would be better equipped to use their land wisely and defend it against schemes to reclaim it. White had great confidence in the power of data, disseminated across the country, to stimulate school improvement; but his suggested "conditioned appropriations" and inspections of schools indicated that he anticipated the necessity of more direct external pressure to achieve his revolution in education. The key to the bureau's success, in White's opinion, would be its administrator. He must be a "Horace Mann," someone possessing "a mind that comprehends the aim and scope of education, its philosophy, its history, its processes, its practical details." [5]

Unlike the N.T.A. plan, Henry Barnard's proposal for a central school agency remained essentially a private creation, an uncompromising attempt to expand the intellectual horizons of schoolmen and guarantee the growth and improvement of public instruction through the work of a federal agency. Throughout the 1860s, he found no reason to change or update the goals and functions of the proposed bureau from those outlined before the American Association for the Advancement of Education in 1854. Indeed, events after 1861 served to strengthen his confidence in the plan's wisdom. Furthermore, he refused to commit himself to a fixed organization for the bureau. Whether it was an independent agency, a branch of the Smithsonian Institution, or a lone clerk working in another federal department mattered little to him. The goal of schoolmen, he cautioned the Ohio Teachers Association in 1865, ought to be the "insinuation" of education in the heart of government, the conscription of federal authority, however nominally at the outset, in the cause of school reform. Although convinced of the value of nationwide data gathering and dissemination, Barnard stubbornly adhered to his view of a national school agency with prerogatives far transcending mere census-taking functions. Nevertheless, his only explicit objection to the N.T.A. proposal concerned White's allusion to Horace Mann as the model school administrator. Barnard complained to the Ohioan that others had served the cause of public education with equal distinction. Beyond this minor point, he accepted the N.T.A. plan for what it was—a narrowed version of his own proposal.[6]

With characteristic exuberance and an eye on Union victory, Charles Brooks revived his plan for a national system of schools in 1864. Weaknesses evident in the original 1839 version remained—for example, the failure to define relations among local, state, and projected federal school agencies; but on the status of the federal agency within the national government, the plan spoke clearly. Needed to mend the Union, Brooks insisted, was a cabinet-level federal school bureau headed by a secretary of public instruction. In addition to collecting and disseminating educational data, the secretary was to (1) superintend a tuition-free system of local schools, state secondary institutions and colleges, and national universities; (2) evaluate the effectiveness and quality of each level and phase of the operation, including curricula; and (3) submit an annual report to Congress. Leaving worrisome details to the federal legislature, Brooks urged Congress to establish procedures for impelling towns and states "to create, support and manage" free schools. Only federal intervention, he warned, could guarantee the education of freedmen, to whom "the national government stands at this time *in loco parentis*," and also European immigrants, "some of whom have opinions and principles adverse to our established institutions, especially on the subject of ecclesiastical rights and sway." He continued: "The Anglo-Saxon blood on this side of the globe must faithfully educate and peacefully lead the other races. It is our destiny, and *we must fulfill it*." To counter arguments that the Constitution forbad federal school legislation, Brooks offered an amendment prohibiting illiterates to marry which he concluded would enable Congress to take the necessary actions and provide a suitable inducement to those otherwise unwilling to benefit from free schooling.[7]

Three campaigns, not one, developed in support of the plans, although Brooks's effort represented, more clearly than the others, a one-man operation. Essentially alike, the Barnard and N.T.A. proposals generated two campaigns principally because each proposal intertwined with efforts in behalf of different candidates for the position of commissioner of the projected bureau. Brooks's campaign included unsuccessful attempts to interest the N.T.A. and the American Institute of Instruction in his plan and countless trips to Washington to hound old friends, such as Charles Sumner, and other congressional and administration leaders with his version of a domestic white man's burden which in his view justified enforcing education on the populace. In time, wearied by what must have been a lonely venture and ridiculed even in the pages of the *Massachusetts Teacher*, Brooks concluded that the country was not yet ready for a national system of education. Unburdening himself to Barnard, an old friend, in a February 1865 letter, he insisted the important issue was not his own plan.

> What I care for is, that when our Constitution is altered, we may insert the angel element of education with a Bureau of Education at Washington and a Minister of Public Instruction who is a member of the cabinet. It can be done and it ought to be done.

Subsequently, Brooks prevailed upon Congressman Nathaniel Banks to present a petition outlining his proposal to the Thirty-ninth Congress, but the plan was never discussed on the House floor. Quite likely, he succeeded more in frightening congressmen away from the idea of a national school agency than in attracting them to it. Next to Brooks's plan, the proposal for a national bureau of educational statistics must have seemed tame indeed.[8]

Charles Brooks's unhinged paternalism contrasted sharply with Henry Barnard's unswerving caution. In his twilight years, the Connecticut educator fondly linked the start of his campaign for a national school bureau with his success in expanding the 1840 census to include educational statistics. His prominence in formulating the plan for such an agency was indisputable, particularly after the 1854 presentation of his scheme before the American Association for the Advancement of Education. However, his efforts remained sporadic at best until 1864. At their annual meeting in August of that year, N.T.A. delegates heard their first formal discussion of the national bureau idea in an address by Illinois schoolman S. H. White, who reiterated the major points found in Barnard's proposal. On motions by White, they approved a resolution endorsing the plan for a national bureau of education and appointed a three member committee to secure the establishment of such an agency during the next session of the Thirty-eighth Congress. As a member of the committee, Barnard, along with White and Zalmon Richards, launched, with energy heretofore lacking, his campaign for a national school bureau.[9]

Spurred on by the thought that at last his decade-old proposal neared realization, Barnard set to work encouraging schoolmen to join him in a massive letter-writing campaign to key congressmen. He dispatched Samuel Bates, a frequent correspondent and pioneer Pennsylvania schoolman, in search of Thaddeus Stevens' famous 1835 speech on education, presumably in order to publish it, thus reminding the House's leading radical of his earlier pronounce-ment on the need for legislative leadership in effecting school reform. An attempt to organize groups of schoolmen from across the country to travel to Washington for the purpose of talking with members of Congress failed. With Bates's assistance, however, Barnard elicited from Pennsylvania Congressman Glenni W. Scofield not only a promise to support the national bureau plan when presented in Congress but also the advice that without an aroused public sentiment in favor of the proposal, Congress could not be expected to respond favorably. Only a few months earlier, in December 1864, Congressman John Pruyn, a Democrat and former regent of the University of the State of New York known for his interest in education, introduced a resolution instructing "the Committee of Ways and Means to inquire into and report upon, the expediency of creating in the Department of the Interior a Bureau on the Statistics of Education." The motion carried, but whether Thaddeus Stevens' Ways and Means Committee ever discussed it is uncertain. The report requested by the resolution was never submitted. Pruyn and Barnard corresponded on occasion, but there is no evidence that Barnard had anything to do with the New Yorker's resolution. The lack of congressional enthusiasm for Pruyn's suggestion at least confirmed Scofield's pessimism about eliciting interest in the bureau from members of the Thirty-eighth Congress.[10]

By April 1865, Barnard was not sanguine about his chances for success. He confided to Elisha Potter that he would be pleased if Congress would simply agree to establish "an American Library of Education," a repository of educational literature in Washington open to all who might come to the capital in search of information on how to improve schools. Renewing the offer he once made to Joseph Henry in hopes of persuading him to create a school bureau within the Smithsonian Institution, Barnard indicated willingness to donate his personal library "as a start."

A month later, he and S. H. White hit upon a strategy which they hoped would give bureau advocates more leverage with political leaders. If state teachers associations would endorse the bureau idea at annual meetings during the summer and fall, the schoolmen reasoned, they might succeed in convincing Congress that the proposal enjoyed strong backing throughout the country. As part of the strategy, Barnard launched a fresh letter-writing campaign directed to state school leaders and attended the summer meeting of the influential Ohio Teachers Association. Unfortunately, he lost the opportunity to head a similar operation sponsored by the N.T.A. when he failed to attend the organization's crucial 1865 gathering.[11]

Like Charles Brooks's effort, Barnard's campaign remained for the most part a lonely and not much more successful affair. His attempt to gain congressional approval of the bureau began during the relatively brief session of the Thirty-eighth Congress, which convened in December 1864, and adjourned three months later. To win support for a measure of such doubtful popularity, Barnard would have been required to start work long before the session began. His correspondence suggests that he did not commence his efforts until after the first of the year. Hence, with justification Scofield advised educators to set their sights on the Thirty-ninth Congress, which would not meet until December 1865. If Barnard hoped to garner administration support during the interim, the strategy was dashed by the immeasurable confusion of celebration and melancholy which enveloped the capital and the Union states in the spring of 1865. Abetted by his long cherished hope of becoming commissioner of education, the Connecticut schoolman continued lobbying for a national educational agency. However, after 1865 the N.T.A. effort acquired fresh leadership.[12]

Neither schoolmen nor political leaders had been much affected by the campaign for the bureau before the N.T.A.'s 1865 meeting. The failure, concluded Andrew Rickoff, outspoken superintendent of Cincinnati's public schools, belonged to the friends of education who had evidenced little energy in pressing the matter upon Congress. Educational organizations, in his view, had been too satisfied with learned discussions, approving resolutions, yet too little committed to extending educational opportunity. If the organizations would intervene effectively, Rickoff suggested, the federal government would learn to recognize common education and school reform as parts of its responsibility for promoting the general welfare. Within three years passions cooled considerably. In the meantime, growing numbers of schoolmen joined the clamor for a national bureau of education.[13]

While Barnard vainly attempted to field a nationally organized campaign of schoolmen and failed to locate a congressional sponsor for his plan, Emerson White, with assistance from Rickoff and Samuel Greene, succeeded in doing both. Letters to congressmen multiplied and resolutions from state teachers organizations endorsing the bureau plan poured into the Capitol. The decision of the new National Association of School Superintendents to meet in Washington brought the campaign to a head. The association gathered on 6 February 1866, just two months after the first session of the Thirty-ninth Congress convened. Congressmen and administration representatives sat in the audience which heard White's discussion of the bureau and the role it could play in reconstruction. They witnessed the debate and subsequent passage of his resolution petitioning Congress to establish the proposed agency. Although no one could argue that the schoolmen's campaign replaced either the Capitol's preoccupation with the politics and economics of reconstruction or the ominous quarrel developing between Andrew Johnson and congressional leaders, few could deny that the issue of a national bureau of education had at last arrived in Washington.[14]

Studied differences separated White's resolution from his earlier remarks before the superintendents. Gone, for example, were references to land reform in the South and the paramount role of external pressure to improve schools. A moderate document intended to placate both schoolmen and politicians fearful of federal intrusion into educational matters, the resolution called upon Congress to establish a school bureau for collecting and disseminating educational statistics. Through its census-taking functions, the statement read, the proposed agency could serve as a force for school reform. Upon approving their resolution, the superintendents directed White, Newton Bateman, Illinois superintendent of public instruction, and J. S. Adams, secretary of the Vermont Board of Education, to deliver it to Congress. Unwilling to leave the matter at that, White authored a bill stipulating the structure and functions of the proposed bureau and deposited both documents with fellow

Ohioan, Congressman James A. Garfield. On 14 February 1866, Garfield presented the resolution in Congress, at the same time introducing a bill calling for the establishment of a bureau of educational statistics in the Department of the Interior.[15]

WHAT THE FARMERS TAUGHT THE TEACHERS AND OTHER PRECEDENTS

Precedent legislation cleared the way for Congress's acceding to the schoolmen's request. Historian Gordon Lee has identified the Land Grant College, Freedmen's Bureau, and Department of Education Acts as precursors of the federal aid to education debate which occupied Congress periodically from 1870 to 1890. The first two pieces of legislation, enacted during the war, also set precedents for the last one. Justin Morrill originally introduced the land grant college bill in 1857 to promote scientific, agricultural, and industrial studies and controlled agricultural experimentation, but found his proposal embroiled in a bitter dispute over the constitutionality of federal involvement in education. The measure narrowly passed both Houses only to be vetoed by President Buchanan. A revised version of the bill, introduced in 1861, enlarged the size of the land grants to be made available to the states and added military tactics to the list of subjects to be taught in the proposed colleges. Further linked to the Union war effort by arguments that the land grant colleges would encourage more efficient farming in the North, now cut off from the products of southern agriculture, the measure easily won congressional and presidential approval in 1862. For schoolmen, passage of the Morrill Act confirmed educational reform as a national priority, a point they had long sought to have ratified.[16]

The Freedmen's Bureau Act, signed by President Lincoln in 1865, did not mention education. Strengthened by subsequent legislation, the bureau in time assumed major responsibility for promoting black education in the South. Lee considered the act relevant to the history of federal aid to education because it represented a new form of federal initiative, approved by Congress for admittedly mixed reasons. Assigned "the supervision and management of all abandoned lands, and the control of all subjects relating to refugees and freedmen from rebel States, or from any district . . . within the territory embraced in the operations of the army," the bureau was to provide humanitarian services, primarily to black people, and promote the loyalty of freedmen to the Union. Its creation, said its supporters, would strengthen the resolve of black men fighting in Union armies and help alleviate the desperate situation of former slaves and white refugees in the South. A federal agency was required, they argued, because the public evidenced little concern for the plight of white loyalists and freedmen and because the problems to be solved surpassed the limited resources of interested individuals or philanthropic organizations. Congressional foes countered that none of the supporting arguments established the bureau's constitutionality, but the specter of the black man also haunted their opposition. Samuel S. Cox, a Democrat from Ohio, viewed the agency as commencing a policy "so latitudinarian that the whole system of our Government is changed" then pressed on to decry "this eleemosynary system for blacks." Complaining of yet another plot of New England humanitarians, wealthy at the expense of western toil, Cox continued:

> No Government farming system, no charitable black scheme, can wash out the color of the negro, change his inferior nature, or save him from his inevitable fate. The irrepressible conflict is not between slavery and freedom, but between black and white; and, as De Tocqueville prophesied, the black will perish.

The Democratic party in the North was not pro-slavery, he insisted, but "anti-intervention." The Republican party by dragging down slavery attacked the very genius of American civil polity, local self-government. Although other congressmen no doubt shared Cox's blatant racism, in the end, pushed by an amalgam of humanitarian feelings and war fever too fine to measure, the bureau won approval in both Houses without a division.[17]

For Cox, the freedmen's bureau bill constituted an unprecedented violation of the states' rights doctrine. That doctrine, historian Arthur Meier Schlesinger once observed, "has never had any real vitality independent of underlying conditions of vast social, economic or political significance." The period beginning with 1865 and continuing two or three years thereafter constituted one of those interludes in which, according to Schlesinger, heretofore unassailable structures and traditions weakened, if only for a while. In the case of

71

the Freedmen's Bureau a sense of urgency bred of the times overwhelmed the constitutional question, hence shortcircuiting congressional allegiance to traditional modes of government action. The new kind of federal initiative thus established served in turn as precedent for a federal school agency, intended, also for mixed reasons, to solve a problem of national proportions, the unequal distribution of educational opportunities.[18]

Later generations forgot, but to schoolmen lobbying for a bureau of education, the Department of Agriculture Act of 1862 became the clearest, and in some respects most bothersome, precedent. The drive for a farm bureau originated in 1839 when the United States Patent Office employed a modest $1000 appropriation to begin collecting and disseminating agricultural data and seeds to the nation's farmers. Ironically, Patent Commissioner Henry L. Ellsworth initiated the program because of his interest in agriculture, not in response to demands from farmers. Strengthened by increased appropriations, the program became the major function of the Agriculture Division of the Patent Office when Congress transferred the latter to the newly organized Department of the Interior in 1849. Henry Barnard, Alonzo Potter, and the friends of education who met in national convention later that year hoped that a bureau of education with functions similar to those performed by the Agriculture Division would be added to the new department. However, their petition urging such action fell on deaf congressional ears.

In the 1850s, agricultural organizations assumed leadership of the campaign for a national farm agency. The United States Agricultural Society, dominated by large land-holding farmers and representatives from farm-related industries, appeared on the scene in 1852, at about the same time educators formed the American Association for the Advancement of Education. The new organization agreed that creation of a bureau of agriculture in the Department of the Interior should become one of its primary objectives. A reluctant Congress soon found itself besieged with petitions from county and state farm groups supporting the society's proposal. While refusing to inaugurate a new federal agency, despite endorsements by Presidents Taylor and Fillmore, Congress dramatically increased annual appropriations to the Patent Office for the promotion of agriculture during the remainder of the decade. By 1862, its mood had shifted. Armed with endorsements from Lincoln, Secretary of the Interior Caleb B. Smith and members of the Agricultural Society in Congress, Illinois Congressman Owen Lovejoy delivered to the House in February of that year a bill calling for the establishment of not a mere bureau, but a sub-cabinet level department of agriculture. After defeating attempts, on the one hand, to house the proposed agency in the Department of the Interior, and, on the other, to grant it cabinet status, Congress agreed to the unusual designation.[19]

The duties of the new department included a broad mandate "to acquire and to diffuse among the people of the United States useful information on subjects connected with agriculture . . . and to procure, propagate, and distribute among the people new and valuable seeds and plants." * In addition, the commissioner of agriculture was to submit an annual report on his work to the president and "special reports on particular subjects whenever required to do so by the President or either house of Congress, or when he shall think the subject in his charge requires it." Allowed to appoint a chief clerk who would assume responsibility for the department in his absence, the commissioner received authority to appoint other employees, including temporary researchers, only "as Congress may from time to time provide." Both principal officers were required to post bonds with the United States treasurer. Thus, Congress carefully defined the commissioner's power to enlarge his staff, while encouraging him to initiate investigations into matters related to the work of his agency. Later, it failed to give similar attention to the department of education bill. Ratified by overwhelming majorities in both Houses, the department of agriculture bill became law on 15 May 1862.[20]

Compared with their farm counterparts, who valued their prerogatives and independence as much as the next man, school leaders vacillated throughout the war years on the question of creating a national bureau of education. Troubled by possible intrusions into privately encircled jurisdictions, they nonetheless cast covetous eyes over the favors Congress bestowed on farmers. Clearly, the farmers taught the teachers a lesson in practical politics. Moreover, the success of their campaigns for a federal agricultural agency contained an irony the schoolmen should have been able to appreciate. Initially, at least, it was spearheaded, like the common school movement itself, from the top, by "gentlemen agriculturalists"

* See Appendix 2 for a copy of the Department of Agriculture Act.

not the masses of farmers with their modest acreages. The prevailing attitude of the latter toward the federal government tended to be a curt "For God's sake let us alone." They got their department anyway, a victory won through effective lobbying by farm organizations and the support of presidents and leading politicians. In 1862, the Agricultural Society counted among its members five ex-presidents, Abraham Lincoln, Justin Morrill, and Horace Greeley. Also influential, in a diffuse sort of way, although for that reason not to be discounted, was a popular attachment to rural imagery. Americans thought of themselves as a nation of farmers, as indeed they were at the time. Thus, while the Department of Agriculture was not a "pulse quickening subject in those days," especially within the farming community, the idealized farmer was. Even if he was not exactly sure he wanted it, he had a slot in the federal bureaucracy.[21]

A relatively solemn lot, the schoolmen evidenced no awareness of the irony in the farmers' victory. A bureau of education, complained Zalmon Richards in 1858, "has quite as much claim for Government support as that of Agriculture," but he recognized not an intractable Congress but the lack of consensus among schoolmen as the major barrier to an effective drive for a federal school agency. In truth, both contributed to the campaign's difficulties. Nevertheless, Andrew Rickoff repeated the criticism at the 1865 N.T.A. gathering. Suggesting the Department of Agriculture Act as a model for the proposed school agency, Rickoff became the first advocate of a sub-cabinet level educational department. "We need to ask for no higher power for the Commissioner of Education within his department," he concluded, "than is assigned to the Commissioner of Agriculture within his." As it turned out, the Department of Agriculture Act provided the pattern for creating autonomous sub-cabinet federal agencies that was subsequently followed in writing both the freedmen's bureau and department of education bills.[22]

Predictably, the campaigns for a federal school agency tended to coalesce once the bureau of education bill reached the House. Hardly able to conceal his disappointment, Charles Brooks abandoned his own plan, at least for a time, in favor of White's moderate proposal. He viewed the bill as a step in the right direction, although an unconscionably timid one. Barnard intensified his letter-writing effort and, upon accepting the presidency of St. John's College in Annapolis, became a persistent advocate for the bill in the

Capitol. White wrote letters, too, confident that if the measure could be passed, Garfield would see to it.[23]

More apparent than actual, the campaign's unity cloaked differences and overlooked omissions as potentially detrimental to the future of a federal educational agency as schoolmen's now traditional ambivalence about establishing such a bureau in the first place. Correspondence between Brooks, Barnard, White, and their supporters gave the semblance of accord, but their unity derived from the proximate goal. On other, more penultimate, matters—for example, the nature of the crisis to be resolved by school reform; the meaning and urgency of equal educational opportunity and its role in reconstruction; the mode of educational enforcement required to meet the crisis; and the priority of black education among postwar goals—on issues such as these, educators' seeming unity, along with their zeal, would shortly wilt. They assumed, as they always had, that common schooling offered education; and in identifying efficiency as the critical school issue and cultural homogeneity as the goal of inclusiveness, that is, educational equality, they continued to overlook the significance of political variables. The turmoil of the 1860s reflected not so much the limited availability of popular schooling as a special sort of ignorance—the clash of contending values, people's inability to listen across the din of differences, and the externally derived political and economic impotence of particular races and classes. The experience of the black man in white society should have jarred the schoolmen's confidence in their law of external pressure indirectly applied. If his needs justified the creation of a national school bureau, they also transformed the enforcement of education into a direct assault on racism, the elimination of which would involve more than the dissemination of school statistics. The *in loco parentis* doctrine applied to black people promised schooling not commonality, as it did for poor whites, immigrants, and workers. Nevertheless, the case of black people was also unique. Given the opposition to their education, those in the South, particularly, stood a good chance of not getting any schools. They eventually got them, of varying qualities, and in many localities only temporarily, principally through the direct intervention of the Freedmen's Bureau, private philanthropic organizations, and hordes of New England school marms. The case of black Americans reveals, in short, that the schoolmen's goals for federal involvement in school reform and the means

75

proposed for realizing them contained implicit and ironic incongruities. The objectives promised more than would be delivered, or, viewed positively, kept an unrealized vision alive.[24]

Even on a superficial level the schoolmen's cohesiveness had been fragile from the outset. Two campaigns remained after Garfield introduced the education bill in Congress, one supporting the bill and another, equally intense, promoting candidates for commissioner of education. At least two schoolmen, Barnard and White, labored in both.

3 Uncertain Mandate: A Legislative History

THE DEPARTMENT OF EDUCATION BILL IN CONGRESS

The historic and first post-Civil War Congress, the Thirty-ninth, convened on 4 December 1865. One week later Nathaniel Banks routinely filed Charles Brooks's petition. An independent conservative Republican, Banks served as commander of the Union army's Gulf Department from 1863 to 1865. Seeking to instill loyalist sentiments in southern children he reorganized the New Orleans public schools, attempted without success to entice whites to attend them, and encouraged the establishment of schools for freedmen throughout southern Louisiana. Earlier, as an economy-minded prewar governor of Massachusetts, he won grudging respect from New England intellectuals by his support for public education. Never a radical in any sense of the term, Banks presented the Brooks document without endorsing it.[1]

Had the petition received a hearing, at least one House member, Republican Ignatius Donnelly of Minnesota, would have found himself in sympathy with its general thrust. Barely thirty-four years old, Donnelly stood at the beginning of his second term in Congress. In his youth he attended Philadelphia's old Central High School, studying under Alexander D. Bache and later the venerable John Hart, a frequent supporter of the national bureau idea at N.T.A. gatherings. Educated, well-read, and a gifted orator, Donnelly became an unrepentant idealist, in the words of one critic, "a rampant Loco Foco," even before moving to his adopted state as a young man. Known in Congress as an ultra radical, he scorned the "myth" of state sovereignty and in the fall of 1865 conducted a spirited but unsuccessful drive in Minnesota for a state constitutional

Ignatius Donnelly, Minnesota congressman and supporter of the Department of Education. Courtesy of the National Archives (Brady Collection), a U.S. Signal Corps photograph.

amendment granting suffrage to black people. Until his death, he remained a vigorous advocate of civil rights for blacks, despite the unpopularity of his position among voters.[2]

On 14 December 1865, Donnelly took the House floor to move adoption of the following preamble and resolution:

> Whereas republican institutions can find permanent safety only upon the basis of the universal intelligence of the people; and whereas the great disasters which have afflicted the nation and desolated one-half its territory are traceable, in a great degree, to the absence of common schools and general education among the people of the lately rebellious States:
> Therefore,
> *Resolved,* That the Joint Committee on Reconstruction be instructed to inquire into the expediency of establishing in this capital a national bureau of education, whose duty it shall be to enforce education, without regard to race or color, upon the population of all such States as shall fall below a standard to be established by Congress, and to inquire whether such a bureau should not be made an essential and permanent part of any system of reconstruction.

Brooks's plan represented a far-fetched packaging of national university ideas, European schemes for national education, and manifest destiny rationales; Donnelly's resolution, on the other hand, applied with simple force the logic of guaranteed common school opportunities, devised earlier by public instruction advocates to postwar post-emancipation conditions. It contained a single novelty, that the federal government should establish an agency "to enforce education." Not even the early promoters of state school bureaus had dared put the matter so bluntly. No American Congress had received a more radical or single-minded proposal for the upward extension of the public school bureaucracy. Even so, the moment passed all but unnoticed. The House approved the resolution without debate or recorded vote after soundly rejecting Democrat Philip Johnson's motion to table by 37 to 113. The intent of the action, however, remained unclear. Despite the impressive support it apparently enjoyed among House members, Donnelly's proposal produced no direct results. If the Joint Committee on Reconstruction discussed his plan, and there is no evidence that it did, the committee never saw fit to submit a report on the subject to either house. Later, Donnelly persistently interpreted the department of education bill as a step toward goals mentioned in his resolution and, like Charles Brooks, may have succeeded in frightening off more support than he attracted. Privately, he confessed his disappointment that a bill so conservative had reached the House floor.[3]

Congress heard no more about a bureau of education until James Garfield introduced Emerson White's bill two months later. Obvious factors drew the schoolmen's attention to Garfield—he was a rural son of mid-America dislocated by ambition and schooling as well as a former teacher and college president. Undoubtedly, his acquaintance with White sealed the decision that he should shepherd their bill. Also, few other candidates for the job appeared. Garfield had been a somewhat lackluster Union general until his election to the Thirty-eighth Congress. Rutherford B. Hayes found him "a smooth, pleasant, ruddy man, not very strong." His voting record in the Thirty-eighth Congress tended to confirm the radical label to which he attached himself on occasion, but like many of his Republican colleagues who survived the political wars of the late 1860s, he mellowed noticeably during the Thirty-ninth Congress and afterwards. His biographers have pictured him as a "party man" of moderate views who supported radical proposals which he thought safely reflected the attitudes of his constituents. There can be little doubt, however, about his genuine interest in the bureau bill. He defended it mightily and deserved credit for its approval in the House of Representatives.[4]

Four Republicans, Garfield as chairman, Donnelly, James W. Patterson of New Hampshire, and George Boutwell of Massachusetts, and three Democrats, Samuel Moulton of Illinois, Samuel Randall of Pennsylvania, and Charles Goodyear of New York, sat on the select committee appointed to study the bureau measure. Moulton, although a Democrat, tended to vote with Republican moderates, as did Patterson and Garfield. Donnelly and Boutwell were radicals. By virtue of advocating school reforms in their respective states, the four Republicans and Democrat Moulton enjoyed reputations as friends of education. Both Boutwell and Patterson attended the 1866 superintendents meeting in Washington.[5]

Early in March 1866, Emerson White, writing to apprise Barnard of progress in the bureau campaign, explained that "General Garfield and others thought we could get the Bureau just as easily as a clerkship." As White knew, Barnard had been willing to settle for the latter. But it was unlikely that many educators, White and Barnard included, anticipated the bill which Garfield's committee reported to the House a month later. Presented in the form of a substitute amendment, it called for the creation of an autonomous department of education patterned after the new Department of Agriculture. The four sections of the bill, placed on the agenda as H. R. 276, described a federal agency designed to collect statistics showing the condition and progress of education in the states and territories, diffuse information which would aid the people in establishing and maintaining efficient school systems, and, finally, "otherwise promote the cause of education throughout the country." The measure allowed a commissioner of education, appointed by the president, to name a chief clerk and four other staff members. Beyond "management" of the department, the commissioner's duties consisted of submitting an annual report to Congress showing the results of his investigations, summarizing the statistics collected, and listing his recommendations for school improvement. The first report was to contain a review of land grants made by Congress to promote education, indicating how these trusts had been managed, the amount of funds raised by them, and, as far as possible, their annual proceeds. Minimum expenses for the department totaled $13,000, the amount designated for staff salaries, including the commissioner's which was set at $5,000. Operating costs, not mentioned in the bill, would require additional funding.[6]

Inexplicit, hence susceptible to the perils of interpretation, the bill projected, at best, an enabling role for the department. Little more about the agency's purposes penetrated the measure's lofty obscurity. Still, its major flaws derived not so much from inexactness as from omissions. Nowhere appeared definitions of the commissioner's responsibility for fiscal matters, the chief clerk's role vis-à-vis that of the commissioner, or the department's relation to state and local school agencies, particularly in the crucial matter of collecting educational data. Missing, too, were provisions setting conditions for staff expansion and the employment of temporary researchers, a predictable need of an agency responsible for collecting and weighing statistics. Items covering each of these omissions found their way into the Department of Agriculture Act, which presumably served as model for the education bill. Most important, the measure failed to stipulate means for securing and disseminating the data. In the debates following the bill's return from committee, the flaws would be exposed, along with an array of conflicting hopes and fears which the measure excited.[7]

Supporters of the bill shared a conviction that schools qualified for federal attention because they functioned as social reforming agents. Conditions left by the war added the element of urgency. Reconstructing the Union, securing the loyalty of southern whites, and guaranteeing the proper preparation of black people for citizenship necessitated federal promotion of common schooling. The department of education would encourage the spread and improvement of schools, initially, some hoped, merely through the nation-wide collection and dissemination of educational data. Beyond general agreement on these points, the supporters parted company. Some viewed passage of the bill as the completion of the bureaucratic structure begun by common schoolmen a generation earlier, an attempt to foster uniformity among the various state systems of schools, similar, it was argued, to steps already taken in Prussia and France to establish central school ministries. Others expected the department to be involved more directly and forcefully in the spread and improvement of public instruction, and not merely in the South.

Nathaniel Banks, confronted with arguments that the agency would undermine local and state authorities, depicted the department as powerless to centralize school control. With limited

81

funds and a small staff, it represented for him a desirable plan for informing Congress and the nation on school conditions. Although it might serve to influence indirectly and from a distance the reform of schools, the department would never be the primary author of change, given its lack of power and authority. Donnelly, on the other hand, viewed it as a form of active external pressure on local school authorities and a foundation for future school reform legislation. As a symbol of the nation's stake in educational advance, the department without coercing states to establish and improve schools would "illuminate the dark places of ignorance" by publishing accurate accounts of school conditions, thus mobilizing public sentiment for education. It would provide needed incentives for communities to "rise together to the level of the most favored localities," prompting, happily for the nation, the equalization of educational opportunity at the highest, rather than the lowest, level of attainment. Donnelly dismissed constitutional objections as callous attempts to derail legislation promising both relief to individuals heretofore excluded from public instruction and a firm basis for re-establishing the Union. Permitted, if not caused, by inequitable school policies in the South, the rebellion, in Donnelly's view, rendered obsolete states' rights arguments against a federal education agency.

Samuel Moulton agreed only in part. Acknowledging the reasonableness of constitutional doubts, he maintained that the clause empowering Congress to enact laws necessary for the general welfare, employed previously to justify creation of other federal agencies, provided sufficient grounds for establishing a department of education. The caprice of individuals or states should not be allowed to abrogate the natural claim of children to education. Without explaining how the proposed department would guarantee such a right, Moulton insisted that the agency posed no threat to established school authorities. Rather, through the publication of educational data, it would provide a service sought by local and state superintendents. A modest operation, the agency could hardly be classified as an extravagant expenditure of federal funds.

Reinforcing Moulton's final point, Garfield reminded his colleagues of recent appropriations for a railroad survey and the promotion of agriculture which eclipsed the limited funds required for the department of education. With extended quotations from Thaddeus Stevens' 1835 speech before the Pennsylvania legislature, he warned House members not to expect the ignorant to clamor for learning. Initiative for encouraging states to take notice of their schools devolved necessarily upon the federal government. However, Garfield added, not "stolid ignorance" but disjunctive "educational quality" had disrupted the Union. Passing the department of education bill would be a way to guarantee the promotion of schools in which all citizens would be directed toward "industry, liberty, and patriotism."

That the supporters ranged far afield from the bill being debated did not pass unnoticed among the measure's critics. Time and again they returned to three basic reasons for their opposition: a department of education suggested an unconstitutional abridgment of state prerogatives, an unnecessary disruption of local school control, and a waste of federal funds. Without belaboring the point, they denounced as simplistic the portrayal of schools as bearers of patriotism, morality, and social betterment. Such notions ignored one inescapable lesson of the war, namely that highly educated southerners had fomented rebellion. Since the bill proposed merely the collection and dissemination of statistics, not the education of individuals, the consequences anticipated by proponents clearly exceeded the measure's scope. In short, the project issued from a faulty premise. School reform, opponents argued, proceeded from local initiative rather than external enforcement, however subtle or indirect.

Democrat Andrew Rogers of New Jersey rejected as invalid suggested similarities between the Department of Agriculture and the education agency. Accepted practice supported federal promotion of agriculture, whereas a department of education represented an unprecedented threat to state control of schools. Bothered by the potential costs of deploying a new federal agency at a time when economizing seemed necessary, he feared the department would rival the Freedmen's Bureau in power and range of operation. Frederick Pike of Maine, the only Republican to oppose the bill on the House floor, shared Rogers' concern for restricting federal expenditures. Providing offices for the new department, he observed, could lead to a major expense, particularly if construction of new buildings proved to be necessary. Pike, who had supported the department of agriculture bill, indicated willingness to attach a bureau of educational statistics to that agency, but a department of education was too much for him. How were the school statistics to be secured? he asked. If the department utilized reports already compiled by local and state superintendents, it amounted to an unnecessary outlay of federal funds. On the other hand, sending agents into the field to collect original statistics would interfere directly with states' rights and responsibilities. It will be a sad day, he concluded, when education is centralized because the next step will be the centralization of churches.

Samuel Randall readily admitted the need for collecting educational statistics but could not understand the necessity of a separate department to perform the task. Two clerks working under the secretary of the interior could complete the work outlined in the bill. Randall defied proponents to show how a mere data gathering agency could achieve the outcomes they projected. Increased numbers of educated Americans would not result from the bill's passage. Furthermore, the department could not be the head of an educational system, because no single American school system existed. There were rather thirty-six systems, which ought never to be made one.

The brief House debate on H. R. 276 began 5 June 1866, resuming three days later when the first votes were taken. Of the two amendments introduced, one lowered the commissioner's salary to $4,000 and reduced his staff to three clerks. It won approval without a recorded vote. The other, authored by Randall, took the form of a substitute bill calling for the establishment of a bureau of education under the authority of the secretary of the interior. The secretary would appoint two clerks to perform the duties outlined in Garfield's measure. The amendment, which eliminated the need for a commissioner of education, offered an alternative means for collecting and disseminating school data, if that was all Congress desired to accomplish. With 63 members either absent or not voting, the House rejected Randall's proposal 53 to 67, but proceeded to defeat the bill itself 59 to 61, again with 63 not voting. Later the same day, Charles Upson, a Michigan Republican, moved to reconsider the vote, thus postponing the bill's final defeat in the House.[8]

Eleven days later, when the motion to reconsider came before the House, Garfield offered to amend the bill by substituting "bureau" for "department," but several members objected to the alteration. Henry Dawes, a Republican from Massachusetts, suggested that the bill be returned to the select committee to increase the department's power. Acknowledging his colleague's good intentions, Garfield offered to support a plan combining the proposed agency with the Department of Agriculture and a general bureau of statistics, but doubted the House's willingness to approve a more comprehensive bill. In a frank appeal for Republican unity, he added, "I hope the instinct which has moved the other side of the House to vote solidly against this liberal and progressive measure will at least induce this side to save it from defeat." The motion to reconsider was passed 76 to 48, with 58 not voting. Rescued by what appeared to be an impressive shift of sentiment, the bill then won House approval 80 to 44, again with 58 not voting.[9]

Zalmon Richards reported the good news to Barnard and in passing awarded himself a share of the credit for the measure's success. He should not be denied his hour. A Washington resident active in local politics, a government employee, and brother of a municipal police captain, Richards no doubt employed his limited influence in behalf of the education bill. But stronger evidence, including the testimony of none other than James G. Blaine, Elihu B. Washburne, and Frederick Pike, supported Garfield's claim to the major portion of the credit for the bill's passage. During the interval between votes on the bill, Garfield, "by dint of personal entreaty," his colleagues later complained, secured the votes necessary for its approval. The Ohioan accepted his colleagues' assessment. "In the first place," he later explained to Emerson White, "the law was never heartily supported by either house of Congress. It was only by the most persistent efforts on my part that the law was passed at all. . . ."[10]

Worried educators now turned their attention to the Senate. An N.T.A. committee, which included Richards and John Hart, sought supporters in the upper chamber, and the National Association of School Superintendents resubmitted its resolution approved four months earlier. Barnard, by renewing his letter-writing campaign and working in concert with Richards, intensified his personal lobby for the bill. Opponents, real or imagined, found themselves the recipients of special attention. Senators Doolittle and Harris, known to be lukewarm on the measure, faced appeals from Washington clergymen recruited by Barnard himself solely because the senators frequented their churches for Sunday services. Beset by rumors that Senate action had to be taken prior to the close of the first session of the Thirty-ninth Congress, unsettled educators feared their campaign was lost when Congress adjourned without approving the department measure.[11]

On 26 February 1867, late in the second session, the upper house began its debate on H. R. 276. The bill had been referred to Lyman Trumbull's Judiciary Committee and favorably reported back to the Senate without amendment. Republican John Conness of California suggested early in the debate that "bureau" be substituted for "department," explaining that he favored the bill but found the department designation confusing when applied to a sub-cabinet level agency. The wording, Trumbull explained, permitted the commissioner to have autonomy in staff appointments, a power not accorded bureau heads, and offered him at least limited protection from political favorites who otherwise might be employed in the agency without his approval. Senator Grimes thought the educational agency could be combined with the Department of Agriculture but won no support for the proposal. Both Senators Dixon of Connecticut and Sumner of Massachusetts, usually on opposing sides in Senate debates, spoke in favor of the bill as presented by the committee. Ignoring the need for collecting and disseminating school statistics, they argued for a central agency to promote education in the rebel states. Sumner advocated a cabinet position for the commissioner of education, but Daniel Norton of Minnesota, a Democrat elected to the Senate as a Union Conservative, retorted that his support of the bill would be lost if he became convinced that the measure represented a hidden attempt to centralize education. Davis of Kentucky and Saulsbury of Delaware, both Democrats, opposed the bill on grounds that it interfered with states' rights and was therefore unconstitutional.[12]

The Senate approved the bill on 27 February 1867 without a recorded vote. A motion to reconsider by Charles Buckalew, the Pennsylvania Democrat, attempted to delay final approval beyond the close of the session, but on 1 March 1867, the Senate rejected the move 7 to 28, with 17 not voting. With the end of the Thirty-ninth Congress rapidly approaching, the bill was forwarded to the president for his signature.[13]

THE INTENT OF CONGRESS: SHADOWS AND DOUBTS

Nathaniel Banks's description seemed apt. In its final form the department of education bill appeared to be a decent, uncalculated attempt by Congress to inform itself and the nation on school conditions and to encourage improvement by the publication of researches.° But proponents—radicals, moderates, and independents alike—expected the department to stimulate: (1) interest in collecting and reporting school data according to regular schedules; and (2) a reform thrust with measurable impact on local educational practices. Working indirectly, so as not to offend, the new agency was intended to improve schools and render them supportive of national goals. In 1867 such talk meant that schools, for the country's sake, must become inclusive and effective agents of academic, political, and moral instruction. No one should be denied opportunity for learning nor be crippled by inferior schooling. Supporters argued that states and communities left to their own devices could not, and in some cases would not, meet the nation's public school needs. Finally, they foresaw national, not merely regional, consequences if the federal government shunned a direct role in promoting the education of whites and blacks in the South.

The bill referred to none of these points explicitly. For this reason, opponents denounced it outright, demanding, at the least, guarantees that the proposed agency would serve strictly as a statistical bureau. Rather than any crisis justifying the displacement of local school control, they detected in the department of education bill threats to established practice, the proper means of government, even a cherished way of life. Their rhetoric sidestepped the educational policy implications of two chilling issues of the postwar era: the status of black Americans and the inevitable redefinition of federal-state relations. If their reasons—the need for economizing and the sanctity of the states' rights tradition—seemed thin in light of the times, not yet two years after Appomattox, they nevertheless testified to the disparate war and reconstruction views held by members of the Thirty-ninth Congress.

Analyses of votes taken on the department bill indicate that opponents included not merely large numbers of Republicans but also members of all the various Republican sub-groups. Categorizing congressmen as members of one or the other of the two major parties during the Reconstruction period has never been easy. Candidates at times presented themselves as "Unionists," "Independents," "Conservatives," or "Emancipationists." In addition, some Republicans, following the lead of Andrew Johnson, moved into the Democratic

° See Appendix 1 for a copy of the Department of Education Act.

fold after the Thirty-ninth Congress got underway. Even more perplexing has been the task of sorting the Republicans into factions. Too often historians have characterized the Thirty-ninth Congress as "radical" or "radical dominated" on the basis of documentary research alone, for example, records of debates, or, what is more indefensible, unexamined assumptions. Acknowledging the difficulties, reconstruction historian David Donald has classified Republican members of the Thirty-ninth Congress as ultra radicals, Stevens radicals, independent radicals, moderates, and conservatives according to their votes on selected roll calls during the second session. Although limited by approximate, and in a few cases questionable, designations of party and faction affiliation, Donald's categories provide means for analyzing opposition to and support of the department bill in the House. A similar analysis of the lone Senate roll call on a motion related to the department bill deserves less attention in light of the ease with which the motion was defeated.[14]

Early in the first session, House members divided along party lines in voting on the motion to table Donnelly's resolution. Furthermore, the young radical's proposal won overwhelming support from all of the Republican factions—ultra radical to conservative. Without additional evidence, one might be misled into concluding that the great majority of House Republicans favored establishing a federal agency to preside over the nationwide enforcement of equal educational opportunity. The vote on Randall's amendment revealed how far this was from the case. Forty-three Republicans, most of them Stevens radicals and moderates, and ten Democrats endorsed the plan to assign responsibility for gathering and disseminating school data to two clerks in the Department of the Interior. Forty-six Republicans and twenty-one Democrats, representing both the outspoken advocates and opponents of the department bill, teamed up to defeat it. The Republicans represented all of the factions, although more Stevens radicals and moderates supported Randall's proposal than opposed it. Fully one-third of the House members failed to vote, either because they were absent or wished to abstain. One likely explanation for the coalition of department supporters and opponents on the vote might be that the former acted to defend the integrity of their bill, while the latter expressed either opposition to any type of federal school agency or held the view that the department measure would be easier to defeat in its original, and stronger, form.

Despite Garfield's attempt to blame Democrats for the measure's initial defeat, the party of Jefferson and Jackson, holding fewer than one-third of the 183 House seats in the Thirty-ninth Congress, could hardly have achieved such a victory alone. The first roll call on the bill found Democrats solidly in the no column. With 14 not voting, only two supported the measure, while 29 opposed it. Republicans, on the other hand, voted 57 to 32 in favor, with 49 not voting. One-half of the Republican no votes came from Stevens radicals, although none of the Republican factions supported the bill unanimously. The inescapable conclusion: Republicans of all persuasions and Democrats combined to defeat the measure. Eleven days later, the situation apparently had changed dramatically. Republican factions pulled together to pass, first, the motion to reconsider, and then the bill itself. One Democrat voted for reconsideration and two supported the bill.

Assessing the meaning of the successful second vote requires examination of voting shifts on the two roll calls necessary for passage of the bill. In all, 71 congressmen changed their votes, if not their minds. Of these, only six Republicans, five of them Stevens radicals, and one Democrat switched from no to yes; one conservative Republican moved in the opposite direction. The remainder of the changes, half reversals at best, were more ambiguous, the key to understanding them hidden within the meaning of the "not voting" designation. James G. Blaine later confessed that he and a number of other opponents abstained on the second roll call as a personal favor to Garfield, after satisfying themselves that the measure was harmless. Nineteen congressmen, including six Republican moderates and six Democrats, who voted no on the first roll call were recorded as "not voting" on the second. How many of these acted at Garfield's behest remains uncertain. In addition, 25 Republicans, including 14 classified generally as radicals and 5 moderates, who failed to record their position on the first vote, joined supporters on the second roll call. What portion of these rallied not to the bill but to the call for party unity again cannot be determined. The injection of party loyalty into the proceedings raises the possibility that the first vote was more indicative of congressional feeling on the bill than the second, which exhibited the "amazing Republican unanimity" characteristic, Donald has found, of "final votes on virtually all measures relating to the prosecution of the war, slavery, and the reorganization of the South. . . ." In any case a good many congressmen supported the bill, or abstained, for reasons not entirely related to the substantive issue.[15]

The Senate roll call on Buckalew's motion to reconsider evidenced many of the characteristics of the House votes. Only McDougall of California, a Democrat with Republican leanings, joined the 27 Republican supporters of the bill in voting against reconsideration. But among the seven who favored reconsideration and probably opposed the bill were three Republicans, among them Fessenden of Maine and Grimes of Iowa, both highly regarded moderates. The 28 supporters included radicals, moderates, and "Johnson Republicans." That a number of Democrats known to be against the measure abstained on Buckalew's motion can be attributed to Barnard's friend, James Dixon, a Johnson Republican who exacted promises from other Senate allies of the president not to oppose the bill. Dixon himself missed the roll call but took the precaution of pairing his vote with Garrett Davis, an opponent of the measure, who abstained on the motion.[16]

A minor piece of legislation, the department of education bill attracted minimal interest and occupied in turn very little congressional time. Debates on the measure, reflecting Congress's absorption with larger reconstruction issues, skirted questions posed by the bill's loose wording in the rush of supporters and opponents to chart the consequences, salutary or dire, anticipated from the creation of a federal school agency. With the exception of Frederick Pike, a man classified as a Stevens radical by Donald, the speakers served to encourage the thought that here was a bill capable of winning endorsements from both radicals and moderates. All of those who spoke in favor of the bill fell into one of these two camps, while with the exception of Pike, the opponents were Democrats. Instead, the offspring of neither radicalism nor moderation, the department measure splintered all of the Republican factions. It stood, therefore, as at least minor documentation of the difficulty in determining both the ideology and membership of Republican factions in the turbulent postwar years. Apparently the specter of a federal school agency raised hackles of a different order for Republican legislators who with near monolithic solidarity approved the 1866 bill amending the 1865 Freedmen's Bureau Act, the Second Confiscation Act, the 1866 civil rights bill, and the 1867 Reconstruction Act.

After winning congressional ratification, the department bill faced a new threat at the hands of the president. An alarmed

Barnard wrote to Elisha Potter from Washington on 2 March 1867: "It is in peril of a veto from the President—Mr. Dixon is just from him, and he has not decided to sign it." In Washington because of Garfield's plea that he "come over and attend to the bill—it is going to be vetoed," Barnard prevailed upon Dixon to intercede with the president. One of the measure's few supporters with easy access to President Johnson, Dixon convinced him that the bill presented no threat to local and state school authorities. Suspicious of the radical tone of the congressional debate, the president nevertheless signed the measure on the day he received it from Congress, 2 March 1867. Yet to be settled was the appointment of the commissioner of education. With some apprehension, Barnard complained to Potter that the president "will not pledge himself to any nomination for the present—so clouds and darkness rest on the future." [17]

THE RACE FOR COMMISSIONER

The scent of a federal appointment lured a number of applicants for the post Barnard wanted. The salary, higher than that received by Harvard's president, the commissioner of agriculture, or the head of the Freedmen's Bureau, and the chance to participate in the challenging and fascinating efforts of reconstruction rendered the position both attractive and respectable. Idealists and job hunters alike wanted to be the nation's first commissioner of education. Applicants included an Indiana college mathematics teacher, the president of Dickinson College in Pennsylvania, a New Jersey politician, and a Philadelphia school board member. Ignatius Donnelly sought the position for John Hart, his former mentor. One of Johnson's secretaries, Edward D. Neill, applied for the post on executive mansion stationery, enclosing a letter of recommendation from Minnesota Senator Daniel Norton, a consistent supporter of the president's reconstruction policies. Senator Dixon, equally deserving of presidential favors, pressed for Barnard's appointment.[18]

Any number of prominent schoolmen would have accepted the president's offer of the position, but only one national educational leader, other than Barnard, emerged as an active candidate for commissioner. Although no scholar and far from being an original or daring thinker, Emerson White was a quietly intellectual man, the editor of a respected educational journal, and an ambitious, able administrator. In Barnard's opinion, White was "the best school officer in the West." In 1863 White's inaugural address as president of the Ohio Teachers Association presented a strong defense of the common school's responsibility for the intellectual and moral development of individuals and the progress and well-being of society. He included a stinging indictment of the South for failing to educate her people for "citizenship and democracy." Two years later, as Ohio's commissioner of common schools and one of the editors of the *Ohio Educational Monthly*, he demanded federal initiative in establishing schools for freedmen. Repeated acts of terror against teachers of freedmen proved, he insisted, that southerners did not want the former slaves educated. The general government must support and protect schools for black people which later can be returned to the loyal governments of the states.[19]

White's candidacy won endorsements from schoolmen James P. Wickersham and B. G. Northrop and his friend James Garfield. In a letter written just after the general election of 1880, White reminisced with President-elect Garfield over the events surrounding passage of the department of education bill: "You may not know that, as soon as the law was passed, there was a spontaneous movement among the leading educators of the country to secure my appointment to the office. Before their strong testimonials could be submitted to President Johnson, he appointed Dr. Barnard." Time had rounded off the edges of White's memory. In 1868, when the department was barely one year old, he admitted to Garfield that interest in his candidacy originated and derived its primary strength from "prominent educators [in the] East." It was not, however, a spontaneous movement. As early as 17 March 1866, Northrop, in a letter to Barnard describing the national superintendents meeting, announced, "I think White is the man for the National Bureau, if the bill passes." Four months later, just after the bill won House approval, Barnard's old friend John D. Philbrick, superintendent of schools in Boston, commented, "I suppose Mr. White may be looking for it [the commissionership]." Philbrick subsequently confessed he had written his "good wishes" to White in the summer of 1866, before he knew of Barnard's interest in the position.[20]

The competition between White and Barnard seems to have been common knowledge among educators active in the N.T.A. Professor James D. Butler of the University of Wisconsin, whose friendship with Barnard dated from the latter's brief term as university chancellor in the late 1850s, wrote in July 1866, that "Dr. Bateman in Illinois bade me tell you that he and all Western educators would go for you as head of the educational bureau." Later, Butler predicted that White would support Barnard for commissioner, suggesting a compromise could be reached by appointing the Ohioan chief clerk. But N.T.A. President James Wickersham did not appear to have compromise in mind when on 11 March 1867 he wrote to the president endorsing White's candidacy:

> The educational men of the country naturally feel a deep interest in the person who is to be appointed Commissioner under the provisions of the [Department of Education] bill.
>
> As President of the National Teachers' Association and Superintendent of Schools for the State of Pennsylvania, I desire to present to you the name of *Hon. E. E. White*, Columbus, Ohio, as a suitable person for Commissioner; and in so doing, I believe I express the wishes of a large majority of the leading educators of the country. Mr. White was until lately Superintendent of Schools in the State of Ohio, and he is now President of the National Association of School Superintendents. There is no man in the whole country better qualified. If you do not feel at liberty to appoint Mr. White, I beg that you will delay the appointment until the educational men of the country have time to name another man more in accordance with your wishes. A telegram will on any day bring me from Harrisburg to Washington to confer with you, and I feel free to say this because prominent men concerned in education in their States, have authorized me to act for them.[21]

Despite his implicit disclaimer to Garfield in 1880, White actively encouraged the effort in his behalf. Not only did he want the position, but also, he needed it financially, for in 1867 the thirty-seven-year-old educator found himself unemployed. The commissioner of Ohio's common schools was an elected official, and in the summer of 1865, White had been defeated for renomination at the Union party's state convention by, as he complained to Barnard, "a maimed soldier unknown to the friends of education."[22]

Even if the "strong testimonials" White mentioned to Garfield had reached the president, there is little reason to believe they would have persuaded Johnson to appoint him commissioner. The president probably was unaware of White's sharp criticism of his reconstruction policies, but Garfield's endorsement of the educator and the support of eastern schoolmen was doubtless enough to alert Johnson to the inadvisability of appointing him, even if his credentials were impeccable. In all likelihood, the Ohioan never emerged as a strong contender for the post from the president's perspective.

On the other hand, Edward D. Neill did. A college graduate and a Presbyterian clergyman, Neill served as the first superintendent of public instruction for the Minnesota Territory from 1851 to 1853, holding a similar position from 1860 to 1861 after Minnesota became a state. Although relatively unknown within N.T.A. circles, he was not without qualifications for the position he sought. Something of an amateur historian, producing countless tracts of local and Indian history, he was considered, Martin Ridge has reported, "Minnesota's most distinguished scholar." He became one of Lincoln's secretaries in February 1864, and after the assassination served Johnson in a like capacity until 1867. Looking for greener pastures, he wrote the president in the fall of 1866 asking for a "$2500 appointment in the Treasury Department." In the words of one of his biographers, Neill was "rather the promoter than the successful administrator, with more versatility than tenacity of purpose." Nevertheless, discounting the president himself, he could claim two influential allies in Senators Doolittle of Wisconsin and Norton of Minnesota. Edward Neill, not Emerson White, was Barnard's main competition for the job of commissioner; however, it is doubtful that very many of the nation's leading educators, Barnard included, knew this.[23]

Henry Barnard entered the race for commissioner as would a man with a mission. On 14 December 1866 he confided to Elisha Potter, "I want this office, if I can get it." A month later, he explained to Potter, "a novice or a politician can render this department obnoxious and injurious—but I believe that I can make it useful and popular." To Daniel Coit Gilman he wrote, "It is the only office under gift of government I would turn my heel to get, as 30 years study and action have fitted me for this work, and I should like to wind up my educational labors in inaugurating this office." He saw in the commissionership a chance to accomplish what he had been attempting to do alone and with his own funds since launching the *American Journal of Education* in 1855. He saw it as the "final polish" to his schoolman's career. Finally, he wanted to be commissioner because he thought he deserved it.[24]

Many of his fellow educators agreed. Shortly after Garfield introduced the bill in Congress, Barnard began receiving letters encouraging him to seek the position. "There is but one opinion among Western educators," wrote his friend John Hancock from Ohio, "as to your eminent fitness for the place." Added John Philbrick: "I learn you are likely to be appointed Commissioner of the Department of Education, if the bill passes the Senate. If anyone is entitled to the post it is yourself. . . . [I]f you would take it, it belongs to you. . . ." As early as 18 July 1866, Zalmon Richards could observe that "almost every well informed member of Congress knows you are thought of for the place." Only a few weeks before, the editor of *Nation* had predicted the Connecticut educator's appointment "should the bill become law." [25]

Barnard actively sought supporters from school and political leaders representing a broad political spectrum, including many who were closely allied with the president. The point, he impressed upon Potter, was "to take this appointment out of the category of politics," by laying before the president endorsements from Democrats and Republicans of all persuasions, North and South, and from prominent schoolmen and scholars, particularly those from western and border states. Coupled with the strong and influential support of Senator Dixon, the endorsements won by Barnard and his friends telegraphed the desired message: here was a qualified man whose politics at worst offered no threat to the president and at best might make him an ally.[26]

Before the department bill had cleared the Senate, White complained to Barnard: "The trouble in securing active assistance from educators is the *President*. Some fear that he will destroy the efficiency of the Bureau by an injudicious appointment." But several educators supported the bill primarily because they anticipated Barnard's appointment. Gilman confessed to Barnard that he had remained cool toward the bill because he feared "the whole project would fall into bad hands," adding that he would help the cause if "there is any reasonable security that you can be made the Commissioner with sufficiently ample powers." Famed naturalist Samuel S. Haldeman, writing more than likely at Barnard's request, informed Senator Cowan that although he doubted the "propriety" of establishing a national educational agency, he thought "concomitant evils might be lessened by the appointment of a man like Henry Barnard. . . ." [27]

Two questions concerning Barnard's appointment deserve particular attention. Why did some of the most prominent educators, including N.T.A. leaders, oppose his being named commissioner, and why, in the end, did the president appoint the Connecticut educator rather than Edward Neill, his secretary? Neither question has been adequately explored in other accounts of the founding of the Office of Education, although answers to each shed needed light on criticisms lodged against the commissioner during the initial years of his agency's operation.[28]

Barnard had been in office less than eighteen months when White confided to Garfield: "I knew Dr. Barnard would fail. He is not the man (between us) for such work. He scatters too badly—undertakes too many schemes." White, whose opinion was shared by others in the N.T.A., made a similar evaluation of Barnard in an earlier letter to Garfield. Since 1855, Barnard's journal had occupied the major portion of his time, interest, and energy, so much so that his every attempt since that year to hold a permanent position had ended in failure. Knowing this and anticipating that Barnard stood a good chance of being named commissioner, White, in August 1866, urged him to stop publishing his journal since he had "neither time nor the means to carry it through." [29]

Added to Barnard's tendency to undertake too many projects and his preoccupation with his journal were his frequent illnesses with which some of his fellow educators came to have little sympathy. In Wisconsin, for example, he left behind a number of bitter critics when illness and repeated, prolonged trips to his home in Hartford cut short his term as chancellor of the university. There may have been some illegitimate reasons for opposition to Barnard's candidacy within educational circles, professional jealousy, for one, but there were legitimate ones, also.

The president's decision to appoint Barnard rather than Neill is more difficult to explain because hard evidence is lacking. With both candidates politically safe, the major difference between them was Barnard's stature as an educational statesman and the impressive list of scholars and schoolmen endorsing his nomination. With very few reasons for selecting Dixon's nominee over Norton's, the president seemed intent upon effecting a compromise between the two, which the senators themselves may have worked out. He would appoint Barnard commissioner, if in turn Barnard would name Neill as his chief clerk. It must have seemed an ideal solution. In any case some sort of arrangement very similar to this one was acceptable to Neill, for he withdrew his application for the post. Barnard, on the other hand, was dumbfounded when the president suggested the plan. The educator claimed not to have committed himself, but as Dixon later warned, Johnson came away from the meeting under the impression that an agreement had been reached. On 11 March 1867, he announced Barnard's nomination. Five days later the Senate unanimously confirmed him as the first United States commissioner of education.[30]

Three months afterwards a group of Ohio college students heard Garfield's summary of what had happened: "The Federal Government has established a National Department of Education, for the purpose of teaching young men and women how to be good citizens." Within a year his view changed, but in June 1867, cheerfulness prevailed, not so much because a seasoned political leader had probed the intent of Congress, but because a most green one measured his success too hastily. Touched by a variety of hands, fashioned to serve too many agenda, the department bill gained from its legislative treatment little clarification of the agency's purposes, functions, and powers. In subsequent generations, historians explained the department's founding in terms of Congress's desire for school statistics and reports on federal land grants for education, but both points sadly reduce the hopes and fears accumulated by the bill on its way to enactment. Even conservative proponents expected passage of the bill to result in school improvements. They anticipated, if only vaguely, an active federal educational agency, not a passive census taker. Given the uncertain mandate which launched the Department of Education, chances for realizing the expectations were not bright.[31]

4 Henry Barnard and the Department of Education: Old Wine, Old Wineskins

THE MAN AND HIS PLAN

Yielding to preoccupation with more pressing reconstruction problems and fearful that greater specificity would guarantee defeat, proponents of the department bill entrusted to the commissioner of education the task of detailing his agency's functions and modes of operation. Despite its imperfections, counseled Wisconsin's Senator Howe, the measure represented a sound beginning. The House heard similar advice from Samuel Moulton, who predicted the commissioner would be "a man of national character; of the most enlarged capacity; a man of culture, science, and experience." Few doubted that he spoke of Henry Barnard, in 1866 the nation's most widely known educator.[1]

Esteem for Barnard in recent years resulted primarily from the high regard of scholars and educationists for the *American Journal of Education*. For over a decade, its volumes, set in painfully small type, served as required reading for anyone wanting to keep abreast of educational thought and practice in the United States and abroad.° During the period from 1855 to 1881, when publication ceased, Barnard produced thirty-one massive volumes, each approximately 800 pages long. No other educational periodical at the time, either in the United States or, according to John Stuart Mill, in Europe, matched its scholarship and comprehensive, ecumenical view of education. Although the editor's financial difficulties and procrastination sometimes limited the number of issues in a given

---

° Richard Thursfield's careful study of the journal and the man responsible for it, published in 1945, documents the significance of the project which claimed Barnard's time, energy, and financial resources for almost thirty years. See Thursfield, *Henry Barnard's American Journal of Education*.

year to three or even two, the quarterly journal represented personal journalism at its best and worst. It was Barnard's project, bore his attention to scholarly detail, and revealed its editor's wide-ranging, somewhat disordered interests in all facets of education. Avoiding fads, gossip, partisan and sectional political controversy, all of which typically found their way into other educational periodicals of the time, Barnard brought to his readers a national and international perspective. His intents were to enlarge their thinking about education beyond a preoccupation with American common schools and to encourage their school reforming efforts. Regular features included biographies of leading American schoolmen and scholars, often accompanied with portraits; reports on national gatherings of schoolmen; articles touching on such new reform efforts as the high school, kindergartens, and female education; analyses of reformatory education, higher education, and technical education; reports on and histories of aspects of European education; educational statistics; and often poetry by the likes of Oliver Goldsmith, William Wordsworth, and Washington Irving that reflected an interest in education. Barnard provided American readers with their first significant introduction to Johann Heinrich Pestalozzi, the pioneering Swiss educator who thought education should enhance harmonious moral, physical, and intellectual development in accordance with the pattern of human growth. Pestalozzi's child-focused educational theories and recommendations continued to generate controversy among European and American schoolpeople long after his death in 1827. In addition to a translation of Pestalozzi's *Leonard and Gertrude*, Barnard published Milton's *Tractate on Education*, Horace Mann's *Seventh Annual Report* as secretary of the Massachusetts Board of Education, Calvin Stowe's *Report on Elementary Public Instruction in Europe*, and James G. Carter's pioneering *Essays on Popular Education* which first appeared in 1825. The history of education represented a consistent theme in the journal. Thus, not all of the articles reflected contemporary activity, for example, the educational "classics" just mentioned and Barnard's account of the national meetings of the American Lyceum that were printed long after the organization had passed from the scene. Also evident in the journal were the editor's interests in educational psychology, teacher education, methodology, school philosophy, moral education, and school architecture.[2]

Contributors to the journal included the leading schoolmen and scholars of the time: William Russell, editor of the first and highly regarded *American Journal of Education*, published from 1826 to 1829; Horace Mann; Charles Brooks; William T. Harris; Francis Parker; and countless college presidents, professors, church leaders, and school superintendents. Barnard had no trouble attracting the authors he wanted, many of whom contributed unsigned pieces. To date, subscription lists have not been located among Barnard's surviving papers, but an examination of the schoolman's correspondence has uncovered an impressive array of subscribers. Generally not found among them were school teachers, a fact Barnard found irksome because it implied that his purpose of embracing "only articles of permanent value and interest" aimed too high. It seemed teachers wanted more popular and immediately practical material and pedagogical prescriptions, not "principles of education or long-term professional growth." On the other hand, state and city school superintendents across the country, college and university presidents, foreign and American intellectuals, school principals, and normal school principals apparently received the journal regularly. Leading educational reformers such as Susan Blow, a pioneer in the kindergarten movement; Charles Brooks; Ashbel Smith, Barnard's

100

friend and business associate who was active in school reform efforts in Texas; Emma Willard, an early advocate of female education; and Elizabeth Peabody, Mary Mann's sister and an early leader in the kindergarten movement counted themselves among Barnard's readers. Acclaimed alike by northern and southern school leaders (many of the latter rushed to re-establish their subscriptions following the war), the journal became a standard reference work in American libraries. Wrote G. Stanley Hall in 1886, at the time professor of psychology and pedagogy at Johns Hopkins University, "[It is] probably the most valuable educational periodical ever published in any language, . . . a vast encyclopedia of information on many if not most topics connected with education, but grouped and indexed in a very confusing way." The qualification testified to a Barnard trait that marked not only his journal but also most of his other endeavors. Admittedly, the journal amounted to a bulky collection, verbose, not clearly organized, and devoid of probing critiques of school-society relationships that might have challenged educational reformers' basic premises or touched sensitive political nerves. Capturing in a simple phrase the publication's strengths and limitations, William T. Harris praised it as "in fact a library of education in itself." [3]

With justification, Elisha Potter advised President Johnson in January 1867 that the Connecticut schoolman remained "one of the few Americans who have a European reputation." He could have added more pointedly that in the intense sectionalism of the time, Barnard, unlike other New England educators, still enjoyed a national following. In the popular mind, he placed just below Horace Mann as the nation's ranking public school statesman. Although theirs was a minority view, Charles Brooks and Emma Willard insisted that Barnard's achievements surpassed those of the Massachusetts schoolman, whose reputation, in their opinion, outdistanced reality. As a national figure and frequent European traveler, Barnard knew the leading educators and scholars of his day on both sides of the Atlantic, and he maintained important contacts within influential business and political circles in the United States.[4]

Being well known, however, fell somewhat short of being respected as a leader of men or a skilled administrator. Fond though they might have been of Barnard personally, many of his fellow educators could not ignore their grave doubts about his ability to function as commissioner of education. A. D. Mayo, in his generally uncritical biographical sketch of Barnard revealed more than he

101

probably intended in describing him as "deficient in the great administrative power of Horace Mann, not always accurate in his knowledge of men and reading of public opinion, not indeed a politician, but a splendid scholar. . . ." Announcing his appointment as commissioner, the editor of *Nation* admitted that Barnard's work in Wisconsin had not been successful and that his journal included "much that is unimportant." He thought, nonetheless, that in the Connecticut schoolman one found "a man of unquestioned ability." "The only question is . . . whether his habits of intellectual labor are such as will enable him to endure the drudgery of a 'bureau.' " [5]

Advantaged by wealth, the polish of a Yale education, and influential friends, Barnard, like many of his educational colleagues, entered the school movement laterally, following an initial involvement in politics and a period of vocational uncertainty. Elected to the Connecticut General Assembly in 1837 at the age of twenty-six, he took charge of supervising the state's public schools the next year. By 1849, when he was only thirty-eight years old, he had secured his place among the major leaders of the common school movement, ironically on the basis of his work as the chief school officer in Connecticut from 1838 to 1842 and afterwards from 1844 to 1849 in Rhode Island. During these years Barnard functioned less as an administrator than as an intense, self-sacrificing pioneer endeavoring to sell the idea of state school supervision and control to the two states' somewhat reluctant citizenries. He labored alone and preferred it that way, winning the respect and loyalty of co-workers and friends of education, such as Daniel Coit Gilman and David N. Camp in Connecticut, Elisha Potter in Rhode Island, and Horace Mann in Massachusetts, by his capacity for work, the intensity of his dedication, and the thoroughness of his scholarship. His most stunning successes in Connecticut stemmed from his work as an educational publicist. Following the pattern being forged by Mann, he inaugurated the *Connecticut Common School Journal* and shaped his annual reports into evangelistic weapons. He launched teacher training institutes, traversed the state many times over on school inspection tours, encouraging along the way the formal organization of teachers and supporters of public education, and maintained contact with a growing number of correspondents from across the country. Suspicious of Barnard's Whig connections, and the notion of state school supervision, the Democratic controlled state legislature abolished his position in 1842. The young schoolman was stopped only temporarily. Invigorated by southern and western tours, he transferred his operation to Rhode Island. In each case his assignment, like Mann's in Massachusetts, required the creation of a new state agency. Renown followed his precedent-setting activity. Then, after 1849, came an extended period of difficulty. For a complex variety of reasons, his administrative achievements failed to meet the high expectations of those who employed him.[6]

Perhaps the reverses resulted from Barnard's frequent illnesses. He thought so, attributing his difficulties to "overwork." As early as January 1848, a few months after his marriage to Josephine Desnoyers, a French Roman Catholic from Detroit, he warned Elisha Potter that he would soon resign his Rhode Island position because of "an almost constant headaches [*sic*], especially after any excitement of mind, and a distressing instability of my nervous system." The resignation came a year later amid heightening criticism over his frequent absences from the state. For the remainder of Barnard's long life (he died in July 1900, at the age of 89) he seemed trapped in a vicious circle of work, illness, and return to his home in Hartford. The illnesses were not imaginary—he was frequently felled by acute diarrhea—still, he often returned to Hartford not merely to recuperate from overwork but also to work at home on some self-appointed task before departing on a fresh assignment. Not infrequently the restless search for position began before the completion of a prior commitment. A short six months after professing exhaustion to Potter and before resigning his position in Rhode Island, Barnard exchanged letters with Mann concerning his interest in succeeding the famed schoolman as the secretary of the Massachusetts Board of Education. The negotiations came to naught. A few months after leaving Rhode Island he proposed to the 1849 National Convention of the Friends of Education the need for an exhaustive history of American education, announcing in the process his intention to complete such a study. The same year he served on the committee which reported to the convention the resolution calling for a national bureau of educational statistics. Very few schoolmen appreciated Barnard's insistent appeal for historical study to provide the necessary framework for understanding school statistical data.[7]

The next year found Barnard serving as principal of the Connecticut state normal school and nominal head of the state's common schools, a position he resigned in 1855 because of ill health and a desire to devote himself to "certain educational undertakings of a national character." Launching the *American Journal of Education* in August of that year culminated a half-decade of reflection, study, and lobbying among friends of education directed specifically toward establishing a central school bureau, if not for the nation, at least for New England. After 1855, Barnard rarely kept himself to a single assignment. Usually at least two claimed his energies, one of which remained his journal, and thus Hartford's attraction became even stronger. When he was away from home, separated from his library and the sources needed to edit his journal, the pull of conflicting interests must indeed have been exhausting for one who by his own admission had been "a used up man" since 1850.[8]

The physical and emotional drain stemming from his vocational ambivalence was aggravated by the fact that few of the assignments Barnard accepted after 1855 could be done effectively in Hartford. Wisconsin officials tolerated his absence from the state during his brief term as chancellor of the university in the late 1850s until they discovered that his illness did not prevent him from working on his journal and also editing a memorial volume dedicated to gun manufacturer Samuel Colt while he recuperated in Hartford. In 1866 he accepted the presidency of St. John's College in Annapolis and found himself embroiled in controversy with college officials and faculty who resented his continued work on the journal and frequent trips to Washington to lobby for the department of education bill. Later, during his term as commissioner, congressmen wondered aloud on the House floor whether he had established the new department in his hometown rather than in Washington. The train of failures became all too visible to his colleagues in the educational field, some of whom began looking askance at his frequent illnesses. James Butler warned Barnard shortly after his appointment as commissioner that many of his friends "were far from appreciating your embarrassments." [9]

Emerson White's comment that Barnard "scatters too badly" meant primarily that he attempted to do too much, but the Ohioan could have been referring also to Barnard's difficulty in defining limits to his tasks and his failure to establish and distinguish between immediate and long-range goals. All of his projects seemed enormous, his plans comprehensive and complete. Yet he hardly ever completed them on schedule, if indeed he completed them at all. He was, it seemed, incapable of meeting deadlines and so he rarely set them for himself. Barnard's mismanagement of his journal magnified —and publicized—his deficiencies as an administrator. Thursfield concluded that Barnard had an "utter lack of managerial ability." His disregard of record keeping, his habitual failure to complete and distribute issues on schedule, his casual approach to subscription lists, and his indifference to finances finally drove publisher C. W. Bardeen to explode: "Barnard never will be able to manage his business himself, and will never work out his plans with any satisfaction to himself or others till the pecuniary responsibility is taken out of his hands and put into those of someone who has experience and prompt business habits. . . ." With evident misgiv- ing, Barnard delegated responsibility for his projects and seemed forever suspicious of subordinates' ability to execute plans he had formulated. Finally, he did not receive suggestions well and, according to Thursfield, resented criticism. From all accounts, he was not an easy man to work with.[10]

A loner who preferred his own to someone else's harness, Barnard favored professional independence to the more public and political tasks related to administration. He followed high standards of scholarly excellence and a private accountability. And yet, restless and ambitious, he repeatedly placed himself in positions of authority which required him to do what he found most distasteful—meet deadlines, supervise subordinates, and satisfy the directives of those who employed him. In the process, he left the well-marked trail of a man at war with himself.

Like many of his contemporaries in the common school movement, Barnard espoused conservative positions on matters of property rights and economic questions generally. An anti-Jackson man in the 1830s, he leaned ideologically and temperamentally toward that branch of the Whig party which during the 1850s edged into the Democratic fold. Unlike Horace Mann, however, he remained aloof from political affiliations all during the antebellum period. While not immune to the disjunctions fostered by urban and industrial growth, he abhorred the symptomatic unrest generated by social justice crusades. For Barnard, the new equality, to be permanently secured, required programs more substantial and less immediately disruptive than the higher wages and better working conditions sought by the direct action tactics of labor organizations. He opposed the abolitionist sentiment for the same reason. In

105

Thursfield's words, he deplored slavery but felt bound to acknowledge "the sanctity of propertied interests vested in slaves." In March 1861, with little appreciation for the crisis confronting the Union, he advised Senator Dixon that if the Senate would assist

> the humble teacher in the 80,000 schools of the land in the great work of educating the next generation in . . . an abiding respect for law and the meaning and sanctity of such words as patriotism, justice, duty, . . . then your successors will have a better time in administering the great interests of the American people, however divided and subdivided into confederacies, nations, and states.[11]

Public education, for Barnard, offered a cure for strikes and the means for restoring noble impulses to the victim of poverty, who otherwise would be inclined toward a life of anarchy and crime. It guaranteed the proper and efficient transfer of religious and political morality to the younger generation, immigrants, and other minorities separated from the values and common sense of the dominant society. In brief, it served to remove "the menace of a populace" and to maintain the peace and sufficiency of the status quo.

Far more than an accommodation of conflicted fears with social change, Barnard's faith in education represented a scholar's belief in schooling as a primary medium of communication across class, race, and sex boundaries. Public instruction, the essential ingredient for transforming a horde into a civilization, provided the indispensable cement for a post-Enlightenment, self-governing society. Insisting, therefore, that common schooling promised no half-cure, he denounced with equal force politicians who limited educational appropriations with miserly indifference and incompetent or visionless teachers. He was committed to the proposition that no one should be omitted from education either directly by exclusion or indirectly through inferior schooling. In advance of more ordinary schoolmen, he pressed for the broadening of public education to include kindergartens, high schools, teachers' seminaries, and colleges; championed such unpopular causes as female education; and advocated the development of state structures for the support, control, and supervision of school systems. While other educators debated the value of the classical curriculum and corporal punishment, he publicized the work of Pestalozzi and the rise of technical education in Europe. Recognizing that friends of public instruction needed practical assistance in establishing schools, he turned his attention to school architecture and furnishings, reproducing sketches of buildings, floor plans, and equipment in his journal. Horrified confederates learned that Barnard even endorsed tuition for public schools as a device, however modest the cost, for maintaining parental interest in educational quality. Local interest, for him, stood as the surest guarantee that common education would not slip to the level of the lowest common denominator. He played a major role in shaping the goals of the common school crusade and viewed school bureaucratization and centralization as reforms that could guarantee effective and efficient public instruction programs. Nevertheless, he was apprehensive that a dulling sameness would infect American education. Avoiding this unwanted result required educators' constant attention to keep the promise of learning alive among themselves, politicians, and parents.[12]

For social historian Merle Curti, Barnard's commitment to educational advance saved the schoolman from the fallacy of unrelieved conservatism. If the educator experienced any internal conflict between his political and economic views and his advocacy of public instruction, he never admitted it. There was no reason why Barnard should have made such an admission. His forthrightness as a school reformer emanated neither from a novel humanism nor from radical principles of social justice. Committed more to the protection and fulfillment of existing structures than to the creation of new forms of social organization, Barnard adhered rather to an ageless confidence in rational man. His hierarchical and centralizing plans for the supervision and control of school systems remained consistent with his economic and political views. Together they reflected the essential conservatism of Barnard the reformer. He championed broadly inclusive schools, if not enforced equality of educational opportunity, and the expansion of school systems to include within the public sector new forms, areas, and levels of instruction because he perceived few other means for guaranteeing stability and peaceful social growth.[13]

Early in his career as an educator, Barnard accepted the proposition that responsibility for encouraging states in their educational efforts devolved ultimately upon the federal government. No other public or private agency possessed the resources needed for either collecting and disseminating school information nationally or providing comprehensive direction for the bewildering, often conflicting and qualitatively uneven, public instruction programs being generated on state and local levels. Stopping short of endorsing plans for federal control of public schools, such as suggested by Charles Brooks and Robert Dale Owen, Barnard viewed the federal role in school promotion as one of bolstering state and municipal education officials in their struggle against public apathy and political infighting over school control and educational policy. Staid, dispassionate, and not at all spectacular, his proposals for a national bureau of education possessed, even so, an ephemeral quality. Whether designed for towns, states, regions, or the nation, Barnard's plans for school organization bore remarkable similarities. On a grander scale, the goals and modes of operation he settled upon as a state school officer appeared once more in his plan for the federal educational agency. Once fixed, as they were by 1855, they remained in place, apparently untouchable by secession, civil war, emancipation, or reconstruction. Not even the Constitution could claim such durability. And yet the plan contained a note of singular unreality: he gave the proposed national school agency no sure location. He preferred a public bureau but would not have complained if a private educational organization had sponsored the plan. He enthusiastically supported the department bill and wrote to Garfield after its passage, "The form of your measure is better than I feared you could ever get." Barnard would have accepted a great deal less—a lone clerk working away in the Smithsonian Institution or even two clerks constituting an inconspicuous bureau tucked away in the Department of the Interior. He wanted the chance to put his plan into operation.[14]

Unsteady on this one minor point, Barnard changed his scheme very little over time, except to make it more elaborate and thoroughly rational. Although his personal experience with public education left him bitter, he fashioned the proposal out of the hope that public schools could disburse knowledge and virtue among the people. Remaining consistent with premises supporting the original American Lyceum suggestions and his own Enlightenment faith in the causal relation between the spread and increase of knowledge and social and individual betterment, Barnard's plan never strayed from the core ideas found also in his proposals for local and state school organization. At its center stood the national agent or commissioner whose experience, personal magnetism, and comprehensive knowledge of educational operations in the United States and abroad would qualify him for the task of gathering, interpreting, and disseminating school data. By "pen, print, and voice" the agent would encourage local and state school improvement. Barnard saw him inspecting schools and attending educational gatherings throughout the country, conducting a vast international correspondence with the friends of education, making himself available for interviews and consultations in his Washington office, and utilizing the press to publicize the nation's educational needs. The effectiveness of the agent's work depended fundamentally on the energy and imagination by which he carried out his responsibilities.

In Barnard's original plan, the central agency exerted no direct control over local schools. Perhaps his experience in Washington explained the shifts in his thinking. In 1870, shortly before leaving his post, he suggested strategies, just shy of federal control, for augmenting the influence of published information. Speaking before the National Association of State Superintendents on 3 March of that year, he recommended empowering the commissioner to establish a model school system in the District of Columbia with federal funds, appoint superintendents of public instruction in the territories, and create as rapidly as possible territorial systems of public schools, all the while overseeing the disposal of federal lands set aside for educational purposes. The model institutions, particularly those in the capital, would stimulate local educational improvement by exhibiting the most effective ways of organizing and conducting schools. At this later date, Barnard also endorsed federal grants to states unable to organize their schools into systems, "accompanied with the right of inspection." In brief, he came to see that the success of a central agency depended upon its power, financial resources, and influence. He further saw that the Department of Education Act subverted the agency's reform mission in recognizing the need only of the last: influence through published school data.[15]

These insights came to Barnard at the end of his term as commissioner. During the preceding three years, the preparation of publications consumed his energy. One might argue that Congress through the Department of Education Act and a subsequent directive to survey education in the District of Columbia forced this concentration of time and energy upon him. However, Barnard's 1854 plan for a central agency and his public remarks after assuming his post made clear that he accepted as the commissioner's primary task the preparation of reports. Furthermore, he repeatedly stated his intention to produce not merely statistical summaries of school operations but also historical and comparative studies of significant innovations in education. As he explained to the American Institute of Instruction in 1867:

> It has been my aim to bring to bear the light of past and present experience. My belief is that anything worth preserving has its roots in the past; and to make us grow we need all the light which can be brought to bear from every country. . . . I shall draw from the resources of the latest 15 years of study. It is known that the very work which I am now engaged in doing, is one which I have been trying to do in my own individual way, and at my own individual expense.[16]

His first *Report of the Commissioner of Education*, submitted to Congress one year later, remained consistent with this aim. A "Schedule of Information Sought" published in the report outlined the range of information Barnard wanted: overviews of education in the United States; detailed descriptions of all levels and classes of schools, public and private, including those offering informal or supplementary education; and information on institutions and topics related to education, such as libraries and the influence of parents in their children's moral development. His plan for disseminating information included monthly circulars, each devoted to a selected subject, which would be used to answer inquiries and mailed to persons known to be interested in the topic. He further proposed to issue tracts and documents begun "several years ago" on the history of education, touching in particular on the different types of schools at home and abroad and educational practices in various kinds of localities, such as urban and rural areas. Finally, he intended to produce a quarterly publication which would be a national series of his journal, and submit an annual report to Congress as required by law.[17]

BARNARD AS COMMISSIONER OF EDUCATION

It was evident from the beginning of Barnard's term that his small staff and limited funds would severely restrict chances for actualizing his plan. Furthermore, his weakened physical condition ruled out inspection tours and attendance at educational conventions. Although present for the 1867 and 1868 meetings of the American Institute of Instruction, he failed to attend any N.T.A. gathering during his three-year term. Despite a personal invitation to the 1868 N.T.A. meeting in Nashville from Tennessee school superintendent John Eaton, he chose to return to Hartford instead.[18]

Barnard had long argued that the national school agent would have to win his way initially by personal influence and magnetism. A friend advised him soon after he took office that such personal contact would be essential to securing the help of southern officials and friends of education during the tense postwar period. Northern schoolmen also eyed the new federal department with suspicion. In the important state of Ohio, for example, Emerson White's successor as superintendent of common schools was Captain John A. Norris, the "maimed soldier," who owed his position to state political leaders. An experienced teacher, Norris neither knew Barnard nor shared the national perspective of other Ohio educators long involved with the common school movement and the N.T.A. A cross-country tour by Barnard to meet with state and local officials and discuss personally the aims of the department and the kinds of information desired would have facilitated the task of gathering data and might have helped in creating a broad base of political and popular support for the agency, thus strengthening the commissioner's hand in dealing with Congress. Even if Barnard could have secured funds for such a journey, he would have been stopped by poor health. Instead, he turned to friends, volunteers, and temporary employees to make the personal contacts and inspection tours and to gather the information he wanted, relying in some cases on previously published state and muncipal reports.[19]

His method of disseminating information became equally casual, dictated in part by lack of funds to print his circulars and reports. John Eaton argued many years later that budgetary limitations forced Barnard to use his journal as the primary means of distributing the data he collected. The explanation, however, ignored the commissioner's repeated assertion that his journal represented an integral part of the department's work. For approximately a year after June 1867, he formally relinquished his role as editor to David N. Camp yet remained intimately involved in editing the publication.

Barnard could never admit to any wrongdoing in combining these two interests despite Camp's continuing on the department payroll for six months of the year he served as editor. Barnard saw his publication as a public service. In his view, publishing articles and documents which would later appear in the department's reports and circulars was legitimate and proper.[20]

Despite the refusal of Congress to print his reports or to allocate funds for the massive distribution of monthly circulars, Barnard could have effectively used the press to disseminate information. The commissioner regularly sent his circulars to editors throughout the country—by the wagonload, according to John Kraus, a frequent correspondent, who judged their appearance to be so dull editors would simply discard them. Kraus wanted Barnard to write articles for selected newspapers, in addition to the scholarly treatises found in the monthly circulars, and even tried his own hand at producing popular accounts of the department's work. The point, he argued, was to stimulate general concern for education and to find ways of disseminating information in language capable of carrying a mass appeal without waiting for congressional approval of funds for printing department publications. Given the nation's preoccupation with reconstruction issues, the deepening rift between the president and Congress, and the approaching presidential campaign, whether such an effort would have had much effect was not clear. It was true that Barnard did not aggressively seek out media for the distribution of educational information.[21]

In one area the commissioner remained true to his original plan. Neither illness nor Congress could prohibit his carrying on a prodigious international correspondence with schoolmen and the friends of education. In the autumn of 1867, while subordinates labored in Washington on the educational survey in the capital, Barnard, in Hartford "so much unwell as to be unable to attend to my work," found strength to initiate and answer inquiries concerning school architecture, Indian education, the history of American normal schools, state histories of education, pedagogy, and the organization of national bureaus or ministries of education in other countries. Each of these topics found its way into his first annual report.[22]

That Barnard completed the report was something of a miracle, given his illnesses, the maze of projects in which he was embroiled, and his characteristic procrastination. As it was, during his three–year term he submitted only the one annual report to Congress, plus his survey of education in Washington. In both cases, congressional pressure appeared to be a major factor behind his drive toward completion. Two other studies were begun. He submitted a special report on technical education in different countries to Congress a few months after he left office. A study of national education in other countries was not completed until 1871. These two documents and the Washington survey were subsequently published as volumes of the *American Journal of Education.*

The *Report of the Commissioner of Education*, including what Barnard termed "illustrative documents," was literally, as Garfield complained, a heavy document. Consisting of almost 900 pages, it appeared to be a further installment of Barnard's projected documentary history of education. Yet its comprehensiveness and depth of insight made it heavy in another, far more important, respect. Buried amid long, unwieldy sentences was a truth about the condition and progress of their educational systems which Americans needed to hear.[23]

The Department of Education was assigned the task of collecting and disseminating useful educational information. Completing the task, Barnard admitted at the outset, was well nigh impossible. With no authority to require the cooperation of local and state officials and no funds to collect original data or conduct inspections, the department found itself forced to rely upon information provided by local authorities and volunteers. Neither was reliable. States and municipalities followed what might generously be termed a casual approach to educational data, no two using the same organization or schedules. The volunteers, while well-meaning, lacked experience in collecting statistics. Without precise and uniform data, the commissioner observed, comparisons among the educational systems of the various cities and states tended to cloak more than reveal "the amazing deficiencies in our systems, means, and methods of universal education."

Barnard recommended that all states, following the same general plan, inaugurate annual surveys of the condition and progress of public and private education within their borders. He urged the National Association of School Superintendents to undertake the creation of a plan for gathering uniform school data and to work for legislation to secure its adoption in each state. In a sentence typical of the total report, Barnard concluded:

> If he [the commissioner] has been reasonably successful in
> indicating the method by which a national agency, like this
> Department, can obtain a record of the educational systems and
> institutions of the several states, and put himself in communica-
> tion with their managers and teachers—can throw light on the
> deficiencies as well as the excellencies of our systems, and
> impart greater activity to all the agencies which determine the
> education of a people—can contribute in the experience of
> States, systems, and institutions, and in the views of eminent
> teachers and educators, the material for a thorough discussion
> and wise solution of educational problems—he has done all that
> he has thus far attempted, or that could reasonably be
> expected.[24]

There it was in a nutshell: the major problem with Barnard's
report was not that it lacked intelligence or insight; rather, it was
ponderous and profoundly unreadable. His operating premise was
simple—deceptively so. In order to comprehend the condition of
American public education and to institute reforms, one had to know
also its history and the history and condition of private and religious
schools, informal education within the family, the moral structure of
the surrounding society, and all of the agencies, institutions, and
forces bearing upon the quality and quantity of learning. In addition,
full understanding required studies of foreign school systems and
societies. Even if statistical comparisons among state and municipal
school systems could be effected, Barnard argued, they would prove
meaningful only if supported by the historical and contextual
information necessary for interpreting them. Lacking reliable statistics, the department could still be useful by making available to key
public officials and school authorities materials designed to stimulate
recognition of the value of education, of which the American people
were still not convinced, Barnard insisted, and the search for
intelligent solutions to school dilemmas.

Barnard's premise made clear why he had such difficulty
completing his report, for in truth arbitrary termination points could
not be imposed on inquiry aimed at understanding education broadly
conceived. Hence the documents accompanying his report served
literally to illustrate the kinds of information one needed to grasp the
educational situation, rather than to exhaust the study of systems and
institutions. The range of subjects included teacher education, school
architecture, secondary and elementary schooling, taxation for public

114

schools, and female education. References to European school practices appeared in several of the documents, and one consisted solely of a discussion of public secondary instruction in Prussia. Present also were reviews of the United States' educational land policy, state constitutional provisions dealing with education, and national and state legislation bearing upon the land grants for agricultural and mechanical arts colleges, in addition to a brief report on each of the land grant colleges established up to March 1868. James Garfield's speech delivered during the debate on the department of education bill and a twenty-four page index to Barnard's journal also found their way into the accompanying documents. The commissioner included the speech, a reasoned, closely documented defense of the new agency, for its public relations value. Also, he had helped to write it, gathering Garfield's supporting documentation from back issues of his journal. Inclusion of the index, roundly criticized as blatant conflict of interest, provided a valuable supplement by identifying related materials for the reader interested in pursuing topics found in the report and documents. Five of the documents plus portions of two others, appeared previously in issues of the *American Journal of Education* during 1867 and 1868.[25]

Arrangement of the documents in the pages following the report was loose. Repeatedly the commissioner apologized for the preliminary, incomplete nature of a document, promising fuller reports in subsequent publications. The pagination was haphazard, and the order of the documents lacked clear rationale. Finally, no overarching plan governed the selection of documents, other than Barnard's announced intention to complete his documentary history of education. He included reports on federal land policy and the land grant colleges because Congress had requested them. The review of state constitutional provisions on education offered a timely discussion of pertinent sections in the new constitutions of the former Confederate states, but the commissioner failed to relate the reports on female education and school architecture to current educational interests. More damaging, the report omitted discussion of education for black people and evaluation of the educational efforts of the Freedmen's Bureau and the several private agencies working among black and white southerners.

All of these deficiencies, particularly the lack of organization, telegraphed the report's hurried construction. Barnard keenly felt the impatient demand for visible evidence of his agency's usefulness voiced repeatedly in Congress during the winter and spring of 1868. By attaching so many documents to his report, without much attention to their relevance or how Congress would receive them, he hoped perhaps to offer some justification for the department itself. John Philbrick, who read the report but not the documents, understood the causes of his friend's anxiety but spoke to him with characteristic bluntness:

> It is in one respect the most remarkable educational document I ever read. I have never seen before so comprehensive a survey of the whole field of educational inquiry condensed into so small a space. . . . Nobody can complain that you have not undertaken enough. It may be said, on the other hand, that you have attempted too much. . . . Some will think, and with some reason, perhaps, that what you are trying to do the first year or two would be enough to occupy the present force of your department for a dozen years at least.

A preliminary draft of the twenty-four page report was presented to Congress early in June 1868; the final statement with the 856 pages of documents appeared one month later. While the Senate showed some interest in the report and the documents, at least to the extent that it approved printing 3000 copies of the former and 1500 copies of the latter, the House, decidedly unenthusiastic, chose to print only the report.[26]

Garfield felt betrayed by Barnard's failure to win congressional favor with the report. Fearing the worst, he had urged the commissioner to omit many of the documents, especially the index and his own speech, but Barnard had refused. The man was "utterly destitute of administrative ability," Garfield complained to White, "and has made the impression on Congress that his faults are far worse than that." Repeating the criticism to B. G. Northrop, he added:

> While Dr. Barnard is no doubt an able man, he seems utterly to have misconceived the purpose and object of the Bill creating the Department. He ought to have remembered that his work was to be subjected to the scrutiny of a body of men many of whom must see a money value in any publication in order to appreciate its worth. The outlines of his scheme as exhibited in his Report, have terrified Congress, and it will be with the

greatest possible difficulty if we save the Department from utter destruction.

The Ohio Republican admitted to his old friend Burke Hinsdale, however, that "to a scholar and educator his [Barnard's] Report will always be a most valuable summary of important material." In the report Garfield thus beheld a multitude of contradictory sins, among which the major trespass apparently derived from Barnard's miscalculation of congressional attitudes toward the department and his consequent error in addressing the report to the nation's educators rather than members of Congress not yet convinced of the agency's value.[27]

White echoed Garfield's complaints. Too comprehensive and too similar to the seventeen volumes of Barnard's journal, the report, in his view, missed the agency's intended purpose.

> Is it the practical, vital work which the Department was organized to accomplish? Order and system need to be brought out of our present chaos of school statistics—a work in which the Department is now evidently failing. . . . What is needed is not so much indefinite and diffuse information as available and reliable statistics which will serve as educational tests and measures; not so much the history of education as the practical lessons of that history; not so much compilation as critical comparison and wise deductions.

Barnard, of course, agreed in general, arguing additionally that data could not be interpreted outside their historical context. White's point, which ignored the difficulty of collecting reliable data in the postwar period, seemed to be that Barnard's attitude allowed him to "scatter" or dilute his energies into endless projects. It was a valid observation, documented by Barnard's inability to draw his inquiries to a reasonable conclusion. Fundamentally, however, the two educators agreed on the proper work of the department—but not on who should be directing it.[28]

Eighteen months passed before Barnard submitted another report to Congress. Beleaguered by illness and squabbles among his staff, harassed by president and Congress alike, he held on to his office only by quelling the temptation to resign. Tenaciousness seemed to provide him with no new sources of strength or

117

imagination. After 30 June 1869, a reduced staff of only two clerks and an appropriation of $600 for expenses effectively rendered the agency inoperative. Still, he dreamed of completing his projected documentary history of education, seemingly oblivious to the chorus of criticism which had greeted his only previous effort. On 22 December 1869, he shared his plan with Potter: a survey of national education, including a report of 300-400 pages "on all the great features and facts of [school] systems in different countries" and five volumes of documents dealing with primary, secondary, and higher education and supplementary schools and agencies. "I shall get the whole work done except my general conclusions in 3 or 4 months," he predicted, "and then I shall retire to my grave or Europe." [29]

Barnard appeared to have forgotten about the still unfinished Washington survey. In mid-January 1870, he received a jarring reminder from the House to submit whatever information had been collected. Away from Washington at the time, Barnard returned to discover that his office with all his books and papers had been moved to different quarters. A few days later, still overwhelmed by the resulting confusion, he heard from Secretary of Interior Cox that President Grant intended to name General John Eaton as commissioner. On 28 January 1870, dismayed by an announcement of Eaton's nomination in the press, Barnard poured out his hurt and frustration to Cox:

118

I could have wished that I had been earlier informed of the
wishes of the President, that I might have retired voluntarily
from a place in which I had worked diligently, if not after the
best plan, and with all the obstacles of an untried movement,
and an utterly inadequate clerical force.

Pleading for more time in which to draw his documents together, he
explained that the report would be delayed by the "displacement" of
his papers. Barnard's request was granted, and in the late spring
1870, Congress received the Washington survey.[30]

Comprehensive in scope, the study was consistent in every
detail with Barnard's premise that meaningful statistics required
historical background and a comparative framework. Unlike his first
report, the Washington survey included statistical tables offering
general population characteristics and school census information,
thanks primarily to the canvass directed by Franklin B. Hough. In
addition, Barnard included a history of public education in the
District of Columbia, descriptions of schools currently in operation,
and a review of relevant school legislation. To facilitate judgments
about the relative efficiency of schools in the capital, he offered brief
reports on public education in every major American city and a
general discussion of education in European cities. At the end of the
report, in concise, blunt language, Barnard recommended the
reorganization of public education in the capital into one school
district embracing every level of learning, including supplementary
schools offering programs in adult and continuing education. Admitting the plan would be costly, he urged Congress not only to provide
the necessary funds but also to establish a board of control with
sufficient authority to create a model, enlightened school system
dedicated to the eradication of illiteracy.[31]

Not surprisingly, a lengthy collection of documents accompanied the report. Two of the most extensive statements dealt with
the education of black people and illustrated the directness and
vision which Barnard brought to his survey. The first, written by M.
B. Goodwin, recounted the long, troubled history of black education
in the District of Columbia, the periodic destruction of black schools
by white mobs, and the persistent efforts of black educators to build
a tradition of learning among their people. The second document
offered a historical survey of the legal status of black education in the
District and every state in the Union. Although unsigned, it appeared

to have been authored by Barnard. Using reports of the Freedmen's Bureau, state school officials, and individual educators, he provided criteria for evaluating the progress of black education in the capital, and along the way catalogued the dreary, familiar story of enforced black illiteracy throughout the nation. He also offered credible evidence to any congressman willing to listen that the Freedmen's Bureau enjoyed no little success in its educational efforts among former slaves. Aware of their value, Barnard urged Congress to print extra copies of the two documents so that they could be widely circulated. No action was taken on the request.[32]

The *Special Report on Education in the District of Columbia* corrected all the shortcomings of Barnard's first report. Readable, well organized, and although long, quite precise in identifying the past, present, and possible future of public education in the capital, it provided a useful model for surveying other urban school systems. Nevertheless, the report was lost in a wave of congressional disregard for the educational agency and Barnard personally. On 16 March 1870, after a last, ignored plea for more time to draw together documents yet unfinished, he relinquished his office to John Eaton and retired to Hartford to complete the reports he had assigned himself. It had been, as he later described it, "a dismal experience."[33]

In many respects the conservatism and timeless dispassion of Barnard's plan suited conditions and moods of the Reconstruction period. Carrying no brief for any segment of the population, it proposed the quiet expansion and revitalization of the movement begun by a previous generation of common school crusaders rather than a radical reordering of educational policy. Grounded in familiar ideas, it offered tested strategies as a means for extending and relating established state school structures. It aimed, in short, to increase and improve educational opportunity by instructing the friends of education, particularly those who controlled and supervised schools.

In executing the plan, Barnard created many of his own difficulties. He held a position demanding the kind of total expenditure of energy and imagination which his responsibilities in Connecticut and Rhode Island had required, and he lacked the heart to give that much of himself again. Furthermore, in his first report he committed an administrative and political error of major proportions by reading the Department of Education Act through the eyes of his own plan. This myopic blunder led him to equate his work as editor of the *American Journal of Education* with that of the new department, and it got him into a great deal of trouble. More fatefully, he ignored, or failed to perceive, warnings that the agency's survival remained an open question from the start. Its enemies, an unlikely collection of radicals, democrats, and educators, were never willing to be reconciled to the department or its commissioner. In light of what happened, even Emerson White shed his ambition for Barnard's job.

5 From Department to Bureau: The Politics of Dream Deferral

At the Beginning: Conflict and Opposition

Things went badly from the outset, and neither Barnard's deficiencies as an administrator nor his personal idiosyncrasies fully explained the trouble. Mangled financial arrangements and delayed reports, compromising involvements of a private journal in the work of a federal agency, frequent illnesses and retreats to Hartford—Barnard's deficits and mistakes unquestionably restricted the department's chances for success. More significantly, they provided belated justification to its enemies settled in their opposition even before the first appropriation for the agency won congressional approval. From the beginning, suspicion and hostility stalked the Department of Education. Watchful and gossip-prone, still hopeful that he might be named chief clerk, Zalmon Richards scurried to Barnard, in office not yet a month, with the cryptic alarm to be careful, "someone is trying to make capital against you." At this point, his only activity as commissioner involved a continuing skirmish with the president over the employment of Edward Neill as chief clerk.[1]

Having successfully inserted one of his followers into the Freedmen's Bureau staff, Johnson seemed intent upon effecting a similar arrangement within the Department of Education. In meetings with Barnard on 6 and 25 March 1867, he pressed for his secretary's appointment to Barnard's highest staff position. The schoolman, in the meantime, still aspiring for latitude in the selection of clerks, approached Elisha Potter and Daniel Coit Gilman with offers to join him in the department, admitting to Potter, "I am likely to be embarrassed in my liberty of choice by Presidential interference. . . ." Both men rejected the overture. Barnard's reluctance to accede to the president's demand forced Senator Dixon into an uncomfortable role. Invoking the compromise outlined during Barnard's 6 March meeting with Johnson, and Barnard's seeming acceptance of the plan, Dixon cautioned the schoolman against any unfriendly delay. "[Y]ou must be careful or you will be in trouble," he wrote on 14 March. "Dr. Neil [*sic*] is very unquiet and seems rather to think himself neglected—and from a hint to me from a person near the Pres. (not Dr. Neil), [your] Commission may be held back by the President if Neil is not appointed." Two days later, he added, "The Pres., I find, expects Dr. Neil's appointment." Urging Barnard to "oblige" Johnson, Dixon renewed his earlier warning: "There are certain difficulties which occur to me if you do not." [2]

Wearied by the mounting pressure, Barnard interviewed both Richards and Neill for staff positions on 25 March, after his second meeting with the president, and left almost at once for home, "sick and exhausted," without notifying either what he intended to do. The following week, while still in Hartford, he named Richards to one of the clerk positions, assigning him responsibility for receiving inquiries about the department, but continued to balk at appointing Neill. With Richards as emissary, news of Neill's displeasure now arrived regularly at Barnard's retreat. The man "has great influence and must be dealt with smoothly," he warned in a 6 April letter reporting Neill's anger at not receiving the promised clerkship. Unknown to Richards, Neill still retained his position in the president's office and thus, despite his complaints, suffered no lack of income. At length Barnard gave in. Neill joined the staff as chief clerk in mid-April. An uneasy truce at best set in. Relations between Neill and Barnard proved to be irreparably bruised, aggravated by Richards' resentment over Neill's superior place in the department hierarchy and Neill's restless drive for Barnard's position. Thus, after barely a month, Lyman Trumbull's patient explanation to the Senate for creating an independent education agency rather than a bureau in the Department of the Interior had been deprived of meaning. The wording of the act aside, in practice the commissioner of education lacked autonomy in appointing his own staff.[3]

While the Neill episode ran its course, even more demoralizing assaults on the fledgling department issued from the new Congress. Fearful that an unwatched president would subvert reconstruction programs, the Fortieth Congress convened hard on the heels of its predecessor. Amid deliberations of enabling bills for measures enacted during the closing days of the Thirty-ninth

Congress, including the crucial Reconstruction Act, Garfield on 11 March introduced legislation appropriating funds for the Department of Education. Requesting $9,400 for salaries, the amount stipulated in the act, and only $6,000 for office expenses and supplies, Garfield failed to muster the two-thirds majority needed for an immediate vote on his motion. He then attempted to channel the measure into the Judiciary Committee where George Boutwell and William Lawrence could assist in speeding it back to the House floor. Samuel Randall, still a confirmed foe of the department, objected to the unusual assignment and the House agreed to forward the bill to the less friendly Committee on Appropriations.[4]

While department supporters awaited the committee's report, the House delimited further its interest in education. On 21 March it approved a motion creating a Committee on Education and Labor after rejecting Ignatius Donnelly's appeal for a body to deal exclusively with educational matters. Even with the backing of the Rules Committee, Donnelly could not persuade his colleagues that the new department, combined with the House's responsibility for keeping informed on the state of public instruction, necessitated a standing committee on education. As it turned out, members of the new Education and Labor Committee, announced in November, included formidable allies of both Barnard and the department. They were instrumental in saving the agency when the Neill affair erupted into an ugly and public conflict.[5]

On 25 March Thaddeus Stevens tacked on to a supplementary appropriations bill then under consideration an amendment providing funds for the department in the amount originally proposed by Garfield. The measure quickly won House approval. Two days later, the Senate agreed to the House action but not before correcting an error which would have delayed starting the department even longer. Stevens' amendment failed to specify funds for the remainder of the current fiscal year. The Senate added $3,000 for this three-month period to the $15,400 designated for the fiscal year ending 30 June 1868. With House approval of the insertion, the bill became law on 29 March 1867. To make the department's financial situation even more precarious, Congress on the same day directed the agency to launch a survey of education in the capital. Introduced by Dixon, the resolution provided no funds for conducting the study, and none of its sponsors suggested that it should.[6]

If Barnard needed reasons for being ill during March 1867,

Congress provided him with several. Its appropriation for the initial three months of the department's operation covered salaries and little else. Beyond that, with only three clerks, a meager sum for office supplies, no secretarial help, and no funds for travel or printing, Barnard found himself expected to launch an entirely new federal bureau responsible at least for the nationwide collection and dissemination of school statistics and to complete studies of land grants for educational purposes in the various states and territories and education in Washington, both enormous projects. Forced to accept, in addition, a chief clerk not of his own choosing and with him the reality of political interference in the work of the department, Barnard began his term with few reasons for optimism. Cataloging, with amazing detachment, the obstructions hedging his operation, he cautioned members of the American Institute of Instruction at their August meeting not to expect too much: "[M]y aim will be to carry out literally the provisions of the law,—to collect and disseminate information, so as to show the condition and progress of education in the States and Territories, . . . to aid the people of the United States in establishing school systems." [7]

The Attempt to Abolish: Department to Bureau

Barnard spent most of the summer of 1867 in Hartford, "regaining his strength." As was his custom, he also worked on various projects, including the journal, periodically mailing instructions and assignments to his staff in Washington. Richards wrote with such weekly regularity of his chief clerk's attempts to undermine the work of the department that Barnard likely became dulled to his frequent alarms. Even news of Neill's personal attacks, his rumor-mongering and portrayals of the commissioner as unfit for office, left him unmoved. In September a letter from Ignatius Donnelly reporting his apprehension over growing congressional criticism of Barnard's administration received the commissioner's immediate attention. Acknowledging that over the years he might have offended or disappointed many in his efforts to advance public education, Barnard insisted that he had "no avowed opponents to the general principles and method of public instruction which I have advocated, who do not oppose others on the same ground." He refused to defend himself against charges of personal incompetence not only because the testimony of educational officers throughout the country seemed sufficient to refute them, but also because no words of his could satisfy critics whose real target was the department itself. Offering to change his adopted policies and procedures "for any which can be shown to be better," Barnard concluded with an appeal for understanding:

> Since I accepted this position, I have devoted the working hours of everyday—and many more morning and night hours, to maturing plans for making it useful. I shall do the best I know, ready at all times to receive suggestions and criticisms. . . . Until Congress gives me some means and facilities, beyond those which I now possess (three clerks and a fund to provide room and stationery), to get information and diffuse it, the friends of Education should be charitable in their judgments as to results realized in less than six months of the most unfavorable part of the year.[8]

Barnard remained in Hartford throughout the autumn, turning his attention increasingly to the progress of the Washington survey. He failed to mention in his letter to Donnelly that rather than employ the third clerk allowed him by Congress, he was using the funds designated for that salary to engage part-time researchers scattered around the country to assist him in gathering data and writing documents for his annual report. Two of these temporary staff members worked on the survey, but the others rarely appeared at the department's offices in Washington. With the department's visibility diminished further by Barnard's extended sojourns in Hartford, the entire operation seemed disorganized and, from Neill's perspective, leaderless. Complaining bitterly to both Richards and congressional allies and audibly dismayed at the commissioner's administrative procedures, he demanded to be named acting commissioner during Barnard's stays in Hartford and squabbled with Richards over such issues as who had responsibility for opening mail. Left without direction, Richards proved capable only of adding to the tension. Proud of his reputation as a man with influence in Washington, he never reconciled himself to Neill's presence on the staff. Serving as Barnard's confidant, private secretary, and disbursing clerk would have soothed the injury, except that Neill's

126

belligerence and Barnard's absence frightened him away from claiming such assignments. Most of all, Richards wanted to direct the population canvass for the Washington survey and could barely cloak his irritation when Barnard selected Franklin B. Hough, one of the part-time researchers, for the task. Late in November, Richards' conflict with Neill erupted into a shouting match which left him shaken. The man must go, he wrote to Barnard, and Barnard, finally out of patience with his estranged chief clerk, returned to Washington in mid-December to dismiss him, knowing full well the risk he ran of incurring presidential wrath.[9]

Neill was not to be gotten rid of easily. He took his complaints against Barnard not only to the president but also to Elihu B. Washburne, "the great retrencher," in the House of Representatives. Although intended only to embarrass the commissioner, Neill's efforts contributed to the near destruction of the department itself. Barnard, for his part, seemed bent upon helping him. Disregarding Richards' advice to ready "something to show for his efforts" before Congress reconvened in November after its late summer recess, he let the deadline pass and then compounded his difficulties by submitting a budget request doubling the department's current appropriation for the next fiscal year. On 8 January 1868, Barnard, again in Hartford, heard once more from Ignatius Donnelly:

> I learn that those opposed to you have made an effort to enlist E. B. Washburne of Illinois in some movement against you and your Department. Would it not be well to see him and, *without letting it be supposed you* are posted, remove any evil impression he may have received? Say nothing about this note.

The following day the Minnesotan sent a more urgent appeal:

> You should come at once to the House. Mr. Stevens will introduce a Resolution from the Committee on Education in the District of Columbia for the repeal of the Act establishing the Department of Education.

Richards added his voice to Donnelly's with a telegram on 11 January, urging Barnard to return to Washington. On 3 February, with Barnard again at his desk, Donnelly reported that the House

127

Appropriations Committee had stricken the department's funds. The agency will be abolished, he warned, "if its friends do not show more energy." [10]

Barnard, now alarmed, rushed into a letter-writing campaign, pleading with friends to write Congress in support of his agency. From February through April, reports of letters written in response to Barnard's requests poured into his office. Even with retrenchment "in the air," Charles Coburn predicted, "economy will begin in the Educational Department, and perhaps end there." Barnard agreed, placing blame for his troubles on the Democrats. Gilman hoped that the impending impeachment trial of Andrew Johnson would remove congressional pressure from the agency and allow Barnard time to finish his report; however, no respite occurred. Invoking an eschatology of uncertain origin, Charles Brooks admonished Barnard not to mourn his fate because the "crooked politicians will be made low." More cognizant of the crisis' ambiguous origins, Boston superintendent John Philbrick attempted to clarify the issues confronting his old friend: "I do hope you will be able to save the Department and that the Department will keep you, and yet if there must be a choice it is better that the Department should be saved without restoring you, than both the Department and its incumbent be swept away together." It was not the message Barnard wanted to receive.[11]

As in the struggle over the organic act, so now in the current crisis, the department's most effective opponents were not Democrats, as Barnard suggested, but influential Republicans in the House of Representatives. Barnard eventually followed Donnelly's advice, asking Washburne on 1 February for an opportunity to discuss with him the work of the department "in anticipation of any printed Report." It was a tardy effort, for on that day Washburne introduced the House appropriation bill for the fiscal year ending 30 June 1869 (H. R. 605), which, as Donnelly had warned omitted any appropriation for the Department of Education. It was an admitted attempt to abolish the agency.[12]

Searching for a compromise with appeal for the "retrenchers," Donnelly introduced on 12 February an amendment to Washburne's bill providing $11,400 for the department, maintaining the staff at its present number and salary, and stipulating a trimmed down $2,000 for expenses. The action set the stage for a second congressional probe of the purposes and functions of a federal school agency. However, what followed only partially repeated debates on the original measure. Opponents again depicted the department as unconstitutional, unnecessary for educational reform, and a waste of public funds. Proponents described it as a constitutional expression of the nation's stake in quality public instruction, a service to states in their efforts to improve schools, a means for equalizing educational opportunities in the South, particularly for black people, and hence an instrument for reunifying the country. Opponents countered by observing the department's lack of authority for educating anyone.

Most of it had been said in 1866, but new arguments against the agency, evidencing mood shifts from the postwar enthusiasm which dominated the Thirty-ninth Congress, also found their way into the 1868 debate. One complaint settled upon Barnard's alleged incompetence. The commissioner spent more time in Hartford than in the capital, Washburne charged, with the result that the department in the course of ten months had not yet been put in operation. Incensed by Barnard's request for $30,000 and three additional clerks for the next fiscal year, submitted before completing his report or offering any other evidence of the department's utility, Washburne viewed the education agency as a budget item which clearly could be eliminated. Fernando Wood, the New York Democrat, suggested a less pragmatic reason for abolishing the department. Congress was already doing too much for the former slaves, he charged, "those thousands of lazy, idle negroes, . . . people who do not work, people who will not work, people who are supported out of the public Treasury by appropriations of Congress for illegal and improper purposes." Other opponents saved their ire for Garfield whose personal "persuasion and eloquence," they complained, convinced a reluctant House to approve the department bill in the first place. Donnelly, Garfield, and Spalding, joined by a handful of other supporters, including Democrats John Pruyn and Charles Phelps, warned against impatience and false economy. Their efforts were to no avail. The House rejected Donnelly's amendment 40 to 61 and on 19 February sent H.R. 605 to the Senate without an appropriation for the Department of Education.[13]

Barnard's flights to Hartford resumed during the late winter and spring. Hoping all the while that the commissioner would finish his report Garfield at length sent him a sharp note on 5 May:

> My great interest in the permanence and success of the Dept. of
> Education induces me to suggest to you my fear that nothing

but an early presentation to Congress of the valuable Reports which you have so nearly ready, will enable the friends of education of the Dept. to save it from abolition and to defend you from the charge that is constantly being reiterated, that no good to the Nation is being accomplished by the Dept.—and that you are using the office in the interest of your Journal. Unless we can get an appropriation through Congress, this session, for the support of the Dept. next fiscal year, it will be virtually abolished. I have great faith and hope in the future of the Dept. if it can once show its right to live.

Nothing in this message should have been news to Barnard. He knew of the blunt criticisms leveled against him and his policies in the recent House debate; yet, he seemed incapable of acknowledging the possible validity of the attack. He mailed a reply—confused and apologetic—to Garfield the following day:

I thank you for your note of the 5th—I am overwhelmed with anxiety, as you may suppose—& no earthly consideration could induce me to work on here, but my desire to bring some of my documents to that stage of completion, that they can be brought together—and I think I can see my way to that end at last.

   I left Washington—fearing if I stayed any longer, I should break down—Mr. [Justin] Morrill told me nothing would be done with the appropriation until after the impeachment trial was ended . . . but the very day of my return [to Hartford], I was taken ill, which with my nervous exhaustion has made the last four weeks the most critical of my life, and yet by the greatest care—by rising early—by employing help, I have continued to finish up nearly two hundred and fifty pages, which constitute a portion of my circulars, (and which are part of the several documents which I propose to make up, with additional matter for which the Govt. pays nothing) referred to in my Report.

   These Circulars, except No. 3, 4 & 5 have cost the Govt. nothing.

   As for my poor Journal which I have continued at a pecuniary loss of nearly two thousand dollars, simply to help the object of the Dept.—it is too bad, it should have to bear the sins of the Commissioner! My highest aim is to save the Dept—& if I escape the exhaustion of this year's labor without the utter ruin of my health, I shall be thankful—if I am able to travel, I shall be in Washington at the close of the week—& after I reach [the Capital] all the printing which will have to be done, will not exceed 15 or 20 pages—

Have patience and charity—& I s^hall probably not
trespass on either much longer—
Very truly your friend
Henry Barnard
I am working against the remonstrances of family & friends.[14]

Within a few weeks Barnard forwarded to Congress a
preliminary report. Rather than silence the criticism against him, it
precipitated a fresh round of bitter denunciation. Perhaps Garfield
missed the implication of Barnard's remark about the few pages
remaining to be printed, but the announcement foretold the
impending attack. Edward Neill, made privy to activity within the
department by Augustus Angerer, Barnard's acting chief clerk,
learned soon enough what Barnard had done. On 3 June, Neill
confided to Washburne:

> By the papers today I notice that the Commissioner of
> Education has presented his first report to Congress. If you will
> take the American Journal of Education for the year 1867–8, I
> think you will find, that it is simply a presentation of papers
> *already published* in that journal, including an *index of forty
> pages* covering the contents of that private journal for *17 years*.
> A General Index is a good thing in its place, but many
> suppose that it is not the intention of Congress to advertise in
> this way, private publications.
> The Report, I presume, is not in manuscript, but
> simply the printed pages of the Journal, with a brief note
> attached. These are facts which as a friend of retrenchment you
> ought to know.

Although he overstated the charge, Neill referred to the fact that
almost half of the documents accompanying Barnard's report, or
approximately 400 pages, appeared in previous issues of the journal.
The published material carried identical page numbers in both the
report and volume XVII of the journal. In the report, Barnard
arranged other documents around those which had appeared in the
journal, which might explain its haphazard pagination and unclear
organization.[15]

Washburne used Neill's information to strengthen House
opposition to the department. The Senate, however, remained
convinced of the agency's value. On 24 June it approved without

debate an amendment to H.R. 605 providing the department with a $20,000 appropriation for the next fiscal year. The sum included $9,400 for salaries, which involved no change from the salary appropriation for the current fiscal year, and $10,600 for general expenses and extra clerical help.[16]

The House took up the Senate amendment on 2 July, after Washburne reported the Committee on Appropriations' recommendation of non-concurrence. Supporters of the department, including Donnelly, Garfield, Spalding, and Phelps, now focused their remarks on the agency's contribution to collecting and disseminating educational statistics. Missing from their speeches were references to the department's role in equalizing school opportunity, educating black people, aiding "in the establishment and maintenance of efficient school systems," or otherwise promoting "the cause of education." Unmoved by the retreat, opponents found a strong ally in Thaddeus Stevens, who two years before had voted to establish the agency. Washburne had previously announced Stevens' opposition to the department, and although Donnelly had feigned disbelief that an old friend of education would take such a position, Washburne's revelation surprised few. Donnelly himself had once warned Barnard of Stevens' desire to abolish the department.[17]

In July, Stevens spoke for himself. Although confused about the totals of House votes taken on the organic bill in June 1866, he revealed that he had supported the measure at Donnelly's request and then primarily because he thought it would eventually fail. "It passed, and a man about whom I could speak that which would place him in a different position from that which he now occupies, was appointed instantly to this place." Stevens depicted the department as a misguided attempt to promote education and to help black people. Nettled by Donnelly's far-flung idealism and Garfield's polished and quotable phrases, he heard inflated and fantastic expectations from department supporters. Blacks would not be helped by teaching them Greek and Latin, he argued, in an aside aimed squarely at Garfield's well-known fascination with classical studies, nor prepared for freedom by giving them a "high scientific polish." Such efforts would take too long to help with reconstruction and in the final analysis would be wasted. Needed, according to Stevens, was education for the ballot box, a job for which the department, given to the gathering of facts by a "worn-out man," was patently unsuited.[18]

132

Leaving aside its attack on Barnard, the speech remained consistent with Stevens' position on educational and reconstruction policy. In his public life he had been a strong advocate of common schools as necessary in preparing citizens for a republic. He viewed public education as the initial step required of society in the development of culture and one means of providing opportunities for individual advancement. Only in this limited sense did the public school represent a means of social reform for Stevens, and it certainly could not be the cause of immediate or radical changes in the social order. To be sure, he seemed to have possessed a larger vision of the practical worth of education when in 1838 he supported a state aid to higher education bill before the Pennsylvania legislature:

> It can hardly be seriously contended that liberal education is useless to man in any condition of life. So long as the only object of our earthly existence is happiness, enlarged knowledge must be useful to every intellectual being, high or low, rich or poor, unless you consider happiness as consisting in the mere vulgar gratification of the animal appetites and passions. Then indeed, that man, like the brute, is happiest who has the most flesh and blood, the strongest sinews, and the stoutest stomach.

Thirty years later, still a visionary, but an eminently practical one, Stevens cherished few illusions about the nature of man or his chances for realizing utopian dreams. After the Civil War, in his own inimitable way he sought guarantees that loyal southern whites would not suffer because of their commitment to the Union, that former slaves would receive basic civil rights, and that the southern states would be reconstructed and not merely restored to the Union. That education, particularly common school education, was needed in the South, that it formed a necessary element in his reconstruction plans, Stevens acknowledged repeatedly in his attempts to secure House approval of a bill creating a system of public schools in the District of Columbia. In fact, one of his arguments against the Department of Education was that funds spent on the agency could be used more effectively in establishing common schools in the capital.[19]

Stevens was a long way from agreeing with Donnelly that education served as the *sine qua non* of southern reconstruction. He advocated, rather, a thorough reworking of the social order in the

133

rebel states; otherwise the guarantees he sought could not be securely established. Not optimistic about achieving his goals in any case, he perceived that educated black men, even with access to the ballot box, could be deprived of their civil rights. Black property owners, on the other hand, might prove to be less easily victimized. Their education, initially at least, ought not be a diffuse excursion through the curricula fancied by white men as the means for acquiring gentlemanly characteristics, but that type of schooling which would enable them to resist the entreaties of white politicians more after their votes than the welfare of black people. If Stevens' reconstruction proposals contained a *sine qua non,* it was the breaking up of large southern estates and the redistribution of lands to those formerly excluded from ownership, in brief, a rearrangement of the economic power base. He never succeeded in attracting a majority of Congress to his position. If congressional reconstruction deserved the radical label, it was due less to Thaddeus Stevens than to Andrew Johnson and the terroristic groups which began feeding the cancer of white supremacy even before Appomattox. Johnson's tendency to treat all Republican proposals as radical-inspired contributed significantly to the unification and radicalization of a splintered and essentially moderate political party.[20]

In July 1868, with the failure of the impeachment trial behind him and the eventual failure of congressional reconstruction clear to almost everyone close enough to the situation to have an intelligent opinion, Stevens, desperate and unwell, closer to death than even his colleagues realized, was not likely to keep silent before what was for him a cruel hoax. And to his way of thinking, the Department of Education was precisely that. Its most vocal congressional supporters, some of them fellow radicals, based their arguments on the premise that education provided the key to social reform, the validity of which he questioned. Furthermore, the commissioner of education, whose department presumed to encourage the advance of public instruction, particularly in the South, sat tired and isolated in Hartford, or on occasion in Washington, writing learned histories of education without clear direction and with little attention to the urgency of the times. The nation required schools which would secure for the Union the devotion and intelligence of blacks and loyal southern whites, not cautious comparisons of existing school systems, not Washington-bound activity of government officials, and clearly not dry statistical reports. Such devises could hardly promise the sort of social change Stevens wanted. A hoax, an illusion of action, and a waste of money—that was the judgment of Thaddeus Stevens on the value of the Department of Education.

Stevens' speech provides only limited insight into the sources of House opposition to the department. Detailed analysis of votes taken during the debates is impossible because none was a roll call. Some House radicals probably shared Stevens' distrust of Barnard simply because he was Johnson's appointee; others, such as Pike of Maine, opposed the department as an implicit threat to state autonomy, not because they agreed with Stevens that the times required more direct federal action in establishing schools. Radicals, of course, did not control the Fortieth Congress any more than its predecessor. Even if their opposition had been near unanimous, it would not have been necessarily fatal to the department. However, moderates, too, were divided. Nudged by criticism of Barnard, a great many of those uncomfortable with the plan for a federal school agency from the outset followed James Blaine in defecting from the coalition Garfield put together to pass the original bill. In 1866 Blaine's support had been circuitous at best. He voted against the department initially but joined the bipartisan contingent of House moderates who at Garfield's urging agreed to help the cause by abstaining when the measure returned for reconsideration. Quite likely, he voted against the department's appropriation in 1868. Finally, shifts in national mood produced in the Fortieth Congress the initial signs of impatience with unprecedented, possibly divisive, legislation, and diminished enthusiasm for plans to "do something for the black man." Expressed in appeals for fiscal responsibility and curtailed federal spending, disaffection for social reforming crusades began setting in. The controversial and troublesome Department of Education, although only a minor budget item, provided a too visible target for the narrowed congressional interests. For a host of reasons, a strange combination of Stevens radicals and Democrats, white supremists and retrenchers, tired reformers and disenchanted moderates, reflecting both ideology and the politician's quest for re-election, joined on 2 July to defeat again the department's appropriation in the House of Representatives.[21]

Two days later, Barnard wrote to Potter:

> We still live but may be as near to death as [Daniel] Webster was when he is said to have said it. If I had accomplished

something more permanent in my Department I would go home with exceeding great joy, for I am literally *tired to death* and I am sick of official life here, although Washington has a large number of intelligent men.

Still uncertain whether the department would live or die, Barnard offered a more hopeful note to his son Henry on 9 July:

As to the Department, my belief is, that it will live through the year 1968—and my belief is founded on the great necessity of a government like this having some such agency to do the work which I am attempting to do . . . my faith is a work-inspiring condition of mind.[22]

The agency was saved by the conference committee appointed to reconcile differences between the House and Senate versions of the appropriations bill. The House agreed to $20,000 for the department for the 1868–69 fiscal year on the condition that at the close of the year, that is, after 30 June 1869, it would become an office within the Department of the Interior. The compromise further stipulated a reduction of the commissioner's salary to $3,000. On 12 July 1868, after both houses agreed to the compromise, a jubilant Barnard gave the news to Potter:

We have beat "Old Thad" and the great "retrencher" [E. B. Washburne], and shall live for one year more as a Dept., & after that (the deluge) as a bureau in the Dept. of the Interior, which is probably its appropriate place. But in one year we can do much with the pamphlets now made.[23]

THE EDWARD NEILL CONTROVERSY: BARNARD'S "MALFEASANCE"

Barnard's note revealed his continued lack of interest in the department's administrative structure and undiminished confidence in his plans for the agency. The month of July, however, provided him with few other occasions to celebrate. The House's refusal to print the documents accompanying his first report followed by one week its reluctant approval of the department's appropriation.

Determined more by their length than by the news that they included reprints from his journal, the decision severely restricted Barnard's ability to disseminate information he had gathered. As Garfield confided to Emerson White, the total report was so bulky "that it has been condemned in advance solely on avoirdupois principles." The House action was essentially a retrenchment effort, but it constructed still another barrier to the department's effectiveness. The Senate, by comparison far more supportive of Barnard and his policies, ordered 3000 copies of the report, 1500 copies of the documents, and in an act of good faith 1500 copies of the still unfinished report on schools in the District of Columbia.[24]

This latest evidence of the House's hardening opposition to the department coincided with a recurrence of conflict within the agency's staff. Unable to locate a satisfactory replacement for Edward Neill—the salary was low and the agency's future too uncertain, friends told him—Barnard had appointed Augustus Angerer as acting chief clerk, at the time a translator for the *American Journal of Education*. Unknown to Barnard, Angerer supported Neill's campaign to become commissioner and willingly served as a liaison between the department and its enemies in Congress and the executive branch. When he proved to be incompetent as chief clerk, Barnard asked for his resignation late in July. Angerer refused, threatening him with exposure for the misuse of federal funds. He offered to take a lower salary if he could keep the title of chief clerk. Indignant and hurt, Barnard dismissed him "on the spot," then allowed him to remain with the department as a clerk when Angerer pleaded for continued employment.[25]

Angerer's charge stemmed from Barnard's use of department funds to employ part-time staff members. More to the point, it reflected Neill's displeasure with the commissioner's reliance on a time-honored practice among federal agencies. The practice, a not very clandestine procedure for escaping budgetary confinements on staff size and mid-year program changes, was so well known to Congress that it outlined the conditions under which the commissioner of agriculture could employ it, a precaution not taken in the creation of the Smithsonian Institution, the Department of the Interior, or the Department of Education. Barnard departed from tradition to the extent of using funds specifically budgeted for a clerk's salary to pay the research specialists. The procedure enabled him to enlarge his staff and at the same time gain the services of high caliber men, such as Franklin Hough, Daniel Coit Gilman, and David N. Camp, unable or unwilling to accept permanent positions. Neill found the practice unseemly, but his motives for doing so were suspect. Barnard, on the other hand, managed his department so poorly, particularly the complex financial arrangements necessitated by dividing the $1600 salary among several short-term employees, that he made himself vulnerable to charges of malfeasance. Often, he drew the salary himself, parceling out small amounts to the individuals hired. Furthermore, he made the mistake of using some of the material submitted by these specialists in his journal. At times, the specialists themselves were unclear whether they worked for the department or the *American Journal of Education.* Barnard took none of the confusion to heart. He found the allegations that he acted improperly bewildering and inconceivable. Publishing the journal formed an integral part of his plan for the agency. The necessity of separating it from his work as commissioner escaped him. Your problem, suggested Mary Mann, would be solved by a private secretary you can trust, for example, John Kraus:

> Your experience is worth so much, that you should relinquish details to those who cannot do the other [more important work], provided you can find faithful workers—but what a microcosm of that wicked Washington your Dept. seems to be. Is it possible that it is Anger [*sic*], the Unitarian minister whom Mr. Kraus describes? You need someone to come between you and toil, as my husband did—I could always find lost papers and things when he could not.[26]

Andrew Johnson could have dismissed Neill's complaints as the mutterings of a disgruntled office-seeker, which fundamentally they were. Instead he entered the conflict. Late in October 1868, his personal secretary, William G. Moore, directed the commissioner to submit a list of department personnel employed since he assumed office, indicating the number of months for which each employee was paid, the amount of money received by each, and the number of days each was actually on duty in the office. In addition, the president required confirmation that all of Barnard's employees had signed the oath of allegiance.[27]

Angered at the thinly veiled implications he found in the president's directive, Barnard prepared his reply but hesitated to post it, fearing its bluntness would result in his dismissal and destruction for the department. Indeed, with its detailed reports on trouble caused by Neill and Angerer, the letter was hardly designed to placate the president. As requested, Barnard listed his clerks, including five scholars recruited to perform specialized services for the department, and noted the length of time each had been employed and his monthly and total salary. He described the assignments given the temporary employees, admitting that they had not done their work in Washington because their assignments had not required it. Employee attendance records had not been maintained, he observed, because he had little reason to complain about absenteeism. Acknowledging failure to secure the signed oath of allegiance from his clerks until the matter had been brought to his attention, Barnard refused to force the procedure on temporary employees "as each was in honorable and successful educational engagements in loyal communities or had been in the service of the government." [28]

Even as Barnard polished his letter to final form and worried over the consequences of mailing it, Neill's complaints against him swept into public view. On 18 November the front page of the Baltimore *Sun* carried the news:

> Charges of gross mismanagement are made against Mr. Barnard, Commissioner of Education. It is alleged that for a period of nearly two years he has been absent from Washington about two-thirds of his time; that he has used the clerical force of the department to assist him in editing a private journal at Hartford; and that he has been very irregular in the mode of drawing money from the treasury. The first report of the Commissioner, it is stated will largely be made up of articles that have already appeared in his private journal.
>
> The President, it is presumed, will not take action against a gentleman who has hitherto borne such a high reputation, unless he is satisfied, after the most careful examination, that the charges are correct.

Barnard had not the slightest doubt that Neill and Angerer were behind the article or that they acted with the president's approval. Outraged by the public accusation of wrongdoing, he promptly dismissed Angerer. To friends he explained the affair as the work of disloyal, ambitious subordinates, including Richards, who had resigned 31 October. "How I was brought into such company," he complained to Potter, "I can't see—Three such in the whalesbelly would have sunk even that fish—" Consoled by the view that it represented Neill's latest strategem for winning the commission-ership, Barnard ignored the accuracy of the admittedly brief and incomplete depiction of his administration. He never accepted the possible validity of the attack.[29]

A few weeks later, the secretary of the interior's 1868 annual report added the voice of Orville H. Browning to those seeking to abolish Barnard's agency. Few questioned that he spoke for the president. Introducing no new reasons for opposing the department, the secretary characterized it as an unnecessary federal endeavor and recommended that legislation dealing with the agency be repealed. Reports of the commissioner of public lands revealed the extent of federal land grants for educational purposes, he argued; educational statistics appeared in the decennial census and more frequently in reports of state school officials; and, finally, Congress needed no assistance from a federal school bureau in executing its legislative duties. The agency, in short, performed no unique function. Education fell within the exclusive jurisdiction of the states, in Browning's view; hence, not a federal department but the states' "enlightened and active zeal . . . affords an ample guarantee that systems of common schools will be maintained throughout the country." The secretary closed his report by recommending a $6,000 appropriation for the reconstituted Office of Education in the Department of the Interior, if Congress elected to continue its operation after the current fiscal year. The amount included $3,000 for the commissioner's salary, as stipulated by law, $1,200 each for two clerks of the lowest grade, and $600 for supplies.[30]

Deliberately or not, Browning ignored the central issue of the near half-century-old debate over the national school agency. Not merely more schools, but federally guaranteed, enforced, educational opportunity across state boundaries had stirred the plan's opponents as well as its advocates. White supremists, retrench-ers, and even tired moderates were closer to the mark. They, at least, addressed themselves to the energy and money costs of enforcing education nationally. And they acknowledged the threats implied by such a commitment to established patterns of local and state school control, on one hand, and to sectional loyalties on the other. The issue had never been simply more schools, or even educational

140

enforcement. The issues rather had been what kinds of schools, serving whom, and to what ends. Control had been the issue and it had been raised repeatedly, most recently by secession, war, and Union victory, because local and state authorities, particularly in the South, had been unable or unwilling to guarantee inclusive educational opportunity. Whether the Department of Education had been designed or was functioning in ways to resolve the issue was, of course, a different question, but Browning failed to address it too.

With opposition to the department mounting, the heretofore dormant House Committee on Education and Labor launched an investigation of the charges against Barnard. Convinced, at length, that the complaints were groundless, committee chairman Samuel Cary, a moderate Republican from Ohio, rushed his report to Congress in hopes of forestalling a second attempt to abolish the agency. Completed by mid-February 1869, the report answered Browning's arguments point by point. The department's assignment to study federal land grants for education required the agency to investigate both the extent of the grants, the committee concluded, and also the "manner" in which the states employed them. Furthermore, it added, if the 1870 census fulfilled the secretary's expectations in regard to educational statistics, "it will accomplish what no census of the United States, or the census alone of any other country has yet done." Far transcending the "mere enumeration of the schools, pupils, and teachers," the report noted, borrowing Barnard's words, the responsibility of the department was to "throw light on the internal operations of educational institutions." The committee charged that while Browning could see no reason for the national dissemination of data collected and published by individual states, school officials could and, furthermore, had repeatedly petitioned Congress to establish an agency to perform the task. Browning's insistence that the department's work contributed nothing of benefit to Congress in the performance of its legislative responsibilities was countered with the reminder that the efforts of the Department of Agriculture likewise were not translatable into immediate legislation, and yet no one doubted the value of collecting and disseminating agricultural information. Citing George Washington as its authority, the committee argued that even if education were the exclusive province of the states, no valid constitutional objection could be lodged against the federal government's promoting education through channels not available to any individual

141

association or state. Finally, the committee took note of Browning's optimistic assertion that "enlightened and active zeal" would lead states to adopt common schools: "[U]p to this time more than one-third of the states have failed to adopt such, or any other system of education, and there is not a State in which the executive or the highest school authority is not recommending additional legislation and immediate reforms." [31]

The committee's report fell shy of the central issues, too, although it approached them from a direction opposite to Browning's, namely a desire to save the department. It failed, for example, to consider Stevens' criticism that the structure and procedures of the agency seemed poorly designed to realize the expectations of its supporters. The committee, instead, affirmed the department's school reforming mission and defended Barnard, who in its view, labored against severe budget restrictions and unreasonable, politically motivated, opposition from both Congress and the White House. Speaking to the charges against him, the committee concluded: "They appeared to be either so frivolous as to be unworthy of serious attention, or so malicious as to fail in the least degree to impair the confidence of the committee in the practical wisdom and earnest devotion of the Commissioner. . . ." The report ended on a note of unqualified praise for Barnard and a plea that the department be restored to its independent status and provided with adequate funds and staff.[32]

The annual appropriation bill for the 1869–70 fiscal year (H.R. 1672), as originally introduced in the House, again failed to make provision for the Department of Education. One week after the appearance of Cary's report Glenni W. Scofield, speaking for the Committee on Appropriations, submitted an amendment stipulating $6,000 for the agency, including $3,000 for the commissioner's salary, $1,200 each for two clerks of the lowest rank, and $600 for supplies and miscellaneous expenses, exactly the amounts recommended by Browning. Congressman B. F. Whittemore, a South Carolina Republican, sought to secure a renewal of the current $20,000 appropriation; however, his motion received only nine affirmative votes. During the brief debate, in which neither Garfield nor Donnelly participated, Thomas Jenckes of Rhode Island pointed to the president's harassment of Barnard and the department but failed to convince his colleagues to grant the agency more funds. The House approved Scofield's amendment 81 to 42. He then introduced a second amendment to abolish the department at the end of the 1869–70 fiscal year. The effort failed on a point of order raised by Maryland Democrat Stevenson Archer. Nevertheless, the agency had been effectively neutralized by the meager appropriation.[33]

The House action occurred late in February 1869. Earlier, while the department's future after 30 June remained uncertain, the president attempted to dismiss Barnard. A letter from Edward Neill to E. B. Washburne, dated 26 January 1869, set in sharp relief the behind-the-scenes maneuvering with which Barnard contended during this troubled period:

> Until last week, it had been some months since the President made any reference to the Department of Education, with the administration of which, he has never been satisfied. Col. [William G.] Moore, four or five days ago told me that the President would send in my name to the Senate, as Commissioner in the place of Dr. Barnard, if I felt willing to accept. After many doubts, I at last felt that it would not injure my country, nor the cause of education. Whatever action is taken in the matter I wish may be for the best interests of the public service.

That something was afoot must have been known outside of congressional circles. Mary Mann, at least, got wind of it, for on 7 February she wrote to Barnard for confirmation of the rumor: "Will the President succeed do you think, in cutting your head off? It makes me wrathy [*sic*] to think of Mr. Neill being put in your place." Barnard was not dismissed, and a letter from Neill to Senator Alexander Ramsey shortly after Grant's inauguration in March explained why. Even though nominated by the new president for the Dublin consulate, Neill, ever the promoter, preferred a position in Washington. After discussing the Dublin matter with Ramsey, he voiced again his ambition to replace Barnard:

> Since the adjournment of Congress, I am informed that the Joint Committee on Retrenchment have examined witnesses, and are convinced that the statements made in debate by Hon. E. B. Washburne and others, as to the mismanagement of the Department of Education are true. You are aware, that when this Department was about to be organized, at the request of the late Senator Dixon, a friend and fellow townsman of Dr.

Barnard, I withdrew my application for the place, and wrote a letter in favor of him, the present Commissioner. You and Mr. Washburne are also both aware, that Mr. Johnson last winter removed the Commissioner, and nominated the writer, but that no action was taken by the Senate.

It is very evident that the late investigation will sooner or later lead to his removal, and perhaps if President Grant knew the condition of the Department, and if you were to tell him my position as Supt. of Instruction in Minnesota, until I went out with the first regiment, he would give me the commissionership.[34]

The investigation mentioned by Neill left no record of its conclusions. He eventually departed for Dublin, and Barnard served for almost one year longer in peace and relative obscurity. After 30 June, the department became an office of the Department of the Interior, and President Grant surprised many, perhaps even Barnard, by renaming him commissioner. Secretary of the Interior Jacob Cox, who brought the news to Barnard in July, cautioned against any misreading of the president's action:

I am authorized by the President to state that he does not entertain any present purpose of designating any person but yourself as Commissioner of Education. A commission temporarily appointing you as such officer . . . will therefore be sent to you.

I make this reference to the subject to avoid any misapprehension on your part as to your tenure of the office, should the President hereafter be of the opinion that the public interests would be subserved by making a change.[35]

Given his small appropriation and two underpaid assistants, Barnard accomplished a surprising amount during the nine months remaining in his term. He completed the Washington school study and continued working on the massive survey of education in the United States and Europe outlined in his late December letter to Potter. Although little remained of his office to criticize, Congress continued to harp at him, and he received little personal support from either Cox or Grant. At least they were not committed to the destruction of the office and even publicly endorsed it.[36]

Ironically, the office had become very much like the agency

Barnard had initially proposed in 1854: a small, essentially one-man, operation. The cost, he had suggested to Joseph Henry, would not exceed $3,000. In 1869, Barnard had twice that much. In the meantime, he had begun to perceive flaws in his original plan. His address before the National Association of State Superintendents in March 1870, revealed the necessary changes: an agency designed to exert indirect external pressure on local and state school authorities through educational data collected and published nationwide; model schools in the capital providing standards for emulation; and finally an agency with teeth, powerful enough to establish public schools in the territories, appoint their superintendents, inspect, and hence evaluate, all schools, and withhold or grant federal funds from deficient state school systems. If Congress or the nation's schoolmen were prepared to accept such a federal education agency, and evidently they were not, Barnard was not the man to lead it.[37]

EDUCATORS AND THE OFFICE OF EDUCATION: AN AMBIVALENT CONSTITUENCY

During Barnard's three troubled years as commissioner, educators, individually and through their organizations, ostensibly supported him and his policies. The American Institute of Instruction called upon him for reports at its 1867 and 1868 meetings and rushed endorsements to Congress when Barnard informed delegates of threats to abolish the department. Although the National Teachers' Association failed to meet in 1867, it, too, passed resolutions of support at the two succeeding annual gatherings. Educators from around the country responded with letters to congressmen and senators when in the winter of 1868 Barnard sent out word that his agency was in danger. On a lesser scale, letter-writing campaigns emerged also in 1869 when the department again faced possible abrogation. In truth the efforts, fitful at best, lacked force. Garfield commented that from his vantage point schoolmen appeared not to care one way or the other about their department. Barnard made a similar observation in his reports to the American Institute of Instruction. What the Department of Education needed during these first years was not merely public endorsements. It required practical help in applying pressure on Congress and in collecting data for its reports. Little help of this sort materialized.[38]

The most glaring weakness in the agency's operation was its dependence upon statistics and information voluntarily submitted by teachers, school officials, and other friends of education. The department had no clerks to work in the field to collect data, no funds to finance the gathering of information, and no power to require the cooperation of local and state school authorities. Barnard's harmless subterfuge of employing temporary researchers in various sections of the country rather than a third clerk represented, at worst, a clumsy attempt to circumvent such difficulties. Placed in the context of limited staff, funds, and power, and, in addition, congressional pressure for quick results, his reliance upon previously published state reports and journal articles, including material from his own journal, became both understandable and defensible.[39]

Given the circumstances, no commissioner could have fulfilled the duties of his office without assistance from the nation's educators. Barnard received at best uneven cooperation. Some state school officials refused to provide the information he requested; others wanted to be paid for their efforts. Promised returns arrived too late for inclusion in Barnard's report; some never appeared at all. In several cases, the difficulty was a local one. A normal school principal in Arkansas working diligently to secure a full report on all levels of education in his state confronted a wall of indifference and hostility as he attempted to gather the desired information from local teachers and officials. John Kraus wrote from Texas that a yellow fever epidemic made it impossible to secure a full and reliable report on education in that state. Besides, he added in another letter,

> I find confirmed . . . most everywhere . . . that most persons are teachers from necessity, or misfortune, rather than real love for and devotion to the occupation. Public schools are grossly neglected in Texas and who cares for that. Where education is most needed, there it is always least appreciated and valued.

He concluded by directing Barnard to the *Texas Almanac* for information on schools.[40]

Few of Barnard's fellow schoolmen appreciated the barriers confounding his attempts to launch the new department. Emerson White, in particular, evidenced a singular lack of charity in his criticisms of the commissioner. White was sufficiently cognizant of the difficulties confronting Barnard to celebrate "my good fortune in not being placed in it [the commissionership] at the first." Nevertheless, in letters to Garfield during the initial period of the department's operation he continued to reinforce the congressman's impression of Barnard as a complete failure. Under fire for his original support of the education agency, Garfield, of course, faced troubles of his own. He had not anticipated the opposition, and when even leaders in his own party challenged him on the issue, he found himself in an untenable position for an ambitious young congressman. Ignatius Donnelly, for example, had worked himself into a protracted feud with E. B. Washburne only to learn that the powerful Illinois Republican had successfully undermined his standing with Minnesota's Republican leaders. Washburne won that struggle when Donnelly lost his bid for re-election to the Forty-first Congress. Garfield clearly needed to avoid that kind of conflict if he intended to achieve major House leadership.[41]

Without disparaging valid criticisms against Barnard, one ought nevertheless to remember the context. Although White initially wanted to be commissioner, the ambition quickly paled before the heat of congressional opposition which annually threatened the office's existence. He chose thereafter to watch from a distance. On 9 June 1868, he confided to Garfield:

> Dr. B's ideas of what the Dept. should do are so different from my own that I am unable to judge of his success. What I have feared from the first is that his tendency to "scatter"—to put more irons in the fire than he can attend to would prevent the largest success. His investigations have taken a wide range and seem to be all incomplete.

Two months later, he repeated the criticism adding a special plea that Barnard "must be sustained," but his comments to Garfield appeared ill designed to achieve that end. White correctly assessed Barnard's administrative disabilities; however, his plan for the agency basically agreed with the commissioner's. The congressman's replies, particularly during the winter of 1868 and 1869, when attacks against Barnard grew most intense and personal, revealed an almost desperate search for a scapegoat, and White, intentionally or not, assured him that Barnard was fair game. Unable even in the privacy of a personal letter to admit that Congress itself posed a

147

major barrier to Barnard's effectiveness, Garfield, on the contrary, insisted that all of the department's problems could have been avoided if "we had had the right man at the head." The "right man" for Garfield was Emerson White. Even White realized that opposition to the agency could not be dissolved so easily. Politely and firmly, he rebuffed Garfield's offer to help secure the post for him after Grant's inauguration. Eventually, White admitted that "the past treatment of this Bureau by Congress is well-nigh a national disgrace," but the confession appeared a year after Barnard's departure from office.[42]

The complaints against Barnard rested on solid grounds. His plan for the department failed to anticipate the administrative and political complexities of launching a new federal agency. He had argued initially for limited staff and funds and yet complained bitterly about receiving both. Although he could not be blamed for Edward Neill's presence on the department staff, he managed, on his own, to appoint a number of second-rate men as assistants. He refused to understand how outsiders could view his continued preoccupation with the journal as a conflict of interest. Because of his involvement with his journal and his frequent illnesses, he spent too much time away from Washington. Finally, he misread congressional support for the department and hence failed to heed advice that he would have to show results if his agency was to survive. Although his poor health lent credence to the characterization, he was less the "worn out man" Thaddeus Stevens depicted than the intractable scholar.

Still, the department's troubled start reflected in equal measure its flawed administrator and the complexities of contending values and partisan politics during the Reconstruction years. It began as a hopeful and liberating scheme for guaranteeing public learning opportunities. Within three years, it became considerably less. If social reform projects such as plans for a national school agency appear with the help of the visionary's loose language and his proclivity for tracing hopes with a broad brush, if in short they begin in public, their implementation may occur just as often in history's back alleys. The gradual, often picayune erosion of the dream of federally enforced equal education during Barnard's term remained obscure, in addition, because it lacked interest and importance. In particular, the dream's disintegration was eclipsed by more noteworthy battles between Congress and president, the demise of the

Freedmen's Bureau, and the vise-like refusal of whites to admit blacks into the nation's social and political institutions. Other variables of the dependent variety intervened also: short money, atrophied public interest in social inequities, a concomitant attraction to international affairs, and a spate of low-profile national and school leaders. The swing of the pendulum, invoked by historian David Donald to describe the shaping of reconstruction legislation in the Thirty-ninth Congress, images what happened. With Congress, Andrew Johnson, school leaders, Barnard, and the department staff playing key parts, diffuse aspirations, many of them politically naive to a fault, for guaranteeing equal education and assigning public schools a formal role in social policy-making narrowed to a forgettable federal agency. Buffeted by conflicting values and interests and education's low priority in Washington, the office lacked the authority, staff, and budget needed to realize even its minimal legislative charge to collect and publish educational data. Deferral of social dreams being necessarily, perhaps, a political process, actualization of plans for a national school bureau followed, like the pendulum's arcs, the diminishing differentials of power. Unless the agency gained an independent force of its own, dead center promised to be the path of least resistance. The Department of Education, however, appeared early, not late, in the process. The story remained unfinished, but within three years its basic lines had been set. Although little of the originating hopes survived the compromises effected by 1870, still uncertain was the agency's future, whether it, too, would survive and if so, in what form, given the limited options remaining.[43]

In retrospect a still more significant, long range, consequence of the department's beginning years can be detected. Barnard's deficiencies, combined with the assaults on the agency from both Congress and the president, tended to narrow concern about the department to whether it should be saved or abolished. The agency itself became the center of controversy and debate. All but forgotten were the reasons for ascribing a reform mission to it, particularly those devised after 1861. The oversight might explain why little progress was made in clarifying the office's role in education policy-making or in weighing the probable consequences, for example, for black people, of failing to do so. There are hardly any grounds for optimism that a bureau, at best a minor administrative unit, however efficient, could have set the stage for less racism, greater inclusiveness, and more humaneness in American public schools in the twentieth century. Nevertheless, it is intriguing to speculate on the results had some arm of the federal government acted a century ago to guarantee, rather than merely talk about, equal educational opportunity. Nothing of the sort happened, and it was perhaps just as well. The flaw in the common school movement, which produced plans for a bureau in the first place, was not its goal of inclusive chances for learning at public expense. For well over a century, a number of public school critics have insisted that the dream of equal educational opportunity has constituted at best an elusive fantasy. Their error, of course, lies in their assumption that somewhere in the past vigorous attempts to realize the dream failed. Such efforts are difficult to locate. Perhaps a major problem all along has been the ambivalent rationale supporting the equal opportunity objective. For the sake of the nation and the well-being of its people, popular education was expected both to control and to liberate those whom it touched. That double-edged justification, combined with strategies of imposition—people defining and programming educational opportunity for others—has produced ironically unequal schooling for large segments of the American people. One can view these results as direct effects or simply as correlations. Either way, however, he is faced with the uncomfortable fact of undesired consequences. Whether the flaw could have been corrected during the years after Appomattox had attention not shifted from the federal government's stake in educational reform to the question of the Department of Education's survival remains unknown, but the implications of the possibility, for subsequent generations facing imperatives of their own, are worth pondering.

6

A Federal School Bureaucracy: Permanence at a Price

JOHN EATON: THE BUREAU BEGINS

*E*ven before Barnard's departure, plans for "saving" the Bureau of Education, as it came to be known after 1869, circulated through Congress. Lamenting that the agency "must make a new start or die," Emerson White endorsed Garfield's proposal for combining it with the educational arm of the Freedmen's Bureau. "The passage of General Garfield's bill," he suggested, "will give the department one more opportunity—may we not say *an* opportunity —to demonstrate its utility and importance." As White doubtless knew, the bureau's permanence, as much as its effectiveness, dominated concern about its future. Spearheaded by Samuel Arnell, a New England educated Republican from Tennessee, several bills before the Forty-first Congress proposed to protect the bureau from extinction by joining it with other federal agencies responsible for data gathering and dissemination. None of them, including Garfield's, won enactment. In the first place, restructuring the bureau generated only mild interest. Also its congressional supporters expressed reluctance to act until the new president replaced Barnard with his own man.[1]

Few candidates for commissioner emerged when Grant assumed office. By reappointing Barnard, if only temporarily, the president forestalled active campaigning for the post. N.T.A. leaders readied a drive in behalf of Emerson White and then hesitated to let it surface so long as Barnard held the position. Still a strong advocate of White's appointment, Garfield found the president unwilling to accept the recommendation because Jacob D. Cox, his newly installed secretary of the interior, also came from Ohio. The "embarrassments of geography" failed to materialize when White, claiming the $3,000 annual salary was too low, removed himself from consideration. When the Freedman's Bureau, which he directed, appeared headed for extinction, General O. O. Howard encouraged rumors of his availability for the position. The modest effort came to naught. Howard uncovered little support either in Congress or among leaders in the new administration.[2]

In March 1870 White eagerly announced John Eaton's appointment: "We learn that this change was made to save the bureau, and that its friends in Congress are now quite confident that its discontinuance will be prevented." Whether the agency was indeed "preserved," Garfield counseled the new commissioner, depended "upon the success of this year's work." Ten months later he shared White's optimism: "We have at last conquered in the first stage of the fight in favor of national recognition of education. Only a small vote can now be mustered for abolishing the Bureau and we shall be able to increase the appropriation a little each year. . . ."[3]

The man primarily responsible for changing—or at least softening—congressional attitudes toward the bureau was no scholar, as two of his children later testified. An aunt, Mary D. Andrews, described him as a "selfish, mercenary office-seeker," characterized by "aristocratic notions" and "an innate desire for authoritative office when attended with a good salary." A harsh judgment overall, it received only partial confirmation from co-workers and subordinates who found him at times to be a difficult taskmaster. Ambitious, outgoing, not especially learned, but politically wise, forty-year-old John Eaton appeared by contrast to be an ideal successor to Henry Barnard. A graduate of Dartmouth College and an ordained Presbyterian minister, he viewed education as a means of individual salvation necessary for the Christian, and the common school as an instrument for achieving national unity. Vaguely idealized, salvation and reunion fused in Eaton's mind as objects of a new, postwar, crusade—a second great educational awakening—which he would lead.[4]

Appointed, like Barnard before him, for essentially political reasons (he was Grant's friend and a staunch Republican) Eaton could claim qualifications for being commissioner, despite an initial disinterest in the position. Before entering Dartmouth, he taught school in his native New Hampshire and after graduation in 1854 accepted a series of school administrative posts in Ohio, where he met Emerson White. Although Eaton entered the war as a chaplain (with the Ohio Volunteers), a chance assignment from Grant to organize and care for the "contrabands" burdening the general's camp turned his attention again to education. His work with black people during the war eventually led to his being brevetted brigadier general and appointed superintendent of the army's freedmen department, which had as one of its objectives the establishment of schools for former slaves. His skillful organization of a project he termed "unpleasant" and his tact in dealing with southern landowners won Grant's respect and, in addition, the opportunity to report directly to Lincoln on conditions among black people in the South. Viewing his work for Grant as a model for the projected bureau of refugees, freedmen, and abandoned lands, he lobbied for passage of the freedmen's bureau bill during the fall and winter of 1864 and 1865. Later, he fielded an energetic campaign for the job of bureau commissioner, a post he lost to General Howard. At Grant's suggestion, Howard asked Eaton to serve as one of his assistant commissioners.[5]

Eaton remained with the bureau for less than a year, resigning in December 1865 to return to Memphis where he had established his headquarters while directing the work with freedmen for Grant. Here he started a Union newspaper, the *Memphis Post,* and joined the Republican party. Elected superintendent of schools for Tennessee in 1867, he re-established contact with Emerson White and in August 1868 served as host superintendent to the N.T.A. which met that year in Nashville. With characteristic drive he organized a system of county school supervision for his adopted state, giving particular heed to the importance of collecting and disseminating reliable statistics on the efficiency of public schools. Although generally successful, his efforts were bound to come under close scrutiny in the tangled political environment of postwar Tennessee. The young superintendent's identification with the radical wing of the Republican party and his relatively recent arrival in the state, which made him vulnerable to carpetbagger charges, aggravated his troubles with the state legislature. By early 1869, faced with mounting complaints that his programs were unnecessary and too costly, Eaton held little hope for keeping his office. It was one of the few occasions he allowed himself to be caught on a losing side in the tug of political change.[6]

In microcosm, Eaton's experience in Tennessee paralleled Barnard's in Washington. The issues were uncomfortably similar.

Not enforced education, but changes, real or anticipated, in the level of government effecting enforcement stirred opponents to action. Hints that schools more widely inclusive would follow the alterations increased concern over the weakening role of local elites in school control. Not given to meekness, Eaton dismissed his enemies as weaklings and reactionaries, unschooled in the lessons of Civil War. Noting intense conflicts between rebels and loyalists in Tennessee, the violence perpetrated by such groups as the Ku Klux Klan, and the dangers faced by radicals in western Tennessee, he deposited the problem with his party: "[A]fter the question of negro enfranchisement was settled," he wrote to the 1869 state Republican convention,

> there has been none more obnoxious to our enemies than that of free, universal education, offering to every man as it does the means, however poor, of training his child in the knowledge which shall enable him to think and act for himself intelligently as a citizen. . . . The storm free schools has encountered has been hardly less than that which broke on colored suffrage.

However correct the analysis, Eaton knew that controversy over his promotion of state-wide school supervision dimmed his prospects for future successes in Tennessee. He mailed his convention message from Washington where he had gone in search of a federal appointment.[7]

"I hope you are not among the crowd of office seekers who daily make a rush to see the President and are denied admittance," his wife wrote from Nashville. "I am seeking no office," Eaton replied, "but one for Lucien [his brother], though quite a number have urged me to secure some good place. I have seen Grant three times. He speaks to me as he used to." Lucien, on the other hand, urged him on with warnings that he could not win re-election in Tennessee: "Quietly arrange to get out of your place as honorably . . . as best you can . . . concentrate your efforts on Grant. . . . Secure something or know the reason why. If you fail you are no worse off than now. . . . For God's sake do not neglect yourself at this juncture as you have always done before." Although pleased with his reception by Grant, particularly the appointment to the president's first Board of Visitors to West Point, Eaton desired a more permanent position. After a campaign to become minister to

Turkey generated little enthusiasm, he found himself still unemployed by early January 1870. Grant's offer of the commissioner of education post provided his only chance for joining the new administration.[8]

He won the appointment, Eaton later recalled, because Grant insisted that the Bureau of Education "should have another trial." Characterizing the agency under Barnard "as an asylum for a political favorite and as utterly useless," a former subordinate of Eaton's at the Freedmen's Bureau, rejoiced at his appointment: "[Y]ou will make the office respected (which I fear it has not been) . . . it would otherwise have been abolished." White assured Garfield that he found Eaton entirely suited for the job. N.T.A. President D. B. Hagar advised the new commissioner that he had the endorsement of the country's leading educators, including Barnard's many friends who yet felt it necessary to displace him "as not in all respects adapted to the place he occupied." Taking into account his experience, active Republicanism, easy access to the president, and most pointedly the contrast with his tired and aging predecessor, bureau supporters found much to celebrate in Eaton's appointment. Despite reservations by detractors who favored candidates better known within educational circles, he began his tenure as commissioner amid general confidence that he could save the agency.[9]

The annual N.T.A. meeting in August 1870 accorded Eaton his first opportunity to discuss plans for the bureau publicly. Invited by Hagar to address the gathering, Eaton avoided detailing proposed courses of action for his agency, concentrating instead on the general principles he intended to follow. He offered a history of federal involvement in education, emphasizing N.T.A. contributions in creating the Department of Education, and touched briefly upon such current problems as illiteracy. All this remained peripheral, however, to the core of his remarks: a metaphysic on the national stake in education which defined the boundaries of federal school policy-making, themes entirely familiar to his audience.[10]

The Constitution limited the scope of federal activity in regards to education, Eaton began, and good sense warned against policies calculated to decrease local or individual initiative. Nevertheless, the national government could not tolerate localized or general ignorance. Between these two poles, each restricting the other, resided the area of possible federal involvement in education. The national government retained responsibility for developing schools in the territories, the District of Columbia, and among the Indian tribes with which it had treaties. It could encourage the study of foreign schools and share reports on domestic institutions abroad. It had the power to use federal lands or income derived from their sale for the benefit of education. It could gather school data and communicate what it learned to states and citizens alike. Given these prerogatives, clearly translatable into legislation, the government, Eaton suggested, acted within the limits of the Constitution and practical wisdom in establishing a federal office charged with fulfilling its educational obligations. Finally, he concluded, the government could take "exceptional" action when circumstances required it for the public welfare, assurance of a republican form of government, protection of freedmen's liberty and rights as citizens, the free exercise of the franchise, the equality of all men before the law, and the fitting of any citizen for responsibilities the nation might impose on him. It was a heady list, with hints that the new commissioner, on the one hand, had familiarized himself with his predecessor's plan and, on the other, had not completely renounced the radicalism which got him into trouble in Tennessee. The speech was well received. Still, he brought the schoolmen little that was new, and the vagueness of his announced principles provided only a blurred forecast of what he intended to do as commissioner.

The Constitution, which omitted any mention of education, offered no satisfying definition of the federal government's interest in the subject, except to those who brought to it preconceived notions about either the states' prerogatives in such a matter or the relation of learning to the general welfare. Conflicts between these two groups had emerged annually in Congress since the initial debate on the department of education bill in 1866. Conventional wisdom on the importance of local initiative in school promotion suffered equally from ambiguity, for it reflected both inertia, the inability to veer from policies strengthened by habit and too easily trusted as tradition, and uncritical acceptance of local communities as near paragons of pure democracy. Common school advocates never wanted simply more schools. They set state supervision and the promotion of systems of schools as major objectives both because communities otherwise might not establish public learning institutions and because they might not foster "good" ones. The level of government enforcing education, not enforcement per se, had been the issue and behind it fights over schools' inclusiveness or lack thereof. The goal was commonality: standard and adequate curricula and teaching methods unencumbered by Protestant sectarianism (an anti-Catholic bias was more acceptable); schools open to all segments of the public, a required policy if they were to be effective in promoting nationalism and common morality; objective criteria for evaluating pupils and employing teachers; and regular pupil attendance, an aim which anticipated calls for state compulsory attendance legislation. Schools' commonality, a matter early proponents of public education concluded could not be left to ensconced local elites, informed the school movement's goals and hence its strategies from the outset and explained its long flirtation with plans for a federal educational agency. Argued Kansas Senator Samuel Pomeroy, a Republican, "Let him [the commissioner of education] see to it that there is more uniformity and more system in the schools. That would be an incalculable advantage. . . ." Eaton's reliance on the good sense of local initiative failed, thus, to note that in 1870 conventional wisdom on the matter remained at odds with itself. Schoolmen and even some of their congressional allies knew, if the commissioner did not, about the law of external pressure, the long-standing and widely held conviction of the friends of education that school reform required the weight of a government agency unfettered by local provincialisms and power structures.[11]

In discussing the other pole which he viewed as bounding the sphere of federal school activity, namely the government's inability to countenance localized or general ignorance, Eaton avoided one of the central issues confronting the bureau. Its opponents in Congress never tired of pointing out that the agency lacked the power to educate anyone. As Congressman John Farnsworth, the Chicago Republican, put it a year after Eaton took office, "[W]hat freedman was ever educated by the report of the Commissioner of Education? . . . How does [it] educate a man whose shackles have been struck off and who wants a primer?" The information contained in the bureau's reports, replied Massachusetts Congressman George Hoar, "is needed by those who are organizing schools and other institutions of education for the freedmen, not by the pupil who is studying the primer." Farnsworth remained unconvinced. "[I]f the Government of the United States is to engage in the education of these people," he retorted, "let us go to work and print primers and spelling-books . . . not these learned books, which are intended for the benefit rather of the superintendent and the

157

heads of the academies and seminaries of learning and colleges. . . ." Farnsworth saw that to counteract ignorance, to
promote the growth of common and inclusive public schools, in
short, to enforce educational opportunity from the federal level,
required strengthening the bureau with authority to intrude itself
into educational policy-making processes at state and local levels.
Neither Congress nor schoolmen generally appeared willing to
approve such a step in 1870. Indeed, Farnsworth offered his remarks
not as support for those advocating an expansion of the bureau's
authority. On the contrary, he viewed the nationwide collection and
dissemination of educational data as wasteful of federal funds and
useless in promoting school reform. He would have been happy to
see the agency limited to collecting information for Congress only.
As Barnard complained when he left office, the bureau was expected
to effect school reforms armed only with the power to influence
school policy and practice indirectly through the dissemination of
information. Given the dilemma, what remained for the agency to
do? [12]

Eaton's answers came soon enough. Instituting minor refine-
ments, most notably a shift in emphasis from historical documentation to contemporary aspects of education, he elected to follow the
main outlines of his predecessor's plan. Many years later, in a long
letter to William T. Harris written after Barnard's death, Eaton
acknowledged his debt to the first commissioner's conception of the
bureau's functions and obligations:

> The plan of work, as unfolded by reports, and especially by the
> carefully prepared circulars printed by Dr. Barnard, was most
> comprehensive and seemed to leave little to be desired. . . . I
> could not see how his devices and methods could be essentially
> improved in form. What could be better? I determined in some
> way to find a method of securing publication.

Barnard himself seemed willing to amend it after his experience as
commissioner, but for Eaton, the timeless dispassion of his predecessor's operation, so burdensome and unspectacular in the turbulent
Johnson years, proved adaptable to the drive for permanence. Eaton
confirmed his sympathy for the plan in a long summary of Barnard's
achievements as commissioner:

Of his relation to the shaping of the work of the office I might say perhaps more specifically of his plans and devices: 1) He gave his utmost influence to the establishment of the bureau; 2) he sought to make reports which would be truly national; 3) he sought more carefully to devise valuable forms for statistics and abbreviated statements; 4) he began the publication of circulars giving information in regard to miscellaneous educational topics; 5) he enforced the national obligation to education; 6) he emphasized the need for universal education; 7) he would make the bureau enforce the universal relation of education to all the details of man's improvement; 8) he would make it understood that the laws of education in their relation to man's welfare were the same for all races; 9) he would draw illustrations of educational processes from all nations and peoples; 10) he sought to stimulate improvement by using both the historical and comparative methods, setting over against each other different years and different institutions and systems, by the publication of facts.

Indeed, it will be hardly possible for a national office of education to find anything appropriate to publish which is not included in the plans of Dr. Barnard as touching education and its relations.

An apt obituary, Eaton's praise failed to calculate the price exacted for adhering to a scheme devised with antebellum belief in the possibility of changes in school policy through rational discourse and benign dissemination of educational statistics. Bureaucratic permanence, not new answers to the questions of who controlled schools and to which ends, dominated Eaton's concerns as commissioner. The costs involved never impressed him.[13]

Eaton's success, measured against his limited goals, amounted to a literal adherence to Barnard's 1854 plan for a central school agency. After only two months in office, Eaton conducted an inspection of schools in the South, thus beginning a practice he followed throughout his sixteen-year tenure of personally visiting the nation's schools. He revived the first commissioner's policy of employing specialists to write reports dealing with current school topics, although he did not always acknowledge their authorship. Like Barnard, he initiated an international correspondence with educational leaders, exchanging reports, surveys, or merely items of information, and early set his staff to work enlarging and cataloguing the bureau's library. In addition, he established an educational museum to display recent models of school equipment and apparatus. Barnard, who included both a national educational library and museum in his original plan, aided Eaton's effort by selling his extensive collection of textbooks, school reports, and educational journals to the bureau. Extending his interest in libraries as informal educational institutions, Eaton decided half way through his first decade in office to publish a directory of the nation's public libraries. One result was the monumental *Public Libraries in the United States of America: Their History, Condition and Management* published by the bureau in 1876. An equally significant, although indirect, consequence was the marshalling of librarians from across the country to the task of regularizing their systems of book classification and cataloguing. With equal fervor he supported pioneering programs in the training of nurses, early childhood education, and the campaign against bogus diploma granting institutions. Although Eaton expressed no singular commitment to creating an historical documentary of education, he appreciated the value of the comparative framework in making judgments about schools' effectiveness. As Barnard had done before him, he combined statistical tables with descriptions of actual school practices in his reports, and he encouraged the comparison of school systems across national boundaries. On the other hand, he avoided the kind of detailed historical study which preoccupied and, to some extent, overwhelmed Barnard.[14]

Eaton completed his first annual report a short eight months after assuming office. A hasty compilation of 1860 census data, information gathered by Barnard, and reports on education from abroad and, where available, from state, municipal, and territorial officers, it was intended to depict current educational conditions in the United States and provide comparative descriptions of schools in other countries. Eaton reprinted Edwin Leigh's survey of illiteracy in the United States, which had appeared in Barnard's *Special Report on Education in the District of Columbia,* and in addition offered new material in Elizabeth Peabody's report on kindergartens and J. J. Noah's careful survey of Hebrew education in the United States. Reports on schools for the deaf, medical education, normal schools, and school supervision appeared, along with statistical reports on formal and informal educational institutions, including libraries and prisons, in order to indicate the scope of the bureau's interest in the educational field. Adopting a practice followed by Barnard in his journal and Emerson White in the *Ohio Educational Monthly,* Eaton published abstracts of recent meetings of national and state educational organizations, because in his words, such groups constituted "one of the most important means of advancing all the interests of education, general and local." Belief in the causal relation of illiteracy to crime and the public school's role in eliminating vice (convictions rarely challenged among common schoolmen), found expression in several articles and statistical summaries, most pointedly in those treating education for laboring people and racial minorities. Arguing that the "proscription of races in elementary education" demanded the nation's attention, he recorded the experiences of certain races, particularly black and Asiatic peoples, in being excluded from public schools or offered schooling inferior to that available to local whites. The exclusion of black people from public schools was "most striking" among the former slave states, the commissioner concluded, adding that even there it was predominantly a rural practice.[15]

His forthrightness, tinged with paternalism and uncritical confidence in progress, won Eaton only mixed reviews. Congressmen who felt their districts had been mistreated in the statistical summaries or that sensitive issues had been discussed too openly lodged objections to the report. Complained Delaware Senator Thomas Bayard, "[I]f the part that relates to the other States is as contemptibly false and absurd as that which relates to my own State, it [the report] will only increase the mass of ignorance in the country, instead of lessening it." The galling line, later expunged from the report, suggested that in one school Delaware boys "did not stand in a straight line when they stood up to spell and they spat tobacco juice. . . ." Another senator objected to the news that a district in his state "did not pay a cent of [school] tax in ten years. . . ." To mollify his colleagues' discomfort, Massachusetts Senator Henry Wilson attempted to place the report's offenses in historical perspective:

> I take it that, instead of being an overstatement of the common school system of the States and of the country, it [the report] is altogether an understatement of its inefficiency and its falling short of what it ought to be. . . . There is no State in the Union that has an educational system which begins to be what the interests of education require. I remember, when Horace Mann took the lead, more than thirty years ago in Massachusetts, and

161

exposed the school system of the State, the people were amazed. They denied, they protested, they declared in the Legislature that what he said was not true. They undertook to overturn his statements, and even to overturn the school system. . . .

Added Wisconsin's Senator Timothy Howe, "I do not understand it to be the purpose of this publication to glorify the educational system in any one of the States." Unimpressed, Bayard refused to soften his criticism. The report, he thought, amounted to "a parcel of opinions, in the first place worthless, and in the next place untrue!" [16]

A different kind of complaint came from Senator Eugene Casserly, a California Democrat. Eaton's report revealed, according to Casserly, a blurring of the bureau's focus. The agency's attention ought to be directed toward the common school system not education in general. Its reports ought to be rigorously factual, not given to quaint aphorisms on the importance of education, romanticized views about the role of the teacher, and articles depicting education as a deterrent to crime. They should avoid side excursions into the realms of informal education, for example, in homes and libraries, and certainly have no business glorifying the benefits of learning for laboring people. If it had concentrated on the condition and problems of common schools, Casserly insisted, Eaton's report "could have done its work in a volume of two hundred pages or less."

Instead of that, what have we here? We have a book of five hundred and seventy-nine pages, which should have had on its title page the words *De omnibus rebus et quibusdem aliis—About everything in the world and several things besides.*

Finally, for those who believe that the best workers are uneducated, Casserly noted, in a reference to the treatment of black people, no statistics will help. "The density of intellect that leads a man to such a conclusion would make him laugh at your statistics and your facts. . . ." [17]

The debates produced no motions to abolish or further curtail the bureau. That at least provided grounds for confidence in the agency's future. Grateful for its appearance so soon after the new commissioner had taken office, most of the legislators accepted Eaton's report with relief.

162

Educators too seemed pleased with his efforts. Emerson White registered disappointment that old and previously published data had been used but praised the report, nonetheless, as "practically useful." Although little more than an abbreviated version of Barnard's previous effort, Eaton's report was clearly more readable— for one thing larger type was used—and better organized than that of his predecessor.[18]

Eaton's first report, with its statistical surveys, topical reports, descriptions of present school practices, and multifaceted discussions of education broadly conceived, established the pattern for his subsequent messages to Congress. His comments on black education illustrated both the pattern and its weaknesses. While courageous to the extent of bringing attention to matters schoolmen across the country seemed intent upon forgetting, they remained ineffectual, blunted by the bureau's lack of power to correct the conditions described and Eaton's deference to nineteenth-century notions about the white man's burden. Informed by the kind of perverse soteriology long haunting relations of Christian groups with victims of white racism, Eaton's attitude included the view that Providence brought Africans to the United States and allowed them to experience the shackles of slavery so they might be "saved." While deploring conditions in schools for minorities, he did not press the point with state school officials. To requests for help from black leaders and teachers in black schools, he replied that his agency was empowered only to collect and disseminate educational facts. "This office has no remedy but that of influence," he informed a correspondent anxious about the burning of black schools by white mobs in his state. To have promised more would have been dishonest. Many years later, Nicholas Murray Butler complained that the Bureau of Education had become simply a "bureau of information." It was John Eaton who initiated this focusing of the agency's function, emphasizing the collection and dissemination of school statistics to such an extent that the phrase became a definition of the bureau itself. He accomplished the result deliberately and with no little difficulty in an attempt to overcome threats endangering the agency's existence since its inception.[19]

Powerless to enforce compliance with his requests for information, Eaton set about to win from educators the cooperation he decided was necessary to keep the bureau alive. With the persistence of a politician in search of votes, he labored to establish lines of communication between his office and school officials throughout the country. He sent messages of congratulation to newly elected state superintendents; and to those facing difficulties with their state legislatures, he offered advice and words of encouragement. It is no insult to Eaton to acknowledge that he was an educational politician, and a very good one. By promising copies of his annual reports to cooperative school officials, establishing exchanges of reports with editors and superintendents, and granting small favors such as the publication of a schoolman's article, Eaton created over the years a more or less reliable procedure for securing the information he wanted. In the process he contributed to the development of uniformity in the nomenclature and type of information published in state and municipal school reports—not an insignificant achievement.[20]

Eaton experienced equal success in winning congressional friends for the bureau, primarily because of his ability to move freely among the members of Congress. He became an unabashed lobbyist for his agency and enjoyed the role. Rarely satisfied with the appropriations he received and continually disappointed over the limited number of his reports printed for distribution, Eaton, nonetheless, never encountered the intense congressional opposition which Barnard had faced. His cordial relations with Congress were, of course, strengthened, at least at the outset of his term, by his loyalty to the Republican party and his widely acknowledged friendship with Grant. That he won the confidence of succeeding presidents and even Democratic members of Congress attested his often noted diplomacy. He seemed able to convince even ardent states' rights men that his bureau was worthwhile, or at least that they should leave it alone.[21]

While Eaton consistently argued that collecting and publishing school data were the bureau's primary tasks, he also sought ways of increasing the agency's scope of operation. Emerson White predicted that the commissioner would not endorse the proposals of Congressman George Hoar for national aid to education, but he was mistaken. With a minimum of fanfare, Eaton encouraged Hoar in his effort, and subsequently supported all of the various bills for national aid introduced during his tenure. Convinced that the measures would strengthen the bureau's authority, he concluded as early as the fall of 1871 that only federal funds could remedy the educational ills of the southern states and influence the development of strong school

164

systems in the territories. When Senator Henry W. Blair began his long and almost successful campaign to secure passage of a federal aid to education bill in the 1880s, Eaton armed him with statistics to document his argument concerning the dangerously uneven distribution of educational opportunities among the states.[22]

Although none of the bills was adopted, Eaton succeeded in a less formal expansion of the agency's influence by systematically strengthening ties between his office and the N.T.A., which in 1870 reorganized itself as the National Educational Association. He distributed N.E.A. publications under the bureau's franking privilege and accepted responsibility for planning conferences of the association and its various departments which elected to meet in Washington with increasing frequency. Not surprisingly, the N.E.A. came to consider the bureau as something of an arm of its own organization. For his part, Eaton found a loyal constituency for both the bureau and himself in the association, particularly its state and national leaders. In 1877, 1881 and 1885 as new presidents prepared to take office, the association staged carefully organized campaigns for Eaton's retention as commissioner, using state and county superintendents to distribute petitions throughout the country.[23]

Barnard viewed his successor's work as brilliant, and it was, if measured in terms of dogged single mindedness and expenditure of energy. In William T. Harris's opinion,

> General Eaton was the true founder of the Bureau of Education, in the sense that he established as the chief work of the Bureau the annual collection of statistics, by means of statistical schedules which were sent to all institutions and all general offices to be filled out and returned to the Commissioner from year to year. In this way he trained educators to keep original records of their operations, and made these records available for analysis and comparison.

Harris's observation was clearly valid; however, John Eaton was more the bureau's organizer than its founder. He routinized the agency's functions, presided over the growth of its staff from two to thirty-eight employees, secured ever increasing appropriations from Congress to support his work, won the cooperation of educators, and established a close working relationship with the leading educational organization of his day.[24]

165

Nathaniel H. R. Dawson, commissioner of education, 1886–89. Courtesy of the U.S. Office of Education.

A clear test of Eaton's success came during his final year in office. In November 1885, nine months after the inauguration of Grover Cleveland, the first Democratic president since James Buchanan, Eaton tendered his resignation, claiming as reasons ill health and a desire to accept the presidency of Marietta College. It was, in addition, a courtesy the new president expected. Remaining in office at the president's request, he waited nine months before Cleveland announced a replacement. In the meantime, Eaton moved his family to Marietta, Ohio, returning to Washington only infrequently. The bureau functioned for almost a year without a chief administrator and also without outraged cries from Congress protesting the commissioner's absences.[25]

PERMANENCE: THE DAWSON AND HARRIS YEARS

That the founding period of the Bureau of Education ended with Eaton's term became clear during the subsequent administrations of Nathaniel H. R. Dawson and William T. Harris. Dawson, who hailed from the South where the bureau had never been popular, lacked Eaton's crusading spirit. He attended, nevertheless, to the shoring up of the bureau's operational structure. Harris,

166

nationally known as a scholar and school administrator, brought to
the agency many of the deficiencies that plagued it during Barnard's
tenure. The bureau survived both Dawson's lack of passion for the
educational "cause" and Harris's administrative ineptitude. A brief
examination of their terms shows what happened: an epilogue to the
Office of Education's founding years.

When Eaton made clear his intention to resign, the NEA
shifted its endorsement to Emerson White for commissioner. The
Ohio educator had long ago shed his reluctance to accept the
position. Garfield's election as president in 1880 had given White his
first opportunity after Eaton's appointment to express interest in the
post. White indicated to the president-elect his desire to become
commissioner, if Garfield wanted "to make a change." There is no
record of Garfield's reply, and whether the president would have
replaced Eaton had he lived to complete the organization of his
administration remains unknown. In 1885, after Eaton's resignation,
White eagerly lent support to the NEA campaign in his behalf.
Identification with the Republican party, however, made his appointment by the new Democratic president unlikely. Cleveland keenly
felt the pressure to appoint a member of his own party and received
numerous endorsements for prominent Democratic schoolmen.
Through Secretary of the Interior L. Q. C. Lamar, he offered the
position to J. L. M. Curry, the highly respected agent for the Peabody Fund and an advocate of federal aid to education. Curry, a
southerner and a Democrat, chose instead to become minister to
Spain. At length, on 6 August 1886, Cleveland appointed Nathaniel
Dawson, an attorney and leading southern Democrat from Selma,
Alabama, to whom he had previously promised a place in his
cabinet.[26]

Howls of protest greeted the appointment of a man
unknown in educational circles, although Dawson's southern origins
and his affiliation with the Democratic party aroused as much
displeasure as his lack of preparation for the position. A trustee of the
University of Alabama for over ten years, Dawson could claim no
previous experience in educational administration. A. E. Winship,
editor of the *Journal of Education*, was outraged:

> There were a score of prominent Democratic teachers and
> superintendents mentioned in connection with the office, any
> one of whom would have reflected credit upon all concerned.

President Cleveland did not select any one of these. He ignored the petitions of the multitude of teachers; he forgot that there was an educational system, a school-room science, a teaching fraternity, at the head of which he was to appoint a national leader. He passed over every State that has made a specialty of educational advancement, and took the State that ranks every other in the Union in the intensity of ignorance and the neglect of general education. He passed over every man who has taught, who has supervised, who has studied education, or written thereon, and selected a man who had done none of these things.

With that off his chest, Winship wished Dawson well. His quarrel was with the president not the new commissioner, whom he welcomed to office as a "brained man, a natural leader, and a friend of education. . . ." Dawson later explained to Curry,

My appointment was unsolicited by me and entirely unexpected. It was in a new and untried field, and I would not have sought it. I considered the appointment a great compliment under the circumstances, and accepted it reluctantly at the instance [*sic*] and persuasion of my friends in Washington, who deemed it important that I should not decline.[27]

During his three-year term, Dawson "displayed little sympathy with the black man" and for a while radically curtailed exchanges with foreign educators; other than these, he instituted no major change in the bureau's work. Retaining Eaton's staff, he reorganized the bureau's divisions in an effort to streamline its operation. When Eaton left office, the thirty-eight member staff was rather casually organized into work groups often with overlapping functions. Dawson established three divisions within the bureau: records, library and museum, and statistics, each under the direction of a chief clerk. Subsequently, he created a fourth division to direct the bureau's responsibilities for education in Alaska, an assignment added to the agency's functions at the close of Eaton's term. He continued Eaton's practice of working closely with educational organizations, particularly the NEA, and in time overcame some of the initial displeasure which his appointment had aroused among schoolmen. He was not a total stranger to the historic concerns of professional educators, he confided to A. E. Winship, because his

father and Horace Mann had been "intimate friends" during the
1820s when they were law school classmates.[28]

Dawson's various inspection tours included a trip to Alaska
to strengthen the bureau's work being directed there by the
Reverend Sheldon Jackson. His conviction that a majority of
southerners favored federal aid to education led him to endorse
Senator Blair's bill, although he was never as vigorous in his support
of school aid proposals as John Eaton. At the suggestion of President
F. A. P. Barnard of Columbia University, Dawson promoted the
publication of a series of histories of education in the various states,
one of the projects initially conceived by Barnard. He succeeded in
interesting Herbert Baxter Adams in the project, which was to
emphasize the development of higher education, and named the
Johns Hopkins' historian as its director. William T. Harris later
praised the series as "of enduring value to the student and teacher
and . . . a monument to his [Dawson's] administration." Dawson's
intent, Harris observed in a later report, was to adhere more closely
than his predecessor to Barnard's original plan for the bureau.[29]

Despite the relative success of his efforts, Dawson remained
uncomfortable as commissioner. In October 1888, as the presidential
campaign drew to a close, he attempted without success to win
appointment as minister to Spain, the position which Curry had
recently vacated. When Cleveland lost his bid for re-election to
Benjamin Harrison, Dawson indicated he would not stay "when the
new man comes in." Still, his letter of resignation kept open the
possibility of a reappointment. He explained to Harrison,

> The appointment was offered to me without any application or
> seeking on my part. I am a democrat in politics. I consider the
> Office of Education as non-political, and it may be so regarded
> by your Excellency, but my desire to leave you perfectly free
> and unembarrassed in the selection of the executive agents of
> your administration induces me to write you this letter, to be
> declined or accepted at your discretion.

Despite appeals from a number of educators, including Massachusetts schoolman A. P. Marble, urging the commissioner's retention,
the new president accepted Dawson's resignation.[30]

In the steady bureaucratization of the education agency
following 1870, Dawson's term represented a significant, if brief,

episode. An able administrator, he directed the careful and swift production of annual reports, which he labored to make more accurate and readable, and a well-organized staff honed for efficiency. For the bureau, it was a time of settling down to agreed upon functions rather than dramatic new ventures, presided over by a man known more for gentlemanly grace than frenetic activity. He attended to business without the flair characteristic of John Eaton, but then by the time of his term as commissioner the permanence of the bureau was no longer subject to doubt.

Harrison attempted without success to interest several leading educators in the commissionership, including Nicholas Murray Butler. Butler claimed to have brought the name of William Torrey Harris to the president's attention. After a brief delay to check his political credentials, Harrison offered the position to the prominent educator, who had received the overwhelming endorsement of educational leaders throughout the country. Harris assumed office on 12 September 1889.[31]

The new commissioner came to the bureau with an international reputation as an Hegelian philosopher and educational leader. Although commonly referred to as "Dr. Harris," he never earned a college or university degree. He withdrew from Yale before completing the undergraduate program. A widely read author of educational and philosophical monographs, he gained national prominence as school superintendent in St. Louis from 1868 to 1880, where he was instrumental in establishing the first system of public kindergartens in the United States and in drawing attention to the special needs of urban populations for new school programs. After resigning his position in St. Louis, he devoted his energies to the Concord School of Philosophy, an admittedly experimental program which he hoped would promote a truly American philosophy and eventually establish him as "the Emerson" of his day. The project achieved scant success, and Harris was close to admitting its failure when he was appointed commissioner.

Anna Tolman Smith, who joined the bureau staff under Eaton and remained to serve under both Dawson and Harris, later recalled that Harris's appointment was accompanied by the general expectation among educators that the bureau's authority would be strengthened and expanded under his leadership. His efforts had almost the opposite effect, even though initially his reputation as a scholar, former superintendent, and leader in the NEA succeeded in

170

bringing fresh attention and respect to the agency. Harris, it turned out, possessed little talent for administration. Unable to organize his own work, he relied on the staff to maintain the agency's efficiency, all the while holding tightly to decision-making powers. The staff, many of them elderly Civil War widows, floundered for lack of direction. Harris compounded the confusion in his office by accepting a protégé of Rhode Island's Senator Nelson Aldrich as his private secretary, a man whose devotion to Harris could not compensate for his own lack of organizing ability. For fear of offending the senator and thus turning him against the bureau, Harris refused to replace the young man.[32]

More detrimental to the bureau was the commissioner's aversion to pressuring Congress for increased appropriations, a tactic both Eaton and Dawson found necessary to save the agency from being overlooked. At length, leaders in the NEA's Department of Superintendence intervened with Congress in hopes of securing larger appropriations for the agency. Harris reportedly found the business of asking Congress for money "unseemly and improper." [33]

Both Smith and Frank A. Fitzpatrick, the former superintendent of schools in Omaha who worked closely with Harris during the first years of his term, characterized Harris's administration as personally oriented to the scholarly interests of the commissioner. Harris preferred working independently and at his own pace. An energetic, seemingly indefatigable man, he tightened the bureau's relation with the NEA and dominated both with his conservative, formalistic views on education. The newer approaches to education being propounded by John Dewey and others repelled him. The testimony of A. E. Winship, although intended to be complimentary, pictured Harris as an irascible man, disinclined to ask advice and intolerant of criticism.[34]

The Harris administration, in many ways reminiscent of Barnard's term, brought the Bureau of Education full circle to its founding years. Both men emphasized scholarly endeavors and stubbornly insisted upon shaping the agency's work to their own interests. They also experienced many of the same difficulties with Congress, their fellow educators, and their respective staffs. Both have been accused of nearly destroying the Bureau of Education. However, by the time Harris became commissioner, hopes for a national educational agency had been translated into a plan of operation by Barnard which Eaton, and later Dawson, had made

171

functional. Barnard pioneered the programming of an idea, while Harris, thanks to Eaton and Dawson, inherited a permanent institution.

The cost of permanence was a considerable narrowing of the responsibilities originally envisioned for the bureau and a steady decline in autonomy. Even as a department, the agency depended upon the vagaries of congressional goodwill. In supporting federal aid to education bills, which indirectly at least, would have enhanced the bureau's authority, John Eaton never forgot his agency's tentative hold on Congress. What he sought, and what he received, were annual appropriations and funds to print his reports awarded with a minimum of difficulty. With few other options available, he deliberately courted and secured the bureau's dependency relation with Congress and added another, one with state and municipal school officials and the NEA. Both relations were necessary, Eaton argued, to guarantee the bureau's permanence.

The national educational agency, in Barnard's 1854 plan, was to serve as an indirect pressure from the federal level on local and state school operations to the end that they might be more inclusive, exhibit greater professionalism and efficiency, and be of an increasingly higher quality. Supporters of the plan wanted to infuse American public schools with a national consciousness, thus correcting the intellectual and professional narrowness implicit in their traditional provincialism, and to provide them with a basis for intelligently determining the course of their future growth. They wanted an advocate permanently inserted in the federal government that would "promote the cause of education throughout the country," an agency that would champion public learning through a host of institutions—not merely schools—and deliver to the people and their representatives "knowledge about education," as Barnard phrased it. Success, Barnard learned, required funds and power, in addition to the agency's capacity to influence educators and political leaders through publications and comparative statistics. The two dependency relations cultivated by Eaton tended to reverse the pressure's direction. The reasons so many school officials and members of Congress insisted that the bureau was designed to collect and disseminate school data, and not anything more, were hardly complex. However, under Eaton's leadership the bureau was increasingly powerless to challenge them and in fact showed little inclination for doing so. His success, relied upon by his successors, in developing procedures for collecting uniform school data and influencing the dissemination of educational statistics in a more precise, scientific, form, even in municipal and state school reports, represented solid accomplishment. It also left the traditional localism of American public education virtually intact. The Dawson and Harris administrations confirmed another aspect of the development: the business of school reform, including activities undertaken by the Bureau of Education, had passed into the hands of professional schoolmen. That, too, had been one of Barnard's objectives.

Historian Richard Hofstadter has argued in *Anti-intellectualism in American Life* that Civil War and Reconstruction produced few substantive social reforms. Perhaps their blood ran thin, he said of the postwar reformers: "[H]ow many grave social issues they barely touched upon and how many they did not touch at all. . . ." In the area of education, if one looks beyond mere quantitative increases in the number of schools available, he finds, in addition to support for Hofstadter's judgment, peculiar ironies. The treatment of black people in separate and unequal schools across the nation developed apace the special brand of Jim Crow experienced by immigrant children whose ethnicity was apparently un-American. A powerful federal educational agency in the post-Reconstruction years, helped by commonly held notions about race, foreigners, and what it meant to be American, and by the wondrous capacity of local, elite-dominated common schools to engender unequal chances for learning, might have settled for enforced homogeneity through schooling more firmly and with greater effect than did Eaton's "bureau of information." In short, if Barnard's revised plan had been realized, the aim of guaranteed, that is, enforced, equal educational opportunity might well have been more surely subverted than it was. Another ironical development emerges with greater certainty. By the end of Eaton's term, it was clear that in the crucial matter of educational policy, the South and the past were winning the Civil War.[35]

7 Barnard's Bureau in the 1970s: Notes for the Future

PAST AS PROLOGUE

Beneath disagreements over the extent and mode of federal intervention in education and petty jealousies which weakened their ability to join in a common cause, original proponents of plans for a national education bureau believed unswervingly in schools' power to shape individual values and aspirations as well as the republic's economic and political structures. The common school, learning within every child's reach, could diminish crime and vice and bring peace to quarreling urban multitudes. It could serve as a source of local pride, symbolizing cultural advance, enlightenment on the march. Children of workers, immigrants, and the poor could find access to the benefits of citizenship and chances to improve their social station through the schoolhouse door. In subsequent eras public schooling might be glimpsed as an imperfect panacea; but at the height of the common school movement, in the decades around the Civil War, schoolmen held tightly to their convictions. Not surprisingly, given their premises, they engaged in reform activity designed to achieve linear and quantitative advances, drives to establish more schools, extend public instruction from kindergarten to high school and teacher training, and increase schools' operational efficiency and their effectiveness in producing literate citizens, national unity, and domestic peace. Plans for state and national education bureaus offered mechanisms for securing such reforms.

Understanding the education movement's centralizing tendencies requires, in addition to an appreciation of the reformers' aims, recognition of the antagonists they thought were working against them. Their enemies turned out to be a strange mixture of political and economic conservatives, moderates, liberals, and radicals. Local

174

elites were a constant source of trouble. They rejected the implication that the schools they controlled formally or tacitly excluded religious, racial, social class, or cultural minorities and resisted efforts to incorporate and hold accountable their schools within state systems of education. The schoolmen perceived another group to be arguing with know-nothing insistence that public schools 1) were unnecessary extravagances, 2) were adequate as they stood, 3) functioned effectively only as locally oriented institutions and hence would improve with the evolution of the immediate society, if indeed improvements were needed, 4) would remain impervious to external attempts to engineer reforms because of their local character, and/or 5) were in any case not justified by the needs of society beyond the elementary level. Schoolmen included in the know-nothing group those who rejected schools as agents of social reform in favor of direct assaults on political and economic inequities and those lower class opponents to the spread of public education who, in the schoolmen's eyes, lacked an intelligent perception of their own needs for learning. The schoolmen also saw themselves in opposition to religious groups which advocated public funds to support sectarian education or attempted to block public school development out of fears that the emerging institutions would affect adversely denominational schools.

A fourth set of opponents sometimes identified by schoolmen as inimical to their cause were the friends of slavery, a group some of them mistakenly labeled as southerners. It is difficult to categorize nineteenth-century opponents and supporters of black education, particularly those who were white. Clearly not limited to the South, resistance to the inclusion of black people in public schools extended throughout the nation. Even among those schoolmen who advocated inclusion, whether in integrated or segregated schools, few argued for rigorously enforced equality of opportunity. Most white supporters of black education mustered at best a benevolent paternalism to justify their position. Opponents, however, tended to chart an even more devious course, championing local school control when faced with proposals for state supervision of education and the primacy of states' rights on questions suggesting a federal role in guaranteeing equal educational opportunity. Although not all states' rights and local-control advocates could be fairly classified as friends of slavery, a number of schoolmen, particularly during the Civil War and early Reconstruction periods,

175

interpreted states' rights arguments as attempts to maintain exclusionary school policies. Finally, the schoolmen saw themselves in opposition to "individualists," those who either rejected the notion that they should help finance the education of others' children or accepted the public school concept only to the extent of endorsing minimal schooling for the offspring of low-income or indigent parents.

None of these groups existed in complete separation from the others. There was considerable overlap in terms of their members and objectives. Moreover, none was as perverse or obtuse as the schoolmen often claimed. Nevertheless, their opposition constituted a major deterrent to the schoolmen's cause and for some of the opponents was grounded in a denial of the value or appropriateness of inclusive schools. If the country required an educated citizenry, bound together by national loyalty and a common morality, as the school reformers believed, equal opportunity apparently would have to be enforced. Few of the schoolmen questioned whether their goals could be realized in schools, although a good many of them acknowledged that schools alone would not be sufficient for the task. Libraries, museums, newspapers and other agents of supplementary education would have to be promoted along with schools. They also tended to agree that equal opportunity meant homogeneously tailored learning programs.

Needed for their movement's final victory, the more tenacious of the schoolmen reasoned, was a national agency to collect and disseminate information about schools and publicize the social and individual betterment to be made possible through the nationwide distribution of education. The communications and evaluation network being developed by Mann, Barnard and others on the state level, would, if extended to the national level, influence the adoption of uniform school policies and practices across the land. It would reveal local deficiencies more pointedly and with greater objectivity than the efforts of state and municipal officials, identify and publicize the nation's most effective and efficient schools, thus providing incentives for increased spending on schools, and equip the new education profession with a national platform from which to alert the public to schools' value. Henry Barnard, self-appointed systematizer of plans for a national bureau, detailed the functions of the proposed agency, adding what he perceived to be significant omissions. In his view, a national bureau should serve as an international repository of knowledge about education, including educational history. It should take responsibility for regular assessments of the nation's schools, the promotion of educational experimentation and innovation, and the initiation and supervision of model schools.

The expectations remained for the most part unfulfilled, and not merely because of the impossible claims for schools' reform capability on which plans for a national bureau were founded. Indifference and opposition, from educators, congressmen, and presidents, greeted the Department of Education during its first years of operation. Despite limited authority and funds, the agency confronted demands for immediate results, most pointedly from Congress. Mere survival, bureaucratic permanence, loomed as its most pressing challenge and became its most significant victory. Henry Barnard proved to be unequal to the political complexities engulfing the department; and John Eaton, an affable man experienced in the ways of politics and a competent administrator, failed to grasp important nuances of his predecessor's plan, particularly the significance of promoting educational experimentation and model schools. At the root of more fantastic visions of its nation-building effectiveness, the office's original supporters expected the increase and improvement of American education, reform leadership, to follow in the wake of its establishment. They reckoned without the realities of national partisan politics, complicated still further by the Civil War's tangled aftermath. Radical reconstruction, encompassing an idealistic federalism which made plans for a national school bureau attainable for the first time, began weakening by 1868. The Department of Education had the misfortune to open its doors as a brief era ended. Too weak to enforce the education of black children or challenge local and state school policies which interfered with the nation's desperate postwar need for inclusive schools and educational innovation, the agency became instead a "bureau of information."

Another difficulty, a major one as it happened, derived from the bureaucratic model developed by Barnard in defining the department's functions and limitations. Although initially lacking direct power of control, state school agencies and even federal offices such as the Department of Agriculture proved to be effective in winning quantitative reforms, more schools organized into something approaching statewide systems, in the first case, and more farmers advised of the latest agricultural techniques by a central information clearinghouse, in the other. Barnard's bureau, designed in similar

177

fashion to exert indirect external pressure on state and municipal school officials, proved to be incapable of negotiating the political currents stirred up by its establishment. Its data gathering and dissemination mission failed to provide the agency with resources to satisfy the conflicting expectations of schools and its own effectiveness found among members of Congress or to combat education's low priority among the causes vying for attention in Washington. Finally, it was not equipped to counteract the resistance of local and state school administrators to proposals for change. Rather, the bureau's design served to focus the agency's reform intention on fulfilling its mandate to collect and disseminate educational information and statistics, on the complementary assumptions that ignorance and inertia blocked the path to equal educational opportunity and that its reports could dispel both.

The operational deficiencies, however, should be measured in light of the clearly inadequate test that Barnard's plan received during the agency's founding years. The office never acquired sufficient funds nor authority to function freely even as a bureau of information. Unable to require cooperation of municipal and state officials, it relied on educational data voluntarily submitted. Its annual reports, published in limited numbers, went for the most part to established school leaders and favored congressional constituents and reflected in tone and format the interests of their narrowed audience. The plan to render judgments about schools' quality and to compare state and local systems, offered by the office's original supporters as means for influencing reform, proved frightening to congressmen and schoolmen alike. Had the agency done nothing more (or less) than assess and publicize school conditions, the impact remains, in sum, unknown. More certain is that the office's steady bureaucratization and increasingly professional orientation later in the nineteenth century paralleled similar developments in state offices of education and urban school systems across the country, although establishing clear causal connections between the two developments requires considerable speculation.

THE YEARS BETWEEN: 1906–1970

From 1906, when William T. Harris resigned as commissioner, to 1970, the bureau's budget increased and its activities and staff became more numerous. In some years, the growth was dramatic; in others, barely noticeable. After occupying rented quarters for more than forty years, most of them spent since early in Eaton's term in the Wright Building at the northeast corner of 8th and G streets, NW, the bureau moved into the Post Office Building in 1909. Eventually, in 1961, it acquired a building of its own.

The agency's name and administrative home also underwent changes. It began as a department without cabinet representation. In 1869, it was reconstituted as the Office of Education in the Department of the Interior. Designated a bureau in 1870, its official title again became the Office of Education in 1929. After 70 years in the Department of the Interior, the office was transferred to the Federal Security Agency in 1939, where it remained until the creation of the Department of Health, Education, and Welfare in 1953.

As they did during the agency's founding years, commissioners after 1906 continued to reflect the politics of the president's party, if not in fact at least in terms of ideological inclination. One commissioner who managed to hold office under presidents of different parties was Philander Priestly Claxton. Appointed by President Taft in 1911, he remained to serve under Woodrow Wilson. Warren G. Harding, a Republican, created a minor storm when he requested Claxton's resignation in 1921. The president had sullied education with politics. Two commissioners in recent memory found themselves out of favor with the presidents who appointed them and ultimately out of office. George Zook (1933–34) expected Franklin Roosevelt's New Deal to include direct federal aid to public schools and resigned when it became clear that education would not be emphasized among the administration's economic recovery programs. James E. Allen, Jr. (1969–70) erred first in publicly suggesting that Richard Nixon's encouragement of school desegregation lacked vigor and second in criticizing the president's decision to invade Cambodia in the spring of 1970. On occasion, incumbents clung to the fiction of the office's political neutrality. Earl J. McGrath, appointed by President Truman in 1949, seemed inclined to stay in office after Dwight Eisenhower's inauguration in 1953. Proposed reductions in the agency's budget convinced him to leave.

In another respect, the commissioners have been political appointees. In addition to satisfying a president's partisan expectations, most of them have been elevated from among the ranks of the

179

nation's school administrators. Most could claim strong organizational ties with professional educators, principally through the National Education Association. Among the exceptions, in addition to N. H. R. Dawson, have been John J. Tigert (1921–28), a University of Kentucky professor of philosophy and psychology; George Zook (1933–34), president of the University of Akron and earlier the director of the bureau's Division of Higher Education; Earl J. McGrath (1949–53), professor of higher education at the University of Chicago; Sterling M. McMurrin (1961–62), academic vice president of the University of Utah; and John R. Ottina (1973–), a mathematical analyst for private industry and a corporation president. Elmer Ellsworth Brown (1906–11) and Francis Keppel (1962–66) qualify as partial exceptions, although both enjoyed NEA support. At the time of his appointment, Brown was professor of education at the University of California and a former NEA president. Dean of the Harvard Graduate School of Education from 1948 to 1962, Keppel was never strictly speaking a school administrator. Nor had he been professionally involved in public education prior to his tenure as dean. Of the twenty commissioners who have served since 1867, thirteen had been state or municipal school administrators at some points in their careers.

The increase in appropriations offers the most obvious indication of the office's growth. During John Eaton's tenure, funds for the agency ranged from approximately $25,000 to $55,000, with the major portion going for salaries and rent. By 1890, the appropriation exceeded $100,000; however, half of this amount was earmarked for the Alaska program. The appropriation for 1910 included $61,000 for salaries, and $212,000 for the Alaska program. As World War I drew to a close, the bureau's appropriation increased dramatically, from just over $190,000 in 1918 (excluding funds for Alaska) to approximately $550,000 in 1919. After the war, the budget decreased sharply. By 1921 it had returned to its prewar level of close to $200,000. Although the office's funds rose over the next two decades, not until World War II did they again experience a dramatic increase. Responsible for a number of defense-related educational projects, the agency found its annual budget approaching $2 million during the war years. By 1953, the office administered more than $90 million, over $70 million of which was earmarked for school aid to areas impacted by population increases resulting from the establishment of nearby federal programs, including defense-related installations and industries. Its operating budget for that year stood at approximately $3 million. Seven years later, Office of Education funds totaled $500 million, roughly half of which went to the construction, maintenance, and operation of schools in federally impacted areas. Aid to higher education and for elementary and secondary education, provided for in the National Defense Education Act, amounted to over $150 million. Other major budget items in 1960 included $47.9 million in financial assistance to vocational education and over $10 million for educational research, the greater portion of the latter supporting NDEA related projects. The 1960 appropriation for salaries and expenses fell slightly below $10 million. With the passage of a number of precedent-setting education bills during Lyndon Johnson's administration, including the Civil Rights Act of 1964 and the Elementary and Secondary Education Act of 1965, the office's funds again rose sharply. By 1970 its appropriation exceeded $4 billion.[1]

The office's appropriations history appears to depict an agency with steadily increasing responsibilities and authority. A brief review of its programs since 1906 indicates that such has not quite been the case. The Alaska program represented a possible exception. One of the more intriguing and, according to one observer, "most onerous" of the bureau's activities, the program involved administrative responsibility for education in the territory. Congress assigned the task to the secretary of the interior in 1884 who in turn delegated it to the Bureau of Education. As noted in the previous chapter, one of Nathaniel Dawson's first acts as commissioner was a tour of the distant territory. He returned firmly committed to promoting education there. Initially, the bureau was responsible for administering schools for the entire population. Early in the twentieth century, the education of non-native (white) residents fell to the territorial government, leaving the Bureau of Education in charge of schools for the native population. It constituted one of the few efforts in which the agency took direct responsibility for an educational program. Actually, the task involved more than building and operating schools, which was difficult enough. The bureau also administered the delivery of medical services and various projects related to ensuring the economic well-being of the native peoples. The latter led the agency into the establishment of cooperative stores and a long-term commitment to introduce herds of reindeer into Alaska.[2]

Missionaries established non-native formal learning institutions in Alaska before the bureau arrived on the scene. The agency began its work by underwriting these existing schools. Contracts with various denominational groups stipulated the use of federal funds for teachers' salaries and supplies, leaving the selection of teachers and the actual conduct of the schools to the church organizations. The arrangement resembled that which funneled state funds to the New York Public School Society to operate free schools in the city during the 1830s and early 1840s. Sheldon Jackson, a Presbyterian missionary, supervised the operation as the bureau's general agent in Alaska. Sectarian quarrels led the government to withdraw support from the contract schools in 1895. Subsequently, the bureau entered the business of running its own schools under the direction of the chief of the Alaska division. By 1920, close to seventy schools scattered throughout the territory were being maintained.

With the inauguration of territorial schools, Alaska found itself with two educational systems, one for native children administered by the Bureau of Education and the other, controlled locally, for children of white residents. Children of mixed blood attended either native or territorial schools. It was not uncommon for schools representing both systems to be established in the same settlement. Lack of adequate funding compounded the bureau's administrative difficulties in the Alaska program. Nevertheless, after 1905, appropriations for education in the territory annually exceeded those for operating the bureau itself. In fact, the agency regularly received more funds for purchasing reindeer than it did for gathering statistics, supposedly one of its primary missions.

The bureau's Alaska program, including the schools, medical relief, and strategies for bolstering the native economy, intended to bring civilization to a primitive people who, as William T. Harris put it, "have not yet reached the Anglo-Saxon frame of mind." Rather than attempting to fashion model learning institutions with the cultures of the people and the climate and terrain of the region in mind, the schools followed the curriculum of the American common school with components of vocational training and manual work added. All the children were taught English. At the center of the Alaska "mission" stood the teacher:

He was an outpost of civilization, in many places completely cut off from communication with the outside world for many

months of the year. He naturally assumed the functions of a
community leader, a counsellor, a censor of morals, an arbitra-
tor in disputes, a local observer and reporter of conditions, a
defender of the peace, and a public nurse and consulting
physician. He faced the problems of ignorance, poverty, famine,
immorality, drunkenness, crime, sickness, and pestilence.

How the Alaskan people managed to survive prior to his arrival
remains something of a mystery.[3]

For Commissioner of Education William John Cooper
(1929–34), the program lacked intelligent and persuasive rationale:

In so far as we acted at all for the education of these peoples,
our policy was to expose them to the system of schools which
had grown up in the United States. It had occurred to no one
that there might be a better system of schools for such people.

To foster education among all the various native peoples who had
come under United States rule, Cooper recommended research
endeavors "to discover what kind of schools each particular people
should have." Such efforts "should furnish the basis for a system of
schools adapted to the native people and the environments in which
they find themselves." Although less blatantly paternalistic than the
white man's burden ideology that informed the bureau's Alaska
program, Cooper's views implicitly denigrated the systems of
learning and youth socialization indigenous to Alaskan natives.
Enlightened by contrast, they attracted the attention of Frederick
Keppel, president of the Carnegie Corporation, who helped secure
funds for the first comprehensive study of the social conditions and
educational attainments of Alaskan natives. (Thirty years later, one of
Keppel's sons was commissioner of education.) By 1934 when the
study was completed, Cooper had left the bureau and the agency's
Alaska program had ended. Committed to shaping the bureau into a
research agency, Cooper convinced the secretary of the interior to
transfer the program to the Bureau of Indian Affairs in 1931.[4]

Other Office of Education activities during the period from
before World War I to the 1950s included annual reports on the land
grant colleges; the promotion of Americanization education for
immigrants; a short-lived, highly spirited campaign to promote home
gardening during World War I; and the administration of school aid

183

funds to federally impacted areas. The range of interest extended from kindergarten to higher education and encompassed the education of minority populations; informal educational institutions, for example, libraries; vocational and industrial training; school administration; and comparisons with foreign school systems. Dramatic increases of funds and new programs emerged during the 1917 to 1920 period and the 1940s as the office joined war efforts to promote patriotism and enlist the nation's schools in various defense-related programs. The home gardening campaign and the organization of the School Garden Army, a loosely connected national cadre dedicated to the cultivation of idle lands, constituted major activities of the bureau during World War I. In none of these efforts did the agency play active policy-making roles. Rather, it continued to develop along the lines of a "bureau of information," functioning in the main as a "statistical secretary," to borrow a description employed in a 1967 congressional study of the office.[5]

With over 2,500 employees, a budget ranging around $5 billion, and over 75 programs to administer, the U.S. Office of Education in the 1970s bears little resemblance to the department Henry Barnard launched over a century ago. Propelled by urgent contemporary issues, its period of greatest growth has occurred only in the years after 1957. Of current office programs, over 80 percent were created during the decade after that year. The 89th Congress enacted approximately 40 percent of them during 1965 and 1966. Recipients of office funds now include state educational agencies and commissions, local school authorities, profitmaking and nonprofit organizations, colleges and universities, nonpublic elementary and secondary schools, and individuals. Touching all levels and programmatic aspects of formal education for general and specialized populations, the use of media in education, on-the-job training, and libraries, Office of Education programs encompass and/or through grants and loans support the development of training, services, research, equipment, planning, and construction. The agency is also responsible for ascertaining compliance with civil rights guidelines among the recipients of its services and funds. Uneasy cold war comparisons with foreign, especially Russian, education; dysfunctions of urban school systems, particularly their failures with culturally plural student populations; inability of the property tax in both urban and rural areas to finance local schools; a widely acknowledged need for national goals in the training and development of human skills and resources; the debilitating effects of poverty and racism on the nation's economy and the morale of the people; and difficulties experienced by ethnic minorities in gaining access to the control mechanisms governing local schools—such quandaries, which have sharpened awareness of the nation's stake in its schools, help explain the office's recent meteoric growth. Its origins appear incidental to its present operation, significant primarily in retrospect and uninteresting save to historians.[6]

Amid continuing disagreement and confusion over the agency's functions, authority, and effectiveness, however, links with its past can be perceived. For one, a disquieting similarity exists among the concerns which over the years have prompted demands for federal leadership in the promotion of education. Uneven commitment to the elimination of racism in school policies and practices remains on local and state levels. Ethnic imperialism, resulting from an admixture of fears of cultural differences and naive adherence to the notion that national unity requires cultural homogeneity, still forces children of "colored" minorities through "common" schooling. At the turn of the century those with eastern and southern European backgrounds found themselves similarly labeled and instructed. Excluded minorities, schooling's victims, still seek redress for their grievances, in most cases through appeals for federal intervention and assistance.

A second link with the past can be seen in modes of school reform. As in the earlier period, contemporary patterns of school organization and control tend to follow centralizing models. Twentieth-century massiveness and technology, frequently identified as causes of cumbersome, overgrown state and urban school bureaucracies, cannot alone explain the development. As an examination of the Office of Education's founding years makes clear, uncritical adherence to efficiency and the reluctance of local elites to widen the control base of their schools have also strengthened the centralizing, bureaucratizing tendencies of American public education. With more attention to structural neatness than to the effects of school organization and policy on students, advocates of operational efficiency still propose the dissemination of functional social control mechanisms across the land, quantities of schools acting *in loco parentis*. For them, school reform remains a bureaucratic imposition from the top down. Their effort connects with a long, if not always honorable, tradition and looks to the federal government for reinforcement, as it did a century ago and with the same ambivalence. In short, two concerns about the mode of educational reform remain. One relates to the attempted use of schools as agents of control, an effort that has promoted both bureaucratization and centralization in American education. The other relates to continued reliance on the presumed democratic character of local school authority which tends to hide from view the rather intensive and long-standing centralization of school control that has developed at the local level. Horace Mann, Henry Barnard and other common school leaders attempted to limit local school authority both because they thought it generated exclusive school policies and because they doubted that unchecked local control of education could produce the quantity and quality of public learning programs required by the nation. They thought equal educational opportunity could be bestowed. Later generations have perceived a point they missed, namely that reform imposed from the top and the drive for efficiency collide with the campaign for equal opportunity, the success of which requires the inclusion of excluded minorities in school policy-making.

The office's lack of a clearly delineated mission constitutes a third link with its past. For good or for ill, the Office of Education still lacks broad legislative mandates to assist effectively and comprehensively either the drive for efficiency or attempts to deliver equal educational opportunity, although supporting demands for efficiency through the collection and dissemination of research findings and school data has proved to be easier bureaucratically than enforcing equal opportunity. The agency's appropriations and programs have increased dramatically over the years; yet, the federal relation to education still lacks definition and clarity of purpose. And a valid question is why? Ambivalence over the level of government primarily responsible for enforcing educational opportunity persists, fed by equivocal commitment to the promise of equality, while conflicts over the extent and proper mode of federal intervention in school programs and policy continue. The office's partnership with state and municipal school agencies remains undependable, on occasion nonexistent when federal action threatens a locally ensconced hegemony with influence in Washington. With little attention to the waste and confusion generated by the resulting duplication, Congress has assigned federal education programs to a number of cabinet-level departments and bureaus, including the Office of

Education, thus weakening the possibility of clear federal school policies emerging. Finally, the status of education among national priorities still awaits determination in the form of unequivocal and long-term budgetary commitments. Hastily conceived projects, easily and fatefully publicized, and appeals for more research or the report of yet another presidential commission should not be mistaken for evidence of education's high national priority. Years of rhetoric about schools as laboratories of democracy, their place in the nation's vanguard of social reforming agents, and their primacy in fostering enlightenment and welfare among the people have proved a poor substitute for purposeful federal activity in the educational sphere.[7]

A fourth similarity between the office's present and past derives from its political status as a federal agency. Today, as a century ago, its commissioner functions as a lower-echelon political appointee with limited public visibility and only indirect access to the president. He presides over an agency with a larger budget than eight cabinet-level departments, finds himself subject to the same tests of partisan loyalty required of cabinet members, and receives the brunt of the criticism and antagonism which follows from administering controversial programs. Yet his authority to execute legislative mandates and his ability to respond to immediate or anticipated educational needs with comprehensive planning remain indistinct, dissipated by fears of federal encroachment by local and state authorities, the office's likelihood of being among the first federal agencies to suffer budget cuts when money is in short supply, and the overlapping education and training activities of other federal agencies, including ten cabinet-level departments. In the same way that the secretaries of labor and agriculture typically have represented special constituencies, commissioners of education have tended to be former schoolmen (no women have ever held the post except in an acting capacity). Their authority, however, has never matched that of cabinet members. As in Barnard's day, the commissioner still encounters restrictions on his freedom to appoint senior staff members of his own choosing.[8]

A fifth link with the office's past can be seen in congressional attitudes toward the agency which continue to vacillate between demands that its activities be limited to the dissemination of information, statistical reports, and research and proposals for a cabinet-level department of education. One confronts on the one hand calls for school reform leadership and on the other fears that the concentration of federal educational programs in a single agency will undermine decision-making on local and state levels. The office's sudden and rapid growth in the 1960s notwithstanding, congressional suspicion still greets its programs, with the result that when new responsibilities are assigned to the agency very little thought is given to its comprehensive mission. And yet everpresent is the impatient congressional demand for results, the pressure to "show and tell," as one educator has put it, which ignores both the office's limited authority and the complexity of institutional change processes. Meanwhile the speechmaking continues, following outlines and premises barely altered during nearly two centuries of talk about the necessity of education in a republic. Still being heard are optimistic assertions of schools' salutary role in achieving and maintaining social health voiced by all manner of schoolmen and politicians, including presidents, who nonetheless withhold support from the federal agency which could be designed to test the assertions nationally.[9]

Hampered by limited authority and funds and bureaucratic entanglements, the office's reform tasks involve delivering federal resources needed by state and local educational programs and finding ways to guarantee schools' effectiveness in educating students from diverse races, ethnic groups, and social classes. In brief, the concerns which led antebellum schoolmen to develop plans for a national educational bureau remain. Success, one often hears, requires more knowledge about how and why learning does or does not occur. As Stephen K. Bailey, chairman of the Policy Institute at Syracuse University, testified in 1971 before a subcommittee of the House Committee on Education and Labor,

> [We] are coming to such sobering conclusions as the fact that we simply do not know how to teach poor kids. We really do not know why Johnny can't read: is it because of his mother's diet during the pre-natal period; is it because of inadequate parental play in the early months of life; is it because of "cultural deprivation" in the home—whatever that slippery term means; is it because of the self-fulfilling prophecies of teachers who believed that Johnny was stupid; is it because of poor instruction; is it because of a low self-image reinforced by failure in terms of middle class grading norms; is it because of some ineffable combination of all of these factors?[10]

For over a century, such appeals have struck responsive chords both within the community of professional schoolmen and among congressional friends of education. Plainly, more knowledge about learning and teaching is needed. Disturbing as Bailey's questions may be, there are others, equally distressing, that can be screened from view by appeals for more research. The generations of Johnnys that have not learned to read suggest, in addition to the possibility that no one knows how to teach them, the chance that school personnel, reflecting formal and informal school policies and local attitudes, do not—perhaps can not—care very much whether some of the Johnnys succeed academically. School policies and practices that are dysfunctional to the extent that they contribute to pupil failure also raise researchable issues. Many direct as much attention to the policies themselves and to the school's dependent relations with other social systems and agencies as they do to the learning process and teacher-pupil transactions. More knowledge about how to organize and change learning institutions is needed; however, resolving such issues as institutional racism requires in the final analysis policy changes, that is, political activity which may utilize but clearly goes beyond pedagogical innovation and learning theory research. The question becomes not merely how to teach Johnny to read or even how to correct public schools' racial, ethnic, and social class centrism, but whether for those who control schools, it is important to do either. The question implies that changes in school programs and practices inevitably touch the distribution of political power over schools and tends to deny that schools practice racism, for example, primarily because no one knows how to eliminate it.

My belief, explained Ohio Senator Robert Taft in 1947,

> Is that the Federal Government should assist those States desiring to put a floor under essential services in relief, in medical care, in housing, and in education. Apart from the general humanitarian interest in achieving this result, equality of opportunity lies at the basis of this Republic. No child can begin to have equality of opportunity unless he has medical care in his youth, adequate food, decent surroundings, and, above all, effective schooling. It is the concern of the entire Nation to see that the principles of the Declaration of Independence and of the Constitution are translated into reality.

189

Early proponents of a federal bureau of education would have agreed only in part. They wanted educational opportunity enforced, that is, guaranteed, and thought the nation's future as a republic with its diverse, sometimes warring, population of races, cultures, and social classes required such a strategy. The remainder of Taft's statement succinctly captures the rationale divised by advocates to support plans for a national educational agency. They wanted a federal bureau responsible for seeing that "the general humanitarian interest" and "the principles of the Declaration of Independence and of the Constitution," as they pertain to education, "are translated into reality." Judged in light of the office's founding years, the translations have been timid and incomplete, and not merely because no one is very confident that he knows what can be done at the federal level to correct educational inequities and schools' apparently endemic provincialism.[11]

Enforcing Education in the 1970s

Plans for reforming schools through a federal agency are still appearing. Some propose a refashioning of the Office of Education, others propose a new organization. Despite differences in detail, the proposals' basic objectives have a familiar ring: to affirm the nation's stake in the quality of public education, stimulate educational research and experimentation, provide mechanisms for disseminating results, and employ federal resources in equalizing educational opportunity.

Proposed periodically during the years following the agency's demotion to a bureau within the Department of the Interior in 1869, plans for re-establishing the Office of Education as a department have appeared once again as its funds and authority have increased during the 1960s. If the office is to realize its new statutory responsibilities for ensuring schools' inclusiveness and open-ended educational policies capable of reflecting both social change and new knowledge about the learning process, department proponents argue, it can expect assaults from established school and political authorities. Reform effectiveness, they suggest, requires that the agency enjoy visibility and structural protection within the federal administration, not merely presidential assurances that school improvement occupies a major priority among domestic programs.

190

Lifting the office to cabinet rank would not alone guarantee the needed defense. It would, however, uncloak the political dimensions of the agency's activities and place ultimate responsibility for promoting or undermining them with the chief executive. A department of education might finally lay to rest the fiction of the office's political neutrality and eventually the long-cherished mythical depiction of American public schools as a-political in terms of program content, organization, and control. Departmental organization of federal education programs now scattered among a number of departments and bureaus would also enable the agency's chief administrator to bring order, focus, and planning to the federal involvement in education and tend to render its mission explicit. Finally, a higher quality pool of talent from which to select an administrator would perhaps become available, if the agency were a department rather than a sub-cabinet office.

Opponents of the department proposal fear that concentration of federal education programs in a single agency would undermine local and state authority over schools. They also argue that federal education policy would be more influenced by changes in administration than is currently the case. The point is not particularly persuasive because it ignores the reality of present practice. From Henry Barnard to the current incumbent, commissioners of education have typically secured their appointments only after the evidence was in that their political predilections were compatible with the administration in power. Often their senior staff members have also been required to pass a political test. Other arguments are not so easily dismissed. For one, bringing all federal programs related to education into a single department is easier said than done. Some are unrelated to formal learning institutions and many are dual purposed, falling legitimately within the jurisdictions of other departments, for example, Labor, Health, Education and Welfare, Housing and Urban Development, Agriculture, and Interior. The options would appear to be to restrict the proposed department of education to school-based concerns or to allow duplicated and/or jointly administered programs to continue under the reorganization plan. The former, if it tacitly equates schooling and education, could result in a considerable narrowing of the federal interest in education. The latter would eliminate one of the major results expected from the creation of an education department.

191

A second telling argument against the department plan follows from the desire to stimulate educational research and development from the federal level. A department would combine operational and research functions in a single organization, as the office did until recently. In the past, the office's administrative concerns, reflecting a not surprising preoccupation with proximate goals and day-to-day management, have tended to sap staff energy and funds away from research, with its future orientation, necessarily flexible deadlines, and long-range objectives. A similar weakening of a department of education's research and development arm, say department opponents, would lessen its planning and problem-solving capability, work to undermine its reform mission, and render staff positions unattractive to high caliber scholars. According to researchers and research-minded educationists, avoiding such undesired consequences requires separating the agency's operational and research functions.[12]

Other plans for strengthening the federal role in educational promotion and development have received less attention. A century ago, Ignatius Donnelly insisted that education needed a voice independent of ideology and partisan politics and yet responsive to both. The point remains valid. A national board of education, such as suggested by former Commissioner of Education James E. Allen, Jr., could be designed to soften the influence of any one administration over the office and protect it against the vagaries of congressional goodwill and the demands of special interest groups. Its structure, as proposed by Allen, might encompass lay membership, presidential appointment, and overlapping terms. Similar results could be attained by fashioning the office after federal regulatory commissions and appointing its commissioner for six-year terms.[13]

Implementation of any of these proposals can have little meaning without clarification of the federal role in educational development and policy making. Recent attempts to decentralize Office of Education functions in regional offices may well constitute a retreat from this imperative and an implicit denial of a federal responsibility for education which is unique from that of states and municipalities. Furthermore, as some state and local school authorities have complained, regionalization may result merely in the insertion of a bureaucratic impediment between their agencies and the Office of Education. Decentralization, they suggest, can have little positive effect if decision-making powers are not also disseminated. The latter would raise questions of a different order. At least in terms of guaranteeing equal opportunity, original proponents of a federal educational bureau have been proved correct in arguing that some form of external pressure is required to pry open restrictive local and state policies, whether of the *de jure* or *de facto* variety. Regionalization may signal abdication rather than clarification of the federal role in educational reform.[14]

None of the plans, except for regionalization, which is well underway, stands a strong chance for adoption, particularly in light of legislation passed in June 1972, creating the National Institute of Education. Periodically suggested and discussed by scholars and education research groups since 1958 and recommended to Congress by Richard Nixon in March 1970, NIE is expected to initiate an expanded federal effort in educational research and development intended to uncover, in the president's words, the "new knowledge needed to make education truly equal." Approved with bipartisan support by both the House and Senate, NIE is now housed as a "separate, co-equal" administrative unit alongside the Office of Education within a new Division of Education in the Department of Health, Education, and Welfare. The NIE director and a fifteen-member National Council on Educational Research, responsible for general policies governing the institute, are appointed by the president.[15]

The institute has been established for both positive and negative reasons: to circumvent the bureaucratic barriers to educational research and development found in the Office of Education and to stimulate high quality, focused studies of the nation's major educational problems. It has been mandated "to seek to improve education . . . in the United States." The country needs educational, not merely school, reform, NIE supporters argue, and hence a highly visible research-oriented agency designed to foster investigations into every aspect and level of the learning process. The Office of Education, they conclude, has been unable to field and sustain high quality research because its bureaucratic organization has tended to smother the search for new knowledge in education under the burden of operational problems derived from administering a welter of often competing programs and functions. It has become heavily invested in a limited mission, maintaining and improving existing educational institutions, allowing, as a consequence, its research efforts to "fall into the hands of traditional educational researchers, complete with their second-water abilities and preoccupation with what goes on in schools." With its limited visibility, often inconclusive and unimportant results, and budget restrictions on salaries for technicians and scholars able to join its staff only on a temporary or part-time basis, the Office of Education's research thrust has failed to attract highly talented, research-oriented personnel. Finally, the impatient demand from political and school leaders for immediate results has encouraged hastily conceived and superficially evaluated research and development projects within the office, piecemeal reform efforts, and a series of widely publicized but undelivered reform promises. NIE supporters view the new agency as a clean slate of research capability, unencumbered by the history of failure, unrealistic expectations, broken promises, and bureaucratic entanglements that haunts the Office of Education. With a budget and administrative structure relatively protected from non-research operational concerns, the possibility of in-house research, and the authority to appoint and compensate staff exempt from Civil Service classifications and tenure, NIE is expected to attract to its service distinguished scholars and researchers from a variety of disciplines, some on a temporary or part-time basis.[16]

Like the Office of Education before it, NIE represents a reform strategy. According to a report by Congressman John Brademus' NIE subcommittee of the House Committee on Education and Labor, "The National Institute of Education should have as its principal objectives the provision of equality of educational opportunity, the solution of problems of and the promotion of the reform and renewal of American education at all levels and in all settings." Two other NIE objectives are to stimulate demand for educational improvement among school people and citizens generally and enhance the research capability of school systems, state superintendents' staffs, universities, and regional research and development laboratories. Although mandated to concern itself with education broadly conceived, NIE is expected to focus its research efforts on selected major problems, for example, improving education for the poor, effective use of resources in education, and improving the quality of education. Creation of a National Institute of Education can, in the words of the NIE subcommittee,

> (a) provide a new beginning for research and development at every level of American education, preschool through post

graduate school, in formal institutions of learning and outside them.

(b) provide a focal point for bringing together a constituency of consumers, researchers and interested public for educational research.

(c) provide visibility to the research effort.

(d) provide enough stability in research policy to make it possible to carry out plans and obtain results.

(e) make possible a personnel policy such as exists at the National Institutes of Health and the National Science Foundation in order to insure the highest quality of research.

(f) do for education what the National Institutes of Health are doing for health—increase available resources and provide a focal point for planning and program implementation.

(g) increase the likelihood of getting the results of research and development into education systems.[17]

Fundamentally, the NIE plan constitutes a twentieth-century variant of Barnard's bureau: a device for achieving educational improvements through the collection and dissemination of data and information related to schools and the educational process generally. The data gathering process it proposes reflects the increased sophistication and confidence of the social and behavioral sciences and thus speaks in the modern idiom about research, experimentation, development, and demonstration. In regard to dissemination, however, that is, the implementation of reform proposals, naivete and sheer ignorance of past experience can be detected. Speaking before the subcommittee, which in 1971 conducted hearings on the NIE plan, Daniel P. Moynihan insisted, "When we start acquiring hard knowledge, it will get picked up fast enough. I think this gap [between research and implementation on the classroom level] reflects not on the quality of the classroom teachers, but on the quality of the research that they are being told to get enthusiastic about." Moynihan apparently not only anticipates the effectiveness of reform strategies emanating "from the top" but also advocates them. He confessed to the subcommittee:

> One of the things that distresses me is the sort of increasing hostility to testing, on the grounds that tests are somehow not valid. Well, this is a perfectly fair question to raise. Are they or aren't they? Are they culturally biased? Are they biased toward one group or another?

I think this is the kind of question you can put to National Institute of Education and know you are going to get a straight answer. It may not be the answer you like, but you are going to get an honest answer from the best men who work in the field, and the Congress and school board and PTA and the superintendent can say, "I am following the best practice known. That is where they came out at NIE, and I will stay with their finding. I don't know any better."

It gives officials, mothers and parents a sense of whatever they do they are doing it as the best impartial available practice.[18]

Not all of those who appeared before the subcommittee shared Moynihan's benign confidence in the school reform effectiveness of experts. James Gallagher, director of the University of North Carolina's Frank Porter Graham Child Development Center, warned that the limited attention paid "to the delivery of finished product or discoveries to the educational consumer, to the administrator, the teacher and the student" in NIE plans represented one of their major weaknesses. Needed, he suggested, are specific delivery plans which take into account the complexity of the change process in education and attempt to identify those elements in proposed new programs that "will overcome the fears and anxieties raised by departing the educational status quo." Hendrik Gideonse, a former Office of Education senior staff member and now dean of education at the University of Cincinnati, argued that Gallagher's definition of the "delivery" problem posed difficulties of its own. In his view, to press for a delivery system which implies that educational change is a one way flow "akin to a physical process where things are delivered from a place where they are to a place where they are not" is counter-productive:

The concept suggests a status hierarchy in which research and development personnel have—or are presumed to have—more say as to what kind of innovations should be sought and "delivered." In response to this, educators will tend to resist the low status implications of being on the receiving end of the system: academics and scientists in turn will tend to find confirmed their latent suspicions concerning the professional motives and competencies of the "natives they have come to save." [19]

196

Rather than a delivery system, NIE should, in Gideonse' opinion, concern itself with creating a consumer system, "an effective market, if you will, for educational research and development." His proposal implies a need for policies requiring the principal thrust of NIE sponsored research to emanate from educational problems and issues identified by parents and practitioners, not the "research community." He wants NIE organized so as to open its programs, policies, and objectives to public decision-making processes. He wants it subjected to regular legislative oversight and shaped by advisory panels composed of individuals representing diverse perspectives on education and a wide-ranging reform agenda. Finally, Gideonse advocates the decentralization of "substantial portions of the institute's research and development activities" in order to involve it in strengthening educational research and evaluation capabilities on local and state levels. In brief, he wants policy checks and balances to ensure NIE's public accountability, its reliance on educational practice in defining "what research and development needs to be done," and its commitment "to preserve and enhance a rich plurality and diversity of educational ends and means."

In the manner of common school advocates a century ago, many NIE supporters have adorned their effort with the trappings of a cause, a reform crusade complete with expectations and promise at once hyperbolic and simplistic. The principle behind the institute plan, Stephen Bailey advised the NIE subcommittee, "is almost ridiculously simple. It is that if a man will focus his skills, reason, and humaneness upon his problems, he can markedly improve his condition." If the institute or something like it is not created and adequately funded over time, Bailey concluded,

> we will not get the poor out of poverty; we will continue to spend increasing billions of dollars a year of the taxpayers' money for inflated educational costs without any real change in the quality of educational output. We will have consigned millions of human beings to underutilized or totally inutile lives.

Partisan expectations aside, the NIE plan, particularly in light of the Office of Education's founding years, raises a number of cautionary questions.[20]

197

First, can it realize its reform objectives? The answer, despite the confidence of Moynihan, Bailey, and other NIE advocates, is that no one can be sure. The uncertainty grows partly out of the methodological difficulties of translating research findings into programs and of transporting them from experimental situations to the nation's classrooms. It also stems from the political character of the schooling process itself. Data gathering, research, and experimentation, Henry Barnard assumed incorrectly, would be politically safe instruments for his department to employ in improving schools. He reckoned without what Gideonse terms education's "inseparable linkage to values." Schools touch people; they are expected to assist parents and their children in fulfilling often conflicting and inflated but nevertheless deeply felt hopes and ambitions. From the perspectives of schools' constituents, the people they serve, the basic question about educational research may concern less the adequacy of its design or the competency of the researcher than whether the research ought to be done at all.[21]

"Educational research," according to Gideonse, "is different in character from research in the physical, natural, or biological sciences." The difference, like that of education, is its inextricable "connection to questions of human choice and value." This characterization of educational research remains true, Gideonse argues, "not only in terms of the outcome of the research as in the other sciences, too, but also in the conception and actual conduct of the research itself." When, by intention or by accident, it affects school programs and policies, educational research inevitably enters the political arena. Thus while consensus among professionals in the field and the public may be achieved behind a research focus for the National Institutes of Health or the National Science Foundation, support for an NIE thrust may be more difficult to develop, particularly if the research is to be initiated and conducted by outsiders to the value relation linking a school with its public. Twentieth-century school reformers may imperil their own effectiveness by ignoring the possibility that research intended to correct educational inequities and to serve minority populations may not receive the expected approbation of those to be benefited, and may even be rejected outright. Black people, poor people, Latin Americans, American Indians, and all manner of white ethnic groups are increasingly resentful of research into their complaints about schools. They have learned that the decision to engage in research can be taken in lieu of policy and program changes aimed at correcting schools' institutional racism, social class bias, or heavy-handed attempts at assimilation. Indeed, citizen groups may insist that where research and model testing in their schools are justified, they play significant roles in planning, formulating hypotheses to be tested, and evaluating outcomes. In sum, there are both methodological and political barriers to improving schools through research.

A more basic doubt about the possible success of NIE reform efforts derives from the structural status of schools within society. Functioning as part of a network of other more powerful social systems with effects that are difficult to isolate, schools have proved to be at best limited agents of social change. Because of the inextricable school-society relation, school reform, whether changes in curriculum and pedagogy or new answers to the questions of who controls, pays for, and sets the aims of schools, tends to follow not lead social reform. As Swedish professor Sixten Marklund advised the NIE subcommittee,

> a central institution of educational research may well lead to the reinforcement of single initiatives within limited sectors but . . . this will not be of any substantial importance unless those initiatives are co-ordinated with improvement and reforms of society. Swedish experience has also shown quite conclusively that this work of improvement is altogether inadequate so long as it is confined to service and information. Genuine change calls for political decisions leading to democratic and administrative resolutions by the authorities concerned.[22]

Even if the educational change can be realized through ways proposed in the NIE plan, a second policy question remains to be considered: Should it be done? What benefits and costs can be anticipated from launching a central educational research agency? New knowledge may emerge, and that would be a significant contribution. However, the immediate and long-term impact of that knowledge upon education as practiced in schools remains uncertain. The benefits, in brief, are clouded by the difficulties of transforming research outcomes into programs, the political complexities of educational research and school reform, and doubts about the effectiveness of school-focused change efforts unaccompanied by broader social reforms. The costs, equally difficult to calculate, could be considerable: a transfer of effective control over the aims and practice of public education from the hands of school professionals, where it has increasingly resided during the past century, to social and behavioral scientists shielded from public accountability by both their expertise and lack of constituency beyond the research community. The result could remove schools still farther away from their publics and allow their futures to be shaped by a new quest for homogeneity, not cultural centrism but scientism.

The perils of such a development become clear by noticing the kinds of questions empirical researchers do not, and perhaps cannot, ask. They understandably omit some queries which cannot be translated into testable hypotheses. Others are overlooked because they surface out of perspectives shaped by unique cultural and/or social class experiences which are alien to outsiders however equipped with the tools of social and behavioral science research. Both sorts of unasked questions reflect a research insensitivity to the often subjective and value-laden relations between people and their schools. With their captive sample populations, defined roles, bureaucratic structures, and relatively explicit cognitive and behavioral objectives that lend themselves to quantitative evaluations, schools present ideal research arenas. The question remains: who is served by such activity, even if it results in changes in educational practice?

That question forces consideration of concerns that are essentially philosophical, although they clearly carry policy implications. What kinds and forms of public education do Americans want? Who should ask that question? Who should be involved in answering it? Who should participate in the translation of educational objectives into programs and policies? Are there room and tolerance for diverse answers? Finally, if it is true that portions of the much-decried failure of schools can be attributed not only to lack of knowledge but also to the refusal, explicit or tacit, to deliver equitable educational policies, can research correct for the apparent loss of nerve? It is not clear that researchers, whether highly talented social and behavioral scientists or educationists with "second water abilities," can prove any less reluctant than professional schoolmen to share control over their projects with publics more interested in the effects of research on people and the policy implications of a particular design than in the canons of objective inquiry. Also, encouraging research without marshalling the funds or intention necessary to implement possibly significant findings would betray the NIE reform objective and could result merely in further institutionalizing the pattern of studying problems studied too long already that has rendered research suspicious to minority populations.

None of these questions is offered in opposition to NIE. They do post warnings, not about the value of research qua research, but about research that has been funded publicly on the grounds that it will improve schools and contribute to the equalization of educational opportunity. A great deal depends upon the range of resources marshalled by the agency and its organization, determinations to be made in the final analysis by its director, Thomas K. Glennan, Jr., his staff, and the NIE board of advisors. NIE could evolve as a sponsor of high quality social and behavioral science research. Current plans anticipate the inclusion of a host of other experts, for example, artists, teachers, philosophers, community organizers, historians, and parents in NIE projects. The latter was recommended by Commissioner of Education Sidney Marland (1970–72) as a means for preventing a single or narrow research perspective from dominating NIE. Utilizing such divergent resources may serve to protect the agency from ivory tower isolation, and also enable it to produce more multifaceted, and hence useful, analyses of educational problems. At least partially satisfied in the process will be Gideonse' hope that major portions of NIE initiated research will flow from issues identified by parents, other citizens, and practitioners directly related to educational programs. NIE's reform effectiveness can be further enhanced by formalizing its public accountability through regular legislative oversight, clear definitions of the authority of its advisory bodies in establishing research policy, and guarantees that NIE advisors represent a rich assortment of perspectives on education, races, ethnic groups, and social classes.[23]

Working in tandem, NIE and the Office of Education may be able to generate both new knowledge about the learning process and solutions to the policy issues plaguing American education, assuming both agencies are funded, mandated, and staffed adequately. Discounting—and in light of the office's founding years it may be foolish to do so—the questionable validity of these assumptions, it ought to be clear that research isolated from the political difficulties involved in changing educational institutions offers as little hope for reform as has the Office of Education's century-long effort to maintain and improve schools through data gathering.

Research may produce new knowledge, but can it produce more effective schools? And even if it does, from whose perspective?

In spite of, perhaps also because of, the doubts and questions raised by the various plans to enforce education nationally, one can still confirm the country's need for a federal agency to attend solely to the promotion of school reform, learning, and equal educational opportunity. New procedures for realizing the aims, however, may need to be developed. As a start, the premise undergirding the nineteenth-century drive to enforce education, namely that so called "uneducated" people lack the desire and human resources to plan and improve their own schools, clearly requires modification. If education means only the completion of stated curricula, the reception of instruction, or simply literacy, the premise can perhaps be trusted. If, on the other hand, it includes acquisition of the knowledge, skill, and understanding requisite for nurturing critical intelligence and individual autonomy, if it liberates and not merely transmits what is already known, accepted, and valued from a dominant group to a subordinate one, it calls for democratic, as overagainst unilateral, devices for promoting it in schools and for shaping educational policies, assuming Americans want their schools to be more than maintenance institutions.

Inclusive educational policies do not emerge as gifts from the trained and powerful to the unschooled and deprived. They come into being, if at all, when people demand them. If schools are for people, they are rightly controlled by the intended beneficiaries who, if supplied with the necessary material resources and the technical assistance required for evaluating school outcomes, can then define for themselves equal educational opportunity and chart their own school reform course. Accepting such givens, the federal task becomes one of enforcing policy guidelines for guaranteeing equal learning opportunities among a diverse population with unequal access to the sources of economic and political power. It includes providing the funds and technical assistance necessary to disseminate knowledge about education, as Barnard originally proposed, and to stimulate citizen demand for quality education and research. The federal responsibility does not extend necessarily to the protection of existing schools or those who control them. Neither is it the federal task to acquire direct power over schools, either overtly in a federal bureaucracy or covertly in a federally subsidized "think tank" of research specialists. The federal responsibility in education is primarily to people not institutions, an emphasis justified by the requirement that schools should serve their constituents, not vice versa.

Acknowledging the past as prologue in part at least voices the expectation that the future will be different and better than the past. It now seems clear after a century of effort that federally initiated school reform encompasses, on one hand, the search for new knowledge about learning and ways to disseminate it and, on the other, challenges to bureaucratic fears of change and dusty provincialisms which are choking vitality from schools. It also requires the encouragement, through aggressive programming and technical assistance, of local attempts to promote divergent thinking and to enlarge perspectives and the range of tolerance for differences among people through education. A federal educational agency, whether NIE, the Office of Education, or some new administrative unit, can function in these ways to the extent that it is staffed, funded, and mandated to act as an agent of change. So armed, a federal educational agency, to borrow from Alfred North Whitehead, can lead the assault on the boundaries of the finite, casting about for new meanings of the educational process and broader, more inclusive channels for its control.

The Office of Education in the 1970s is not the agency born a century ago. Time, events, and the changing needs and aspirations of people have taken care of that. Worth perpetuating, in spite of the office's past failures and present inadequacies, is commitment to the founding vision, the ambition to equalize educational opportunity and fashion an intellectual and political force to encourage, shape, and expand American educational progress. How to realize the dream, what it means in terms of federal initiative and activity and actual school policies and programs, and whether in the final analysis Americans prize it are questions yet unanswered.

Appendices

APPENDIX 1: THE DEPARTMENT OF EDUCATION ACT OF 1867

Be it enacted by the Senate and House of Representatives *of the United States of America in Congress assembled,* That there shall be established, at the city of Washington, a Department of Education, for the purpose of collecting such statistics and facts as shall show the condition and progress of education in the several States and Territories, and of diffusing such information respecting the organization and management of schools and school systems, and methods of teaching, as shall aid the people of the United States in the establishment and maintenance of efficient school systems, and otherwise promote the cause of education throughout the country.

Sec. 2. *And be it further enacted,* That there shall be appointed by the President, by and with the advice and consent of the Senate, a Commissioner of Education, who shall be intrusted with management of the Department herein established, and who shall receive a salary of four thousand dollars per annum, and who shall have authority to appoint one chief clerk of his Department, who shall receive a salary of two thousand dollars per annum, one clerk who shall receive a salary of eighteen hundred dollars per annum, and one clerk who shall receive a salary of sixteen hundred dollars per annum, which said clerks shall be subject to the appointing and removing power of the Commissioner of Education.

Sec. 3. *And be it further enacted,* That it shall be the duty of the Commissioner of Education to present annually to Congress a report embodying the results of his investigations and labors, together with a statement of such facts and recommendations as will, in his judgment, subserve the purpose for which this Department is established. In the first report made by the Commissioner of Education under this act there shall be presented a statement of the several grants of land made by Congress to promote education, and the manner in which these several trusts have been managed, the amount of funds arising therefrom, and the annual proceeds of the same, as far as the same can be determined.

Sec. 4. *And be it further enacted,* That the Commissioner of Public Buildings is hereby authorized and directed to furnish proper offices for the use of the Department herein established.

Approved, 2 March 1867.

Appendix 2: The Department of
Agriculture Act of 1862

Be it enacted by the Senate and House of Representatives
of the United States of America in Congress assembled, That there is
hereby established at the seat of Government of the United States a
Department of Agriculture, the general designs and duties of which
shall be to acquire and to diffuse among the people of the United
States useful information on subjects connected with agriculture in
the most general and comprehensive sense of that word, and to
procure, propagate, and distribute among the people new and
valuable seeds and plants.

Sec. 2. *And be it further enacted,* That there shall be
appointed by the President, by and with the advice and consent of
the Senate, a "Commissioner of Agriculture," who shall be the chief
executive officer of the Department of Agriculture, who shall hold his
office by a tenure similar to that of other civil officers appointed by
the President, and who shall receive for his compensation a salary of
three thousand dollars per annum.

Sec. 3. *And be it further enacted,* That it shall be the duty of
the Commissioner of Agriculture to acquire and preserve in his
Department all information concerning agriculture which he can
obtain by means of books and correspondence, and by practical and
scientific experiments, (accurate records of which experiments shall
be kept in his office), by the collection of statistics, and by any other
appropriate means within his power; to collect, as he may be able,
new and valuable seeds and plants; to test, by cultivation, the value
of such of them as may require such tests; to propagate such as may
be worthy of propagation, and to distribute them among agricultur-
ists. He shall annually make a general report in writing of his acts to
the President and to Congress, in which he may recommend the
publication of papers forming parts of or accompanying his report,
which report shall also contain an account of all moneys received and

expended by him. He shall also make special reports on particular subjects whenever required to do so by the President or either House of Congress, or when he shall think the subject in his charge requires it. He shall receive and have charge of all the property of the agricultural division of the Patent Office in the Department of the Interior, including the fixtures and property of the propagating garden. He shall direct and superintend the expenditure of all money appropriated by Congress to the Department, and render accounts thereof, and also of all money heretofore appropriated for agriculture and remaining unexpended. And said Commissioner may send and receive through the mails, free of charge, all communications and other matter pertaining to the business of his Department, not exceeding in weight thirty-two ounces.

Sec. 4. *And be it further enacted,* That the Commissioner of Agriculture shall appoint a chief clerk, with a salary of two thousand dollars, who in all cases during the necessary absence of the Commissioner, or when the said principal office shall become vacant, shall perform the duties of Commissioner, and he shall appoint such other employes as Congress may from time to time provide, with salaries corresponding to the salaries of similar officers in other Departments of the Government; and he shall, as Congress may from time to time provide, employ other persons, for such time as their services may be needed, including chemists, botanists, entomologists, and other persons skilled in the natural sciences pertaining to agriculture. And the said Commissioner, and every other person to be appointed in the said Department, shall, before he enters upon the duties of his office or appointment, make oath or affirmation truly and faithfully to execute the trust committed to him. And the said Commissioner and the chief clerk shall also, before entering upon their duties, severally give bonds to the Treasurer of the United States, the former in the sum of ten thousand dollars, and the latter in the sum of five thousand dollars, conditional to render a true and faithful account to him or his successor in office, quarter yearly accounts of all moneys which shall be by them received by virtue of the said office, with sureties to be approved as sufficient by the Solicitor of the Treasury; which bonds shall be filed in the office of the First Comptroller of the Treasury, to be by him put in suit upon any breach of the conditions thereof.

Approved, 15 May 1862.

Appendix 3: United States
Commissioners of Education 1867–1973

Commissioners	Appointing President	Subsequent Administrations Served	Term of Office
1. Henry Barnard	Andrew Johnson	U. S. Grant	1867–70
2. John Eaton, Jr.	U. S. Grant	Rutherford B. Hayes	1870–86
		James A. Garfield	
		Chester A. Arthur	
		Grover Cleveland	
3. Nathaniel H. R. Dawson	Grover Cleveland		1886–89
4. William T. Harris	Benjamin Harrison	Grover Cleveland	1889–1906
		William McKinley	
		Theodore Roosevelt	
5. Elmer Ellsworth Brown	Theodore Roosevelt	William Howard Taft	1906–11
6. Philander P. Claxton	William Howard Taft	Woodrow Wilson	1911–21
7. John J. Tigert	Warren G. Harding	Calvin Coolidge	1921–28
8. William John Cooper	Calvin Coolidge	Herbert Hoover	1929–33
		Franklin D. Roosevelt	

	Commissioner	President	Term
9.	George F. Zook	Franklin D. Roosevelt	1933–34
10.	John W. Studebaker	Franklin D. Roosevelt / Harry S. Truman / Dwight D. Eisenhower	1934–48
11.	Earl J. McGrath	Harry S. Truman / Dwight D. Eisenhower	1949–53
12.	Lee M. Thurston	Dwight D. Eisenhower	1953
13.	Samuel M. Brownell	Dwight D. Eisenhower	1953–56
14.	Lawrence G. Derthick	Dwight D. Eisenhower	1956–60
15.	Sterling M. McMurrin	John F. Kennedy	1961–62
16.	Francis Keppel	John F. Kennedy / Lyndon B. Johnson	1962–66
17.	Harold Howe II	Lyndon B. Johnson	1966–68
18.	James E. Allen, Jr.	Richard M. Nixon	1969–70
19.	Sidney P. Marland, Jr.	Richard M. Nixon	1970–72
20.	John R. Ottina	Richard M. Nixon	1973–

Notes

Abbreviations
  AJE: *American Journal of Education*
  DAB: *Dictionary of American Biography*
  NEA: National Education Association
  NTA: National Teachers' Association

Author's Note:
  Complete publishing information
  will be found in the Bibliography.

INTRODUCTION

1. Katz, ed., *School Reform: Past and Present*, p. 1; Karier, Violas, and Spring, *Roots of Crisis*, p. 5.
2. Katz, *Class, Bureaucracy, and Schools*, p. viii.
3. Butts, *The Education of the West*, pp. 3–13.
4. Greene, "Identities and Contours: An Approach to Educational History," paper presented at the American Educational Research Association annual meeting, February, 1973, pp. 19–22.

CHAPTER ONE

1. Richardson, ed., *A Compilation of the Messages and Papers of the Presidents: 1789–1908*, 1: 66; Coram, *Political Inquiries* in *Essays on Education in the Early Republic*, Rudolph, ed., p. 113; Jefferson, *Bill for the More General Diffusion of Knowledge*, in *Social History of American Education*, Vassar, ed., 1: 109.
2. Richardson, 1: 202, 409.
3. Rudolph, ed., pp. 212–18, 319–22; Hansen, *Liberalism and American Education*, pp. 63–89, 168–76; Du Pont de Nemours, *National Education in the United States of America*, pp. 151–53; and in *Correspondence Between Thomas Jefferson and Pierre Samuel du Pont de Nemours*, Malone, ed., pp. 8–26. Plans for national systems of schools including suggested central educational agencies were much discussed in Europe during the final quarter of the 18th century. See, *e.g.*, Rackauskas, "The First National System of Education in Europe," *Lituanus* 14, 4 (1968): 5–53.

Notes

4. Rush, "Of the Mode of Education Proper in a Republic," in *The Selected Writings of Benjamin Rush*, Dagobert D. Runes, ed., p. 92; Webster, "On the Education of Youth in America," in *Turning Points in American Educational History*, Tyack, ed., p. 96; and Webster, "Letter to a Young Gentleman Commencing His Education," in *A Collection of Papers on Political, Literary, and Moral Subjects*, p. 302. The Daniel Webster quotation is taken from Tyack, p. 126.

5. Wright, "Lecture on Existing Evils and Their Remedy," in Vassar, 1: 240–42; Commons *et al.*, eds., *A Documentary History of American Industrial Society*, 5: 165–77.

6. For a provocative analysis of the ambiguous origins of American public schooling, *see* Katz, *The Irony of Early School Reform*, especially, Part 1, "Reform by Imposition," pp. 19–112.

7. White, "Introductory Discourse," American Institute of Instruction, *Lectures and Proceedings*, 8 (1837): 3; Bishop Potter's comment is quoted in Schlesinger, *The Age of Jackson*, p. 221. *See also* Hansen, *Early Educational Leadership in the Ohio Valley*, p. 21; *Western Academician*, 1 (1837): 3; Bates, "Moral Education," American Institute of Instruction, *Lectures and Proceedings*, 8 (1837): 69.

8. Hansen, *Early Educational Leadership*, pp. 24, 31; White, American Institute of Instruction, *Lectures and Proceedings*, 8 (1837): 21.

9. Carlton, *Economic Influences Upon Education Progress in the United States, 1820–1850*, pp. 39–48. Carlton's claim cannot be documented, but the "labor-education myth" which Carlton, and later Philip Curoe, articulated has only recently been opened for critical review. *See* Pawa, "Workingmen and Free Schools in the Nineteenth Century," *History of Education Quarterly* 11 (1971): 287–302.

10. Lewis, "The Expediency of Adopting Common School Education to the Entire Wants of the Community," *Western Academician* 1 (1837): 531.

11. Brooks, *History of the Introduction of State Normal Schools in America*, pp. 6, 12; undated notebook in the Henry Barnard Collection (Watkinson Library, Trinity College, Hartford, Connecticut), Box 8. Cited hereafter as Barnard Collection.

12. George C. Mann, ed., *Life and Works of Horace Mann*, 4: 341–403; Mary Peabody Mann, *Life of Horace Mann*, p. 259; Mann to S. J. May, 22 September 1848, quoted *ibid.*, p. 271; Mann to Mr. and Mrs. George Combe, 15 November 1850, quoted *ibid.*, pp. 335–39; Mary P. Mann to Charles Sumner, [n.d.], Henry Barnard Manuscript Collection (Fales Library, New York University, New York), Item 8906. Cited hereafter as Barnard MSS. For accounts of Mann's 4 July 1842 Oration and his "re-entry" into politics, *see* Messerli, *Horace Mann*, pp. 374–78, 452–57.

13. *Ibid.*, pp. 412–21, 309–15, 328–32; Brooks, *A Prospective System of National Education for the United States*, p. 18.

14. Quotations from the Stevens speech are taken from Knight and Hall, eds., *Readings in American Educational History*, pp. 350, 353. *See also*, Brodie, *Thaddeus Stevens*, p. 62.

15. *Ohio Educational Monthly*, 13 (1864): 287.

16. U.S., *Register of Debates in Congress*, 21st Cong., 1st Sess., 1829, 6: 475.

17. U.S., *Register of Debates in Congress*, 25th Cong., 2nd Sess., 1837, 13: 49.

18. *Connecticut Common School Journal*, 1 (1839): 150; Bode, *The American Lyceum: Town Meeting of the Mind*, pp. 117–19.

19. Hayes, *The American Lyceum: Its History and Contributions to Education*, pp. viii, 7–9; *American Annals of Education and Instruction*, 1, pt. 2, No. 6 (1831), 274–76.

20. Richardson, ed., 1: 202.
21. U.S., Congress, Senate, *Public Documents*, 26th Cong., 1st Sess., 1840, 4, Doc. No. 181; American Institute of Instruction, *Lectures and Proceedings*, 8 (1837): xvi, xviii.
22. Brooks, *A Prospective System of National Education for the United States*, pp. 15–18; Barnard, "The American Lyceum," *American Journal of Education*, 14 (1864): 553–57. Cited hereafter as AJE.
23. National Convention for the Promotion of Education in the United States, *Proceedings* (1840), pp. 2–10. *See also*, Bache to Barnard, 17 March 1840, 15 May 1840, and 26 May 1840, Barnard MSS, Items 381, 418, and 1908.
24. AJE, 19 (1870): 837; *ibid.*, 30 (1880): 193; Mayo, "Henry Barnard as the First U.S. Commissioner of Education," *Report of the Commissioner of Education for the Year 1902*, 1: 893; and "Memories of Presidents," undated notebook in the Henry Barnard Collection, Box 7.
25. Alfred E. Wright to Barnard, 5 December 1848, and 19 December 1848, Barnard MSS, Items 2116 and 2129; *Massachusetts Teacher*, 2 (1849): 160; National Convention of the Friends of Public Education, *Proceedings* (1849), pp. 3–25.
26. U.S., Congress, House, *Journal*, 21st Cong., 1st Sess., 1850, p. 407; American Institute of Instruction, *Lectures and Proceedings*, 37 (1866): 50–54.
27. National Convention of the Friends of Public Education, *Proceedings*, Second Session (1850), pp. 65–66; American Institute of Instruction, *Lectures and Proceedings*, 21 (1850): v–vii, xii–xiii; *ibid.*, pp. xxv–xxvi; John Batchelder to John D. Philbrick, quoted in Isaac M. Wright, "History of the United States Bureau of Education," p. 3; American Association for the Advancement of Education, *Proceedings*, Fourth Session (1854), pp. 10, 15–16; AJE, 1 (1855): 15–16, 134–36.
28. Barnard to Dixon, 14 March 1862, Barnard Collection, Box 9, Miscellaneous Letters Sent.
29. National Teachers' Association, *Proceedings*, 2 (1858): 57. Cited hereafter as NTA, *Proceedings*.
30. The quotations are taken from the speech of Senator James M. Mason of Virginia opposing Justin Morrill's land grant colleges bill in 1859; *see* U.S., *Congressional Globe*, 35th Cong., 2nd Sess., 1859, 28, 718.

CHAPTER TWO

1. AJE, 30 (1880): 193n.
2. American Institute of Instruction, *Lectures and Proceedings*, 32 (1861): lixf; *ibid.*, 34 (1863): 63; *ibid.*, 36 (1865): 16; Greene, "The Educational Duties of the Hour," AJE, 16 (1866): 231–32.
3. Brooks quoted *ibid.*, p. 243; *Ohio Educational Monthly*, 14 (1865): 268, 271–72.
4. AJE, 16 (1866): 241; E. E. White, "National Bureau of Education, AJE, 16 (1866): 184–85.
5. White, AJE, 16 (1866): 177–86.
6. *Ohio Educational Monthly*, 14 (1865): 268–72; White to Barnard, 3 March 1866, Barnard MSS, Item 2-8090.
7. Brooks to Barnard, 23 November 1864, 8 February 1865 and 29 July 1865, Barnard MSS, Items 7413, 7497, and 7778; Brooks, *A Prospective System of National Education for the United States*; Brooks *et al.*, "Free Education in

the United States," U.S., Congress, House, *Miscellaneous Documents*, 39th Cong., 1st Sess., 1866, Mis. Doc. No. 5.

8. American Institute of Instruction, *Lectures and Proceedings*, 36 (1865), 107–108; Brooks to Barnard, 8 February 1865, Barnard MSS, Item 7497; *Massachusetts Teacher*, 20 (1866): 12–16.

9. S. H. White, "A National Bureau of Education," AJE, 15 (1865): 180–84; "Proceedings of the National Teachers' Association, 6th Session, August 10–12, 1864," AJE, 14 (1864): 597.

10. Bates to Barnard, 11 February 1865, 13 February 1865, 15 February 1865, and 21 February 1865, S. H. White to Barnard, 2 March 1865, Barnard MSS, Items 7513, 7517, 7523, 7537, and 7558; U.S., Congress, House, *Journal*, 38th Cong., 2nd Sess., 1865, p. 68; Pruyn to Barnard, 27 March 1867, Barnard MSS, Item 8501.

11. Barnard to Potter, 24 April 1865, S. H. White to Barnard, 25 April 1865, and 13 May 1865, Barnard MSS, Items 7618, 7619, and 7647.

12. Bates to Barnard, 21 February 1865, Rickoff to Barnard, 1 November 1865, Barnard MSS, Items 7537 and 7881.

13. N.T.A., *Proceedings*, 7 (1865): 220; *Ohio Educational Monthly*, 14 (1865): 343.

14. *Ohio Educational Monthly*, 15 (1866): 90–92; AJE, 16 (1866): 389.

15. U.S., Congress, House, *Miscellaneous Documents*, 39th Cong., 1st Sess., 1866, Doc. No. 41.

16. Lee, *The Struggle for Federal Aid: First Phase*, pp. 15–22; U.S., *Congressional Globe*, 37th Cong., 2nd Sess., 1862, 32: 2625–34, 2770.

17. U.S., *Congressional Globe*, 38th Cong., 1st Sess., 1864, 34: 568, 570, 709, 712, 773–76, 2799, 2801–03.

18. Schlesinger, *New Viewpoints in American History*, p. 243.

19. Harding, "Some Landmarks in the History of the Department of Agriculture," *Agricultural History Series*, 2 (1942): 1, 10, 16, 29–31; Dupree, *Science in the Federal Government*, pp. 47, 110–12, 149–50; Richardson, ed., *Messages and Papers of the Presidents*, 5: 18, 85–86, 127–28; U.S., Congress, Senate, *Journal*, 31st Cong., 1st Sess., 1850, pp. 64, 93, 158, 190, 195, 200, 218, 235, 240, 278, 304, 371. None of these petitions originated from a southern state and only one came from a border state.

20. U.S., *Congressional Globe*, 37th Cong., 2nd Sess., 1862, 32: 855–57, 1690–91, 1755, 2017.

21. Harding, pp. 29–34.

22. Richards, "The Agency of the Association in Elevating the Character and Advancing the Interests of the Profession of Teaching, NTA, *Proceedings*, 2 (1858): 57; Rickoff, "A National Bureau of Education," AJE, 16 (1866): 310; U.S., *Congressional Globe*, 38th Cong., 2nd Sess., 1865, 35: 564.

23. Brooks to Barnard, 12 January 1866, Hancock to Barnard, 19 February 1866, Brooks to Barnard, 31 March 1866, and Richards to Barnard, 25 April 1866, Barnard MSS, Items 8001, 8066, 8129, and 8164.

24. See Bond, *The Education of the Negro in the American Social Order*, pp. 37–57; Bond, *Negro Education in Alabama*, pp. 73–119; DuBois, *Black Reconstruction*, pp. 637–69; Hyman, ed., *The Radical Republicans and Reconstruction: 1861–1870*, pp. 189–229; and Swint, *The Northern Teacher in the South: 1862–1870*. Swint's criticism of the teachers aside, his description of their efforts brings to mind the Peace Corps, another idealistic crusade launched a century later.

CHAPTER THREE

1. U.S., Congress, House, *Journal*, 39th Cong., 1st Sess., 1866, pp. 37, 93, 183, 690, 721, and 946; Harrington, *Fighting Politician*, pp. 45, 50, 95, 108–10.
2. Ridge, *Ignatius Donnelly*, pp. 5, 36, 47, 80, 81, 93–94; McKitrick, *Andrew Johnson and Reconstruction*, p. 59.
3. U.S., *Congressional Globe*, 39th Cong., 1st Sess., 1865, 36: 60; Ridge, p. 101.
4. Caldwell, *James A. Garfield*, pp. 21–29, 162, 200–03; McKitrick, p. 283; Taylor, *Garfield of Ohio*, pp. 95–124; W. H. Wells (former Superintendent of Schools in Chicago) to Barnard, 21 January 1867, Barnard MSS, Item 8463; Garfield to General S. C. Armstrong, 9 February 1871, James A. Garfield Papers, Letters Sent, Manuscripts Division, Library of Congress (hereafter cited as Garfield Papers); Donald, *Politics of Reconstruction*, pp. 89, 103.
5. *Ibid.*, pp. 100–03; *Ohio Educational Monthly*, 15 (1866): 91–92.
6. White to Barnard, 3 March 1866, Barnard MSS, Item 8090; U.S., *Congressional Globe*, 39th Cong., 1st Sess., 1866, 36: 2966.
7. *Ibid.*, pp. 2966–68, 3044–49.
8. *Ibid.*, pp. 3051, 3053.
9. *Ibid.*, p. 3070.
10. Richards to Barnard, 20 June 1866, Barnard MSS, Item 8230; U.S., *Congressional Globe*, 40th Cong., 2d Sess., 1868, 39: 1140; Garfield to White, 26 December 1868, Garfield Papers, Letters Sent.
11. U.S., Congress, Senate, *Journal*, 39th Cong., 2nd Sess., 1867, pp. 151, 218; Richards to Barnard, 30 June 1866, Butler to Barnard, 10 July 1866, Swett to Barnard, 17 July 1866, Richards to Barnard, 18 July 1866, Barnard MSS, Items 8241, 8252, 8255, and 8261.
12. U.S., *Congressional Globe*, 39th Cong., 2nd Sess., 1867, 37: 853, 1842.
13. *Ibid.*, pp. 1893, 1950.
14. Donald, *Politics of Reconstruction*, pp. 53–82, 91–105; Trefousse, *The Radical Republicans*, pp. 3–33, 338–40. *See also*, Weisberger, "The Dark and Bloody Ground of Reconstruction Historiography," *Journal of Southern History* 25 (1959): 427–38; Krug, *History and The Social Sciences*, p. 157. Donald incorrectly labels Latham of W. Va. as a Democrat and Spalding of Ohio as a Republican.
15. U.S., *Congressional Globe*, 40th Cong., 2nd Sess., 1868, 39: 1140; Donald, *Politics of Reconstruction*, p. 6.
16. U.S., *Congressional Globe*, 39th Cong., 2nd Sess., 1867, 37: 1950; Richards to Barnard, 18 July 1866, Barnard to Potter, 2 February 1867, Barnard MSS, Items 8261 and 8465.
17. Barnard to Potter, 2 March 1867, Barnard MSS, Item 8487; Steiner, *Life of Henry Barnard*, p. 108, n. 13; AJE, 30 (1880): 197.
18. John L. Campbell to Hugh McCulloch (Secretary of the Treasury), 2 March 1867, and Campbell to Andrew Johnson, 12 March 1867, Department of the Interior Records, Appointments Division, National Archives, Washington, D.C., Tray 111 (hereafter cited as Interior Records, AD 111); H. M. Johnson to Andrew Johnson, 2 March 1867, Gordon to Andrew Johnson, 9 March 1867, Petition from John Hill *et al.* to Johnson, 26 February 1867, Neill to Johnson, 5 March 1867, Dixon to Johnson, 26 February 1867, all in Interior Records, AD 111; Dixon to Johnson, 8 July 1866, Andrew Johnson Papers, Manuscripts Division, Library of Congress, Washington, D.C., ser. 1, vol. 77 (hereafter cited as Johnson Papers); Ridge, p. 101.
19. On White's contribution to the campaign for a national bureau of education, *see*

Notes

AJE, 16 (1866): 389–90; Lee, p. 23; Warren, *Answers to Inquiries About the U.S. Bureau of Education*, pp. 9–11. Also Barnard to Gilman, 29 June 1865, Barnard MSS, Item 7738; *Ohio Educational Monthly* 12 (1863): 235–38; *Ohio Educational Monthly* 14 (1865): 182–84; Anderson, "Biography of Emerson E. White," pp. 40f, 148ff.

20. Garfield to White, 26 December 1868, Garfield Papers, Letters Sent; White to Garfield, 13 November 1880 and 16 August 1868, Garfield Papers, Letters Received; Northrop to Barnard, 17 March 1866, Philbrick to Barnard, 3 July 1866, and Philbrick to Barnard, 1 March 1867, Barnard MSS, Items 8112, 8243, 8489.

21. Butler to Barnard, 10 July and 8 October 1866, Barnard MSS, Items 8252, 8333; Wickersham to Johnson, 11 March 1867, Interior Records, AD 111.

22. White to Barnard, 1 January 1867 and 4 February 1867, and Gilman to Barnard, 9 February 1867, Barnard MSS, Items 8438, 8467, and 8473; White to Barnard, 3 March 1866, Barnard MSS, Item 8090.

23. Ridge, p. 178; Neill to Johnson, 20 November 1866, Johnson Papers, ser. 1; Buck, "Edward Duffield Neill," DAB 13: 408; Neill to Johnson, 5 March 1867, Interior Records, AD 3.

24. Barnard to Potter, 14 December 1866 and 14 January 1867, Barnard MSS, Items 8401 and 8447; Barnard to Gilman, 10 January 1867, Gilman Papers (Johns Hopkins University, Baltimore, Maryland).

25. Hancock to Barnard, 19 March 1866, Philbrick to Barnard, 3 July 1866, Richards to Barnard, 18 July 1866, Barnard MSS, Items 8113, 8243, and 8261; *Nation* 2 (1866): 722.

26. Barnard to Potter, 21 January 1867 and 2 February 1867, F. A. P. Barnard (president of Columbia University) to Hugh McColluch, 31 January 1867, W. H. Wells to Barnard, 31 January 1867, Wells to Samuel Moulton, 31 January 1867, John Andrews to Barnard, 5 February 1867, J. B. Lindsley to Barnard, 9 February 1867; Barnard MSS, Items 8455, 8462, 8463, 8464, 8465, 8468, and 8474; Memorial from Gov. Brownlow (of Tennessee) *et al.* to Johnson, 11 February 1867, Interior Records, AD 3.

27. White to Barnard, 4 February 1867, Gilman to Barnard, 9 February 1867, Haldeman to Edgar Cowan, 24 December 1866, Barnard MSS, Items 8467, 8473, and 8409.

28. *See,* Mayo, "Henry Barnard," *Report of the Commissioner of Education for the Year 1896–97,* 1: 769–810; Mayo, "Henry Barnard as first U.S. Commissioner of Education," *Report of the Commissioner of Education for the Year 1902,* 1: 891–901; Harris, "Establishment of the Office of the Commissioner of Education of the United States, and Henry Barnard's Relation to It," *ibid.,* pp. 901–26; Blair, *Henry Barnard,* pp. 73–84; Smith, "A History of the United States Office of Education, 1867–1967," pp. 21–43.

29. White to Garfield, 6 August and 9 June 1868, Garfield Papers, Letters Received; White to Barnard, 18 August 1866, Barnard MSS, Item 8285.

30. *See,* Wells to Barnard, 31 January 1867, and Wells to Moulton, 31 January 1867, Barnard MSS, Items 8463 and 8464; Barnard to Potter, 2 February 1867, Item 8465; Neill to Alexander Ramsey, 27 April 1869, Interior Records, AD 111; "Memories of Presidents," Barnard Collection, Box 8; Dixon to Barnard, 14 March and 16 March 1867, Barnard Collection, Box 7.

31. "College Education: An Address Delivered before the Literary Societies of the Eclectic Institute at Hiram, Ohio, June 14, 1867," Garfield Papers, Public Utterances: 1866–1869. *See also,* Beard and Beard, *The Rise of American Civilization* (1936), p. 816; Morrison and Commager, *The Growth of the American Republic* (1962), 2: 116; Butts and Cremin, *A History of*

Education in American Culture, pp. 425–27; Edwards and Richey, *The School in the American Social Order*, p. 624.

CHAPTER FOUR

1. U.S. *Congressional Globe*, 38th Cong., 1st Sess., 1866, 36: 3044; *ibid.*, 2nd Sess., 1867, 37: 1843.
3. Buisson, *Rapport sur l'instruction primaire a l'Exposition universelle de Philadelphie en 1876*, p. 18, n. 1; AJE, 14 (1864): 554–57; and Thursfield, *Henry Barnard's American Journal of Education*, pp. 73–79, 106–31, 151–67, and 300.
3. *Ibid.*, pp. 82–89, 269, 270, and 271–303; on pp. 303–07 Thursfield indicates the limits of the journal's influence.
4. Potter to Johnson, 27 February 1867, Interior Records, AD 111; Thursfield, p. 112; Curti, *The Social Ideas of American Educators*, p. 144.
5. Mayo, "Henry Barnard," in *Report of the Commissioner of Education for the Year 1896–97*, 1: 782; *Nation* 4 (1867): 230.
6. No adequate biography of Barnard exists; for sketches of his life and work, *see* three early biographies, Blair, *Henry Barnard*; Mayo, "Henry Barnard"; and Steiner, *Life of Henry Barnard, The First U.S. Commissioner of Education, 1867–1879.*
7. Thursfield, pp. 26, 27, 59–60, 71, 72; Barnard to Potter, 4 January 1848, Barnard MSS, Item 1799; *see also*, Barnard to Potter, 4 March 1848, and Josephine D. Barnard to Potter, 14 December 1848, Barnard MSS, Items 1850, 2123; Mann to Barnard, 13 September 1848, Barnard MSS, Item 2008; Steiner, pp. 68–69.
8. Barnard used this phrase to describe himself on a number of occasions; *see*, Barnard to Potter, 24 November 1950, quoted in Blair, p. 58; *also*, Thursfield, p. 72, and Starr, DAB 1: 623.
9. U.S., *Congressional Globe*, 40th Cong. 2nd Sess., 1868, 39: 1139; Butler to Barnard, 12 April 1867, Barnard MSS, Item 8509.
10. Thursfield, pp. 46, 48; *see* testimony of David N. Camp in Steiner, p. 130.
11. Thursfield, p. 128.
12. Steiner, p. 89; Blair, pp. 93–94.
13. Curti, p. 168.
14. Barnard to Garfield, 28 February 1867, Garfield Papers, Letters Received.
15. "Memorandum of Paper read before American [National] Association of State Superintendents, Washington, March 3, 1870," Barnard Collection, Box 3.
16. American Institute of Instruction, *Lectures and Proceedings*, 38 (1867): 45.
17. U.S., Department of Education, *Report of the Commissioner of Education with Circulars and Documents Accompanying the Same (1868)*, p. xiii.
18. Eaton to Barnard, 24 October 1867 and 23 March 1868, Barnard MSS, Misc. Files: letters, 1867, 1868.
19. J. S. Bacon to Barnard, 10 May 1867, White to Barnard, 26 June 1865, Barnard MSS, Items 8527 and 7734; *Ohio Educational Monthly* 14 (1865): 345.
20. Eaton to William T. Harris, 29 May 1901, in Harris, "Establishment of the Office of the Commissioner of Education . . . ," in *Report of the Commissioner of Education for the Year 1902*, 1: 905.
21. Kraus to Barnard, 24 August 1868, Barnard MSS, Item 9192.
22. *See* Coburn to Barnard, 28 December 1867, Barnard MSS, Item 8885.
23. Garfield to White, 26 December 1868, Garfield Papers, Letters Sent.

Notes

24. *Report of the Commissioner of Education . . . 1868*, p. xii.
25. *See* AJE, 17 (1867): 11–63, 65–76, 81–124, 337–68, 385–400, 435–518, 658–820. Identical pages are found in Barnard's Report; *see also* "Memories of Presidents," Barnard Collection, Box 8.
26. Philbrick to Barnard, 17 May 1868, Barnard MSS, Item 9125.
27. Garfield to White, 26 December 1868, Garfield Papers, Letters Sent; *also*, Garfield to White, 26 July 1868, and Garfield to Northrop, 12 January 1869, Garfield Papers, Letters Sent; Smith, *The Life and Letters of James Abram Garfield*, 2: 783.
28. *Ohio Educational Monthly*, 18 (1869): 26.
29. Barnard to Potter, 22 December 1869, Barnard MSS, Item 9396.
30. Barnard to Cox, 28 January 1870, Interior Records, AD 111.
31. *See* AJE, 19 (1870). This volume consists of Barnard's Report, "Education in the District of Columbia." *See also, Special Report of the Commissioner of Education on the Condition and Improvement of Public Schools in the District of Columbia* (Washington, D.C.: Government Printing Office, 1871).
32. [Barnard], "Legal Status of the Colored Population in Respect to Schools and Education in the Different States," AJE 19 (1870): 301–400; Goodwin, "Schools and Education of the Colored Population in the District," *ibid.*, pp. 193–300; Barnard, "Education in the District of Columbia: Letter of Commissioner of Education," *ibid.*, p. 6. Constance Green's complaint that Barnard's history of black education was uncritical and the figures on black illiteracy were too low are well taken. Barnard's historical studies tended to be descriptive and chronological, rather than analytical. *See* Green, *Washington*, 1: *Village and Capital, 1800–1878*, pp. 307–08.
33. Barnard to Jacob D. Cox, 16 March 1870, Interior Records, AD 111; "Brief Review of My Life Work," Barnard Collection, Box 7; Blair, p. 83.

CHAPTER FIVE

1. Richards to Barnard, 6 April 1867, Barnard MSS, Item 8504.
2. For a discussion of the Johnson "spy" episode, *see* Bentley, *History of the Freedmen's Bureau*, p. 118; *also*, McKitrick, p. 285, n. 29. Barnard to Potter, 2 March 1867, Barnard to Gilman, 16 March 1867, Gilman to Barnard, 22 April 1867, Barnard MSS, Items 8487, 8495, and 8517; Potter to Barnard, (n.d.) Barnard Collection, Box 7; Dixon to Barnard, 14 March and 16 March 1867, Barnard Collection, Box 7; "Memories of Presidents," (n.d.), Barnard Collection, Box 8.
3. Richards to Barnard, 6 April 1867, Barnard MSS, Item 8504; Andrew Johnson to Neill, 25 April 1867, Johnson Papers, ser. 3B, p. 151; *see also*, Dupre, *Edward Duffield Neill*, p. 68; Richards to Barnard, 26 April 1867, Barnard MSS, item 8518.
4. *Congressional Globe*, 40th Cong., 1st Sess., 1867, 38: 61.
5. *Ibid.*, pp. 264, 739, 784. Members of the first House Committee on Education and Labor included Samuel F. Cary (R-Ohio), chairman, Jehu Baker (R-Ill.), Thomas Cornell (R-N.Y.), George W. Julian (R-Ind.), George S. Boutwell (R-Mass.), Stephan F. Wilson (R-Pa.), Demas Barnes (D-N.Y.), Joseph J. Gravely (D[?]-Mo.), and Frederick Stone (D-Md.).
6. *Ibid.*, pp. 338, 376, 437, and 443.
7. American Institute of Instruction, *Lectures and Proceedings* 38 (1867): 41–42.

8. *See,* Richards to Barnard, 10 May and 16 August 1867, Barnard MSS, Items 8528 and 8530; Dupre, pp. 102–05; "Edward Duffield Neill," *DAB* 13: 408; Barnard to Donnelly, 19 September 1867, Barnard MSS, Item 8692.

9. Richards to Barnard, 27 September and 3 October 1867, Barnard to Gilman, 20 November 1868, Richards to Barnard, 25 November 1867, Barnard MSS, Items 8709, 8715, 9269, and 8815.

10. Neill to Andrew Johnson, [14 December 1867], Johnson Papers, Ser. 1, Vol. 120; Richards to Barnard, 23 August 1867, Donnelly to Barnard, 8 January and 9 January 1868, Richards to Barnard, 11 January 1868 (telegram), Donnelly to Barnard, 3 February 1868, Barnard MSS, Items 8927, 8929, 8932 and 8984.

11. John Hart to Barnard, 20 February 1868, Newton Bateman to Barnard, 25 February 1868, Bateman to Senator Lyman Trumbull, 25 February 1868, B.G. Northrop to Barnard, 6 March 1868, John Swett to Barnard, 21 March 1868, Coburn to Barnard, 4 February 1868, Barnard to Potter, 20 February 1868, Gilman to Barnard, 26 February 1868, Brooks to Barnard, 21 April 1868, Philbrick to Barnard, 4 May 1868, Barnard MSS, Items 9016, 9019, 9021, 9043, 9069, 8988, 9014, 9025, and 9027.

12. Barnard to Washburne, 1 February 1868, Elihur B. Washburne Papers, Library of Congress, Manuscript Division, Washington, D.C., vol. 56 (cited hereafter as Washburne Papers); *Congressional Globe,* 40th Cong., 2d Sess., 1868, 39: 920.

13. *Ibid.,* pp. 1138, 1140, and 1252.

14. Garfield to Barnard, 5 May 1868, Garfield Papers, Letters Sent; Barnard to Garfield, 6 May 1868, Garfield Papers, Letters Received.

15. Neill to Washburne, 3 June 1868, Washburne Papers, Vol. 59; compare AJE 17 (1867): 11–63, 65–76, 81–124, 337–68, 385–400, 435–518, and 658–820 and *Report of the Commissioner of Education . . . 1868,* pp. 11–63, 65–76, 81–124, 337–68, 385–400, 435–518, and 658–820.

16. *Congressional Globe,* 40th Cong., 2d Sess., 1868, 39: 3431.

17. *Ibid.,* p. 3784.

18. *Ibid.*

19. Stevens' 1838 speech quoted in Wickersham, *A History of Education in Pennsylvania,* p. 337; *Congressional Globe,* 40th Cong., 2d Sess., 1868, 39: 11, 443, 537, and 3888.

20. Brodie, pp. 21, 211, McKitrick, pp. 99–101, 295–96; Wood, *Black Scare,* pp. 106–10; McPherson, "The Ballot and Land for The Freedmen, 1861–1865," *Reconstruction,* Stampp and Litwack, eds., pp. 141–55.

21. *Congressional Globe,* 40th Cong., 2d Sess., 1868, 39: 3705; Barnard to Potter, 4 July 1868, Barnard MSS, Item 9150; Cox and Cox, "Negro Suffrage and Republican Politics," Stampp and Litwack, pp. 156–72; W. R. Brock, "The Waning of Radicalism," Stampp and Litwack, pp. 496–99, 508–15; Trefousse, pp. 436–48; *also,* the chapters on radical reconstruction and social equality in Wood, pp. 103–55.

22. Barnard to Potter, 4 July 1868, Barnard to HDB (his son), 9 July 1868, Barnard MSS, Items 9150 and 9151.

23. *Congressional Globe,* 40th Cong., 2d Sess., 1868, 39: 3958; Barnard to Potter, 12 July 1868, Barnard MSS, Item 9156.

24. Garfield to White, 26 December 1868, Garfield Papers, Letters Sent; *Congressional Globe,* 40th Cong., 2d Sess., 1868, 39: 4501.

25. Coburn to Barnard, 9 December 1867, Hancock to Barnard, 18 December 1867, "Memorandum," 2 December 1868, Barnard MSS, Items 8839, 8860, and 9274.

Notes

26. *See* Department of Agriculture Act, Appendix 2; *also,* Hoyt to Barnard, 30
    December 1867, and Gilman to Barnard, 26 February 1868, Barnard MSS,
    Items 8890 and 9025; U.S. Department of Education, *Report of the
    Commissioner,* 1868, pp. xxiii–xxv; Mary Mann to Barnard, 4 October 1868,
    Barnard MSS, Item 9239.
27. Moore to Barnard, 29 October 1868, Johnson Papers, Ser. 3A, p. 415.
28. Barnard to Johnson, 9 November 1868, Barnard to Gilman, 20 November 1868,
    Barnard to Potter, 22 November 1868, Barnard to Gilman, 24 November
    1868, Barnard MSS, Items 9262, 9269, 9270, and 9271.
29. *The Sun* (Baltimore), 18 November 1868, p. 1; Barnard to Gilman, 20 November
    1868, Barnard to Potter, 22 November 1868, Richards to Barnard, 3
    January 1869, Barnard MSS, Items 9269, 9270, and 9295.
30. *Report of the Secretary of the Interior,* House of Representatives, 40th Cong., 3d
    Sess., 1868, Executive Documents, 2: iv–vi. Blair mistakenly attributed this
    report to Jacob D. Cox, Browning's successor; *see* Blair, p. 78.
31. U.S., Congress, House, Committee on Education and Labor, *Report: Department
    of Education,* 40th Cong., 3d Sess., 1869, Report No. 25.
32. *Ibid.,* p. 8.
33. *Congressional Globe,* 40th Cong., 3d Sess., 1869, 40: 1541–42.
34. Neill to Washburne, 26 January 1869, Washburne Papers, Vol. 64; Mann to
    Barnard, 7 February 1869, Barnard MSS, Item 9306; Neill to Ramsey, 27
    April 1869, Interior Records, AD 111.
35. Cox to Barnard, 8 July 1869, Letters from the Secretary of the Interior,
    Department of the Interior Letter Book, Miscellaneous Division, National
    Archives, Washington, D.C., Vol. 5, pp. 207–208; Barnard to Cox, 10 July
    1869, Barnard MSS, Item 9344.
36. Barnard to Potter, 22 December 1869, Barnard MSS, Item 9396; Richardson, 7:
    41.
37. "Memorandum of Paper read before the American [National] Association of State
    Superintendents, Washington, D.C., March 3, 1870," Barnard Collection,
    Box 3.
38. American Institute of Instruction, *Lectures and Proceedings* 38 (1867): 47;
    American Institute of Instruction, *Lectures and Proceedings* 39 (1868):
    75–76; NTA, *Proceedings* 9 (1868): 687; NTA, *Proceedings* 10 (1869): 700.
39. American Institute of Instruction, *Lectures and Proceedings* 38 (1867): 40–42.
40. J. D. Geddings to Barnard, 15 April 1867, H. T. Morton to Barnard, 3 July 1867,
    Richards to Barnard, 15 July 1867, G. W. Atherton to Barnard, 19
    September 1867, Richards to Barnard, 24 September 1867, Kraus to
    Barnard, 13 May and 17 May 1868, Barnard MSS, Items 8512, 8574, 8589,
    8693, 8703, 9118, and 9126.
41. White to Garfield, 9 June and 6 August 1868, Garfield Papers, Letters Received;
    Congressional Globe, 40th Cong., 2d Sess., 1868, 39: 2349–54; Ridge, pp.
    112–114.
42. White to Garfield, 9 June and 6 August 1868; Garfield Papers, Letters Received;
    Garfield to White, 26 July and 26 December 1868, 26 January and 21 April
    1869, Garfield Papers, Letters Sent; *Ohio Educational Monthly* 20 (1871):
    30. White s recollection of these years faded with the passage of time. *See*
    White to Garfield, 13 November 1880, Garfield Papers, Letters Received.
43. Donald, *The Politics of Reconstruction,* pp. 64–65.

Chapter Six

1. *Ohio Educational Monthly,* 19 (1870): 61–62; Garfield to White, 17 January 1870, Garfield Papers, Letters Sent; Arnell to Eaton, 4 October 1869, S. N. Clark to Eaton, 3 March 1870, John Eaton Papers, University of Tennessee Library, Special Collections, Knoxville, Tennessee, Items 595 and 788. Cited hereafter as Eaton Papers.

2. Garfield to White, 26 December 1868, Garfield Papers, Letters Sent; Northrop to Garfield, 8 January 1869, Garfield Papers, Letters Received; Garfield to Northrop, 12 January 1869, Garfield Papers, Letters Sent; White to Garfield, 9 February 1870, Garfield Papers, Letters Received; Clark to Eaton, 10 February 1870, Eaton Papers, Item 766.

3. *Ohio Educational Monthly* 19 (1870): 98; Garfield to Eaton, 16 March 1870, Garfield Papers, Letters Sent; Garfield to White, 18 January 1871, Garfield Papers, Letters Sent.

4. *See* testimony of John Quincy Eaton and Elsie Eaton Newton in Alexander, "John Eaton, Jr.—Preacher, Soldier, and Educator," p. 8; Andrews quote in Bentley, p. 51; Eaton to W. H. Ruffner, Virginia State Superintendent of Schools, 30 September 1870, Eaton to John Hart, 17 October 1870, Eaton to George Geddes, 17 January 1878, and Eaton to Carl Schurz, 14 April 1880, Outgoing Correspondence of the U.S. Commissioner of Education, National Archives, Washington, D.C. (cited hereafter as Bureau Letters Sent); and Ford, "The Educational Contributions of the U.S. Commissioners of Education, 1867–1928," p. 46.

5. Alexander, pp. 40–48; McMurry, "John Eaton," *DAB* 5: 608–09; U. S. Grant to A. Lincoln, 11 June 1863, in Alexander, p. 178; Bentley, pp. 50–51; Howard, *Autobiography of Oliver Otis Howard,* 2: 225; Eaton, *Grant, Lincoln, and the Freedmen,* pp. 240–46.

6. *Ibid.,* p. 248; White to Eaton, 5 February 1869, Eaton Papers, Item 352.

7. Eaton to Chairman and Gentlemen of the Republican Convention, 20 May 1869, Stillwell to Eaton, 2 August 1868, L. B. Eaton to Eaton, 23 May 1869, I. W. Fuller to Eaton, 16 February 1869, and Eaton to Alice Eaton, his wife, 4 March 1869, Eaton Papers, Items 466, 227, 470, 358, 378.

8. Alice Eaton to Eaton, 15 March 1869, Eaton to Alice Eaton, 19 March 1869, Fred Eaton to Eaton, 8 May 1869, Lucien Eaton to Eaton, 23 May 1869, Clark to Eaton, 25 November 1869, A. J. Roper to Eaton, 27 January 1870, Eaton Papers, Items 392, 398, 448, 470, 643, and 735.

9. Eaton, p. 258; Clark to Eaton, 10 February 1870, Eaton Papers, Item 766; White to Garfield, 9 February 1870, Garfield Papers, Letters Received; Hagar to Eaton, 14 March 1870, Eaton Papers, Item 796.

10. Eaton, "The Relation of the National Government to Public Education," NTA, *Addresses and Journal of Proceedings* 10 (1870): 111–30.

11. *Congressional Globe,* 41st Cong., 3rd Sess., 1871, 43: 1466.

12. *Congressional Globe,* 42nd Cong., 1st Sess., 1871, 44: 669.

13. Eaton to Harris, 29 May 1901, in Harris, "Establishment of the Bureau of Education," *Report of the Commissioner of Education for the Year 1902,* 1: 905–06.

14. Eaton to Alice Eaton, 13 May 1870, Eaton Papers, Item 854; Eaton to Barnard, 2 April 1873, Bureau Letters Sent, Miscellaneous File; *Ohio Educational Monthly* 20 (1871): 280.

15. *Report of the Commissioner of Education Made to the Secretary of the Interior for the Year 1870 with Accompanying Papers,* pp. 9, 38–55, 61–62, 64, 337–39;

Notes

Eaton to Mrs. Spencer, 24 March 1876, and Eaton to John C. Covert, Assistant Editor, Cleveland *Leader,* 12 November 1877, Bureau Letters Sent.

16. *Congressional Globe,* 41st Cong., 3rd Sess., Part 11, 1078, 1133–35.

17. *Ibid.,* Part 111 (Appendix), pp. 296–302.

18. *Ohio Educational Monthly* 19 (1870): 354–55; White to Garfield, 4 February 1871, Garfield Papers, Letters Received.

19. Eaton to General Clinton B. Fisk, 6 April 1877, Bureau Letters Sent, Miscellaneous File; Eaton to George Geddes, 17 January 1878, Bureau Letters Sent; Butler, "The Future of the Bureau of Education," *Educational Review* 21 (1901): 526–27; Eaton to Edward Young, 12 June 1872, and Eaton to J. L. M. Curry, 9 February 1871, Bureau Letters Sent. The two brief histories of the bureau published during Eaton's administration repeatedly asserted that the agency was originally designed to collect and disseminate school data, "to act as an educational exchange," to use the words of Charles Warren, one of the authors. Both pamphlets relied on quotations from leading school officials throughout the country affirming this view of the bureau's mission. *See* Warren, *Answers to Inquiries about the U.S. Bureau of Education,* pp. 5–12; and Shiras, *The National Bureau of Education,* pp. 4–12.

20. Eaton to Ruffner, 30 September 1870, Eaton to Warren Johnson, Maine State Superintendent of Schools, 11 May 1872, Eaton to Duane Doty, Detroit Superintendent of Schools, 16 December 1874, Eaton to Daniel Leach, Providence, Rhode Island, Superintendent of Schools, 11 January 1878, Eaton to A. F. Biggers, Lynchburg, Virginia, Superintendent of Schools, 15 January 1878, and Eaton to Barnas Sears, 30 January 1868, Bureau Letters Sent.

21. Eaton to E. D. Mansfield, 22 June 1872, and Eaton to Neil Gilmour, New York State Superintendent of Public Instruction, 15 October 1878, Bureau Letters Sent; *Report of the Commissioner of Education for the Year 1884–1885,* pp. xiv–xxiii.

22. *Ohio Educational Monthly* 20 (1871): 30; Eaton to Hoar, 6 September 1872, George F. Hoar Papers, Massachusetts Historical Society, Boston (cited hereafter as Hoar Papers); Eaton to Hoar, 4 October 1870, Eaton to Senator Henry Wilson, 24 February 1871, Eaton to Ruffner, 9 March 1872, Eaton to Robert Ritchie, 15 December 1885, Bureau Letters Sent.

23. Eaton to W. D. Henkle, 7 February 1876, Eaton to the Reverend James McCoch, 14 December 1877, and Eaton to Edwin H. Fay, Louisiana State Superintendent of Public Instruction, 20 January 1880, Bureau Letters Sent. Commissioner of Education Elmer Ellsworth Brown (1906–11) later characterized the bureau as "in a sense the child of the National Association." *See* Brown, "A Message from the U.S. Bureau of Education," NEA, *Journal of Proceedings and Addresses* 48 (1910): 88; *also,* Wesley, p. 52. Petitions for the retention of John Eaton are deposited in Interior Records, AD 158 and 273.

24. Ethel Osgood Mason, "John Eaton: A Biographical Sketch," in Eaton, *Grant, Lincoln, and the Freedmen,* p. xxii.

25. Eaton to Cleveland, 25 November 1885, Interior Records, AD 111.

26. *Journal of Education,* 24 (1886): 117; White to Garfield, 13 Nobember 1880, Garfield Papers, Letters Received; White to Holcombe, 25 December 1894, Interior Records, AD 409; Rice, *J. L. M. Curry: Southerner, Statesman, and Educator,* pp. 122–23; Alderman and Gordon, *J. L. M. Curry: A Biography,* p. 280; Curry, *National Problem of Southern Education,* pp. 14–16.

27. *Journal of Education* 24 (1886): 117; A. E. Winship, "In Remembrance of William T. Harris," *Journal of Education* 82 (1915): 595; Dawson to Curry, 29 November 1886, N. H. R. Dawson MSS, Southern Historical Collection, University of North Carolina Library, Chapel Hill, N.C. (cited hereafter as Dawson MSS).

28. Leidecker, *Yankee Teacher*, p. 487; Wright, p. 39; *Report of the Commissioner of Education for the Year 1886–1887*, pp. 11–13; Dawson to Winship, 29 October 1886, Bureau Letters Sent, 1886; "Methods of Conducting Business," n.d., Bureau Letters Sent, 1887; "Job Descriptions," memorandum dated 10 November 1887, Bureau Letters Sent, 1887.

29. Dawson to Curry, 29 November 1886, Dawson MSS; "Resolution on the Death of N. H. R. Dawson," 2 February 1895, Interior Records, AD 273; Harris, "Establishment of . . . ," *Report of the Commissioner of Education for the Year 1902*, 1: 904.

30. Dawson to William S. Thorington, 4 October 1888, Dawson MSS; R. M. Nelson to Thomas F. Bayard, Secretary of State, 1 October 1888, Dawson MSS; Dawson quote in memorandum from H. E. Shepherd to Dawson, n.d., Dawson MSS; Dawson to Harrison, 29 March 1889, Interior Records, AD 273.

31. For petitions supporting Harris, *see* Interior Records, AD 409; Butler, *Across the Busy Years*, 1: 189–90; Leidecker, pp. 456–62; and Winship, "In Remembrance of William T. Harris," pp. 593–96.

32. Anna Tolman Smith, "Expansion of the Bureau of Education," *Educational Review* 43 (1912): 310; Fitzpatrick to Isaac Miles Wright, 12 April 1916, in Wright, pp. 229–32. Fitzpatrick was former superintendent of schools in Omaha, Nebraska, and president of the National Council of the NEA.

33. *Ibid.; also, Journal of Education* 82 (1915): 599; and Leidecker, pp. 469–71.

34. Winship, "In Remembrance of William T. Harris" pp. 593–96; *also,* Leidecker, pp. 478–79, 493–94; and Butler, 1: 191–93.

35. Hofstadter, *Anti-intellectualism in American Life*, pp. 172–79.

CHAPTER SEVEN

1. *See* Darrell H. Smith, *The Bureau of Education*, pp. 130–41; U.S., Congress, House, Committee on Education and Labor, *Study of the United States Office of Education*, 90th Cong., 1st Sess., 1967, House Doc. No. 193, pp. 769–77, and *Budget of the United States Government for 1972*.

2. Smith, *The Bureau of Education*, pp. 47–55, 79–93; and Anderson and Eells, *Alaska Natives*, p. 215.

3. Harris to Julia Ward Howe, 22 January 1901, Bureau Letters Sent; and Smith, *The Bureau of Education*, p. 50.

4. Anderson and Eells, pp. vii and 89–91.

5. *Study of the U.S. Office of Education*, p. 24.

6. *Ibid.*, pp. 23–25, 451–54.

7. For a discussion of the "Chicago incident", a recent encounter between the Office of Education and local authorities, *see* Glenn Smith, "A History of the U.S. Office of Education: 1867–1967," pp. 262–64.

8. Timpane, "Educational Experimentation in National Social Policy," *Harvard Educational Review* 40 (1970): 547–48; Allen, "An Interview with James Allen," *Harvard Educational Review* 40 (1970): 533–46; *also, Study of the U.S. Office of Education*, pp. 30–32, 451–54.

9. *Ibid.;* David Krathwohl, "Hopes for the National Institute of Education," *Phi Delta Kappan,* 52 (1971): 575.
10. U.S., Congress, House, Committee on Education and Labor, Select Subcommittee on Education, *Hearings: To Establish a National Institute of Education,* 92d Cong., 1st Sess., 1971, pp. 51–52.
11. U.S., Congress, Senate, Subcommittee of the Committee on Labor and Public Welfare, *Hearings: Federal Aid to Education,* 80th Cong., 1st Sess., 1947, p. 40.
12. See, *Study of the U.S. Office of Education,* pp. 451–54; and Harry F. Silberman, "Why NIE," paper presented at the American Educational Research Association annual meeting, April, 1972, pp. 1–3.
13. See Allen, *Harvard Educational Review* 40 (1970): 533–46.
14. *Study of the U.S. Office of Education,* pp. 380–400.
15. Richard M. Nixon, "Education Reform," *Weekly Compilation of Presidential Documents,* 9 March 1970, pp. 304–14; U.S., Congress, House, Committee on Education and Labor, *Higher Education Act of 1971,* 92d Cong., 1st Sess., 1971, Report No. 92-554, pp. 60–70; *Congressional Record,* 92d Cong., 2d Sess., 1972, 118: H5409.
16. See Silberman, pp. 1–4, 6; U.S., Congress, House, *To Establish A National Institute of Education,* pp. 31–35.
17. U.S., Congress, House, *Higher Education Act of 1971,* pp. 64, 62. For a more comprehensive statement of projected NIE objectives and programs, *see* "National Institute of Education: Preliminary Plan for the Proposed Institute," a report prepared for the Department of Health, Education, and Welfare by the Rand Corporation, Roger E. Levien, Study Director, R-657-HEW, February, 1971.
18. U.S., Congress, House, *To Establish A National Institute of Education,* pp. 24, 19.
19. *Ibid.,* pp. 34, 38–39, 230.
20. *Ibid.,* pp. 50–52; *see also* Sidney P. Marland, Jr., "A New Order of Educational Research and Development," *Phi Delta Kappan* 42 (1971): 576–79.
21. U.S., Congress, House, *To Establish A National Institute of Education,* pp. 230–31, 318–23.
22. *Ibid.,* p. 650.
23. *Ibid.,* pp. 230–31, 498. For a helpful—and hopeful—discussion of NIE purposes, functions, and anticipated effects *see* Ronald G. Havelock, "A Utilization Strategy for the National Institute of Education," a paper prepared for the Symposium, "The Impact of the National Institute of Education on Practice Improvement," American Educational Research Association annual meeting, April, 1972.

Selected Bibliography

Books and Articles

Albree, John. *Charles Brooks and His Work for Normal Schools.* Medford, Massachusetts: Press of J. C. Miller, Jr., 1907.

Alderman, Edwin Anderson, and Armisstead Churchill Gordon. *J. L. M. Curry: A Biography.* New York: Macmillan Co., 1911.

Alexander, Philip Wade. "John Eaton, Jr.—Preacher, Soldier, and Educator." Ph.D. dissertation, George Peabody College for Teachers, 1933.

Allen, James E., Jr. "An Interview with James Allen." *Harvard Educational Review* 40 (1970): 533–46.

Anderson, Kenneth C. "Biography of Emerson White." Ed.D. dissertation, Western Reserve University, 1952.

[Barnard, Henry.] "Education:—A National Interest." *American Journal of Education* 17 (1867): 41–48.

Barnard, Henry. "The American Lyceum." *American Journal of Education* 14 (1864): 553–54.

Barnes, William H. *History of the Thirty-Ninth Congress of the United States.* New York: Harper and Brothers, 1868.

Bates, Joshua. "Moral Education." American Institute of Instruction, *Lectures and Proceedings,* 8 (1837): 51–69.

Bentley, George R. *A History of the Freedmen's Bureau.* Philadelphia: University of Pennsylvania, 1955.

Billington, Ray Allen. *The Protestant Crusade.* New York: Macmillan Company, 1938.

Blair, Anna Lou. *Henry Barnard: School Administrator.* Minneapolis: Educational Publishers, Inc., 1938.

Blauch, Lloyd E. "To Promote the Cause of Education." *School Life* 25 (1953): 117–19, 123–24.

———. "To Promote the Cause of Education." *School Life* 25 (1953): 134–35.

Bode, Carl. *The American Lyceum: Town Meeting of the Mind.* New York: Oxford University Press, 1956.

Bond, Horace Mann. *Negro Education in Alabama.* Washington, D.C.: Associated Publishers, Inc., 1939.

———. *The Education of the Negro in the American Social Order.* New York: Octagon Books, 1966.

Boorstin, Daniel J. *The Americans: The National Experience.* New York: Random House, 1965.

Boutwell, George S. *Reminiscences of Sixty Years in Public Affairs.* Vol. 2. New York: McClure, Phillips, and Co., 1902.

Brodie, Fawn M. *Thaddeus Stevens: Scourge of the South.* New York: W. W. Norton and Co., 1959.

Brooks, Charles. *History of the Introduction of State Normal Schools in America.* Boston: John Wilson and Son, 1864.

———. *A Prospective System of National Education for the United States.* Boston: John Wilson and Son, 1864.

———. "School Reform, or Teachers' Seminaries." American Institute of Instruction, *Lectures and Proceedings,* 8 (1837): 161–79.

——— et al. "Free Education in the United States: Petition of the Town of Medford, Middlesex Co., Massachusetts, for Government Aid in Securing Free Education to All the Children in the United States." U.S., Congress, House, Miscellaneous Document No. 5. 39th Cong., 1st Sess., 1866.

Buisson, Ferdinand Édouard. *Rapport sur l'instruction primaire à l'Exposition universelle de Philadelphie en 1876.* Paris: Imprimerie Nationale, 1878.

Butler, Nicholas Murray. *Across the Busy Years: Recollections and Reflections.* Vol. 1. New York: Charles Scribner's Sons, 1939.

———. "The Future of the Bureau of Education." *Educational Review* 21 (1901): 526–27.

Butts, R. Freeman. *The Education of the West.* New York: McGraw-Hill Book Co., 1973.

Caldwell, Robert Granville. *James A. Garfield: Party Chieftain.* Hamden, Connecticut: Archon Books, 1965.

Campbell, John Lyle, ed. *The Teacher's Indicator and Parent's Manual for School and Home Education.* Cincinnati: Moore, Wilstach, Keys and Co., 1859.

Carlton, Frank Tracy. *Economic Influences Upon Educational Progress in the United States, 1820–1850.* New York: Teachers College, Columbia University, 1965. (First published in 1908.)

Cash, W. J. *The Mind of the South.* New York: Vintage Books, 1941.

Commons, John R., et al., eds. *A Documentary History of American Industrial Society.* Vol. V. Cleveland: Arthur H. Clark Co., 1910.

Cremin, Lawrence A. *The American Common School: An Historical Conception.* New York: Bureau of Publications, Teachers College, Columbia University, 1951.

Culver, Raymond Benjamin. *Horace Mann and Religion in the Massachusetts Public Schools.* New Haven: Yale University Press, 1929.

Curoe, Philip R. V. *Educational Attitudes and Policies of Organized Labor in the United States.* New York: Bureau of Publications, Teachers College, Columbia University, 1926.

Curti, Merle E. *The Social Ideas of American Educators.* New York: Charles Scribner's Sons, 1935.

226

Curry, J. L. M. *National Problem of Southern Education.* Richmond: Dispatch Steam Printing House, 1882.

Donald, David H. *Charles Sumner and the Coming of the Civil War.* New York: Alfred A. Knopf, 1960.

————. *The Politics of Reconstruction, 1863–1867.* Baton Rouge: Louisiana State University Press, 1965.

DuBois, W. E. B. *Black Reconstruction in America.* Philadelphia: Albert Saifer, Publisher, 1935.

Du Pont de Nemours, Pierre Samuel. *National Education in the United States of America.* Translated by B. G. Du Pont. Newark, Delaware: University of Delaware Press, 1923.

Dupre, Huntley. *Edward Duffield Neill: Pioneer Educator.* St. Paul: Macalester College Press, 1949.

Dupree, A. Hunter. *Science in the Federal Government: A History of Policies and Activities to 1840.* Cambridge: Belknap Press of Harvard University Press, 1957.

Eaton, John. *Grant, Lincoln, and the Freedmen.* New York: Longmans, Green, and Co., 1907.

Exton, Elaine. "The Office of Education in Its 85th Year." *The American School Board Journal* 125 (1952): 27–30.

Ford, Thomas Benjamin. "The Educational Contributions of the U.S. Commissioners of Education, 1867–1928." Ph.D. dissertation, American University, 1933.

Franklin, John Hope. *Reconstruction: After the Civil War.* Chicago: University of Chicago Press, 1961.

Gay, Peter. *The Enlightenment: An Interpretation,* Vols. 1 and 2. New York: A. A. Knopf, 1966 and 1969.

Goode, G. Brown. *An Account of the Smithsonian Institution: Its Origin, History, Objects, and Achievements.* Washington, D.C.: Smithsonian Institution, 1895.

Greene, Samuel S. "The Educational Duties of the Hour." *American Journal of Education,* 16 (1866): 229–43.

Grimsted, David. "Rioting in Its Jacksonian Setting," *The American Historical Review,* 127 (1972), 361–97.

Hansen, Allen Oscar. *Early Educational Leadership in the Ohio Valley.* Journal of Educational Research Monographs, No. 5. Bloomington, Illinois: Public School Publishing Co., 1923.

————. *Liberalism and American Education in the Eighteenth Century.* New York: Macmillan Co., 1926.

Harding, T. Swann. "Some Landmarks in the History of the Department of Agriculture." Agricultural History Series, No. 2. Washington, D.C.: U.S. Department of Agriculture, 1942.

Harrington, Fred Harvey. *Fighting Politician: Major General N. P. Banks.* Philadelphia: University of Pennsylvania Press, 1948.

Harris, William T. "Establishment of the Office of the Commissioner of Education of the United States, and Henry Barnard's Relation to It." In *Report of the Commissioner of Education for the Year 1902,* 1: 901–26. Washington, D.C.: Government Printing Office, 1903.

Hayes, Cecil B. "The American Lyceum: Its History and Contributions to Education." U.S. Office of Education Bulletin, No. 12. Washington, D.C.: Government Printing Office, 1932.

Henry, Joseph. "Report on the Smithsonian Institution." American Association for the Advancement of Education, *Proceedings*, 3 (1853): 99–108.

Hofstadter, Richard. *Anti-intellectualism in American Life*. New York: Alfred A. Knopf, 1963.

Howard, Oliver Otis. *Autobiography of Oliver Otis Howard*. Vol. 2. New York: Baker and Taylor Co., 1908.

Hyman, Harold M. *The Radical Republicans and Reconstruction, 1861–1870*. Indianapolis: Bobbs-Merrill, 1967.

Johnson, Kenneth R. "N. H. R. Dawson: United States Commissioner of Education." *History of Education Quarterly* 11 (1971): 174–83.

Katz, Michael B. *The Irony of Early School Reform*. Cambridge: Harvard University Press, 1968.

Kendrick, Benjamin B. *The Journal of the Joint Committee of Fifteen on Reconstruction*. New York: Columbia University Press, 1914.

Keppel, Francis. *The Necessary Revolution in American Education*. New York: Harper and Row, Publishers, 1966.

Knight, Edgar W., and Clifton L. Hall, eds. *Readings in American Educational History*. New York: Appleton-Century-Crofts, 1951.

Krathwohl, David. "Hopes for the National Institute of Education." *Phi Delta Kappan* 52 (1971): 575.

Krug, Mark M. *History and the Social Sciences: New Approaches to the Teaching of Social Studies*. Waltham, Massachusetts: Blaisdell Publishing Co., 1967.

————. *Lyman Trumbull, Conservative Radical*. New York: A. S. Barnes and Co., 1965.

Kursh, Harry. *The United States Office of Education: A Century of Service*. Philadelphia: Chilton Books, 1965.

Lee, Gordon Canfield. *The Struggle for Federal Aid: First Phase*. New York: Bureau of Publications, Teachers College, Columbia University, 1949.

Leidecker, Kurt Friedrich. *Yankee Teacher: The Life of William Torrey Harris*. New York: Philosophical Library, 1946.

Leopold, Richard William. *Robert Dale Owen: A Biography*. Cambridge: Harvard University Press, 1940.

Lewis, Samuel. "The Expediency of Adopting Common School Education to the Entire Wants of the Community." *Western Academician and Journal of Education and Science* 1 (1837): 531.

Lincoln, Solomon. "Memoir of the Rev. Charles Brooks." *Proceedings of the Massachusetts Historical Society* 18 (1880–1881): 174–78.

McKitrick, Eric L. *Andrew Johnson and Reconstruction*. Chicago: University of Chicago Press, 1960.

McPherson, Edward. *The Political History of the United States of America during the Period of Reconstruction*. Washington, D.C.: Philip and Solomons, 1871.

Madsen, David. *The National University: Enduring Dream of the USA*. Detroit: Wayne State University Press, 1966.

Malone, Dumas, ed. *Correspondence Between Thomas Jefferson and Pierre Samuel du Pont de Nemours*. Boston: Houghton-Mifflin Company, 1930.

Mann, George C., ed. *Life and Works of Horace Mann*. Vol. 4. Boston: Lee and Shepard Publishers, 1891.

Mann, Mary Peabody. *Life of Horace Mann*. Washington, D.C.: National Education Association of the United States, 1937.

Marland, Sidney P., Jr. "A New Order of Educational Research and Development," *Phi Delta Kappan* 52 (1971): 576–579.

Mayo, A. D. "Henry Barnard." In *Report of the Commissioner of Education for the Year 1896–97*, I, 769–810. Washington, D.C.: Government Printing Office, 1898.

———. "Henry Barnard as First U.S. Commissioner of Education." In *Report of the Commissioner of Education for the Year 1902*, I, 891–901. Washington, D.C.: Government Printing Office, 1903.

Messerli, Jonathan. *Horace Mann: A Biography*. New York: Alfred A. Knopf, 1972.

Morant, R. L. "The National Bureau of Education in the U.S." Great Britain: Board of Education, Special Reports on Educational Subjects, I (1896–97): 647–65.

Morison, Samuel Eliot. *The Oxford History of the American People*. New York: Oxford University Press, 1965.

Morris, Richard K. "Parnasus on Wheels." *Teacher Education Quarterly* 18 (1960–61): 45–57.

———. "The Barnard Legacy." *Teacher Education Quarterly* 18 (1961): 93–105.

National Institute of Education: Preliminary Plan for the Proposed Institute. Report prepared for the Department of Health, Education and Welfare by the Rand Corporation. Roger E. Levien, Study Director. R-657-HEW, February, 1971.

Packard, Frederick A. *The Daily Public School in the United States*. Philadelphia: J. B. Lippincott and Co., 1866.

Pawa, Jay M. "Workingmen and Free Schools in the Nineteenth Century: A Comment on the Labor-Education Thesis." *History of Education Quarterly* 11 (1971): 287–302.

Philbrick, John D. "The National Teachers' Association: Its Nature and Objects." *American Journal of Education* 14 (1864): 49–60.

Rackauskas, John A. "The First National System of Education in Europe: The Commission for National Education of the Kingdom of Poland and the Grand Duchy of Lithuania (1773–1794)." *Lituanus* 14 (1968): 5–53.

Rantoul, Robert, Jr. "The Education of a Free People." American Institute of Instruction, *Lectures and Proceedings* 10 (1839): 1–33.

Rhees, William J. "James Smithson and His Bequest." Smithsonian Miscellaneous Collections, 21: 32–49. Washington, D.C.: Smithsonian Institution, 1881.

Rice, Jessie Pearl. *J. L. M. Curry: Southerner, Statesman, and Educator*. New York: King's Crown Press, 1959.

Richardson, James D., ed. *A Compilation of the Messages and Papers of the Presidents: 1789–1908*. Vols. 1–7. Washington, D.C.: Bureau of National Literature and Art, 1908.

Rickoff, Andrew Jackson. "A National Bureau of Education." *American Journal of Education* 16 (1866): 299–310.

Ridge, Martin. *Ignatius Donnelly: The Portrait of a Politician*. Chicago: University of Chicago Press, 1962.

Rudolph, Frederick, ed. *Essays on Education in the Early Republic*. Cambridge: Belknap Press of Harvard University Press, 1965.

Runes, Dagobert D. *The Selected Writings of Benjamin Rush*. New York: Philosophical Library, 1947.

Schlesinger, Arthur M., Jr. *The Age of Jackson*. Boston: Little, Brown and Co., 1954.

Schlesinger, Arthur Meier. *New Viewpoints in American History*. New York: Macmillan Co., 1937.

Shiras, Alexander. *The National Bureau of Education: Its History, Work, and Limitations*. Washington, D.C.: Government Printing Office, 1875.

Smith, Anna Tolman. "Expansion of the Bureau of Education." *Educational Review* 43 (1912): 310–13.

Smith, Darrell H. *The Bureau of Education: Its History, Activities, and Organization*. Baltimore: Johns Hopkins Press, 1923.

Smith, Leonard Glenn. "Founding of the U.S. Office of Education." *The Educational Forum* 21 (1967): 307–22.

———. "A History of the United States Office of Education, 1867–1967." Ph.D. dissertation, University of Oklahoma, 1967.

———. "John Eaton, Educator (1829–1906)." *School and Society* 97, No. 2315 (1969): 108–112.

Smith, Theodore Clarke. *The Life and Letters of James Abram Garfield*. 2 vols. New Haven: Yale University Press, 1925.

Stampp, Kenneth M. and Leon F. Litwack, eds., *Reconstruction: An Anthology of Revisionist Writings*. Baton Rouge: Louisiana State University Press, 1969.

Steiner, Barnard C. *Life of Henry Barnard, the First U.S. Commissioner of Education, 1867–1870*. U.S. Bureau of Education Bulletin, No. 8. Washington, D.C.: Government Printing Office, 1919.

Stevens, M. [pseud.] "The National Bureau of Education." *The School Journal* 16 (1898): 743–50.

Still, Bayrd. "Patterns of Mid-Nineteenth Century Urbanization in the Middle West." *The Mississippi Valley Historical Review* 28 (1941): 187–206.

———. "The History of the City in American Life." *The American Review* 2 (1962): 20–34.

Stowe, Calvin E. "Queries on Education." *The Western Academician and Journal of Education and Science* 1 (1837): 147–53.

Swint, Henry Lee. *The Northern Teacher in the South, 1862–1870*. Nashville: Vanderbilt University Press, 1941.

Taylor, Howard Cromwell. *The Educational Significance of the Early Federal Land Ordinances.* New York: Teachers College, Columbia University, 1922.

Taylor, John M. *Garfield of Ohio: The Available Man.* New York: W. W. Norton & Co., Inc., 1970.

Thursfield, Richard Emmons. *Henry Barnard's American Journal of Education.* Baltimore: Johns Hopkins Press, 1945.

Timpane, P. Michael. "Educational Experimentation in National Social Policy." *Harvard Educational Review* 40 (1970): 547–66.

Trefousse, Hans L. *The Radical Republicans: Lincoln's Vanguard for Racial Justice.* New York: Alfred A. Knopf. 1969.

True, Webster P. *The First Hundred Years of the Smithsonian Institution, 1846–1946.* Washington, D.C.: Smithsonian Institution, 1946.

Tyack, David B., ed. *Turning Points in American Educational History.* Waltham, Massachusetts: Blaisdell Publishing Co., 1967.

Vassar, Rena L., ed. *Social History of American Education.* Vol. 1. Chicago: Rand McNally and Co., 1965.

Wade, Richard C. *Slavery in the Cities: The South, 1820–1860.* New York: Oxford University Press, 1964.

———. *The Urban Frontier: The Rise of Western Cities, 1790–1830.* Cambridge: Harvard University Press, 1959.

Warren, Charles. *Answers to Inquiries about the U.S. Bureau of Education, Its Work, and History.* Washington, D.C.: Government Printing Office, 1883.

Webster, Noah. *A Collection of Papers on Political, Literary, and Moral Subjects.* New York: Webster and Clark, 1843.

Weisberger, Bernard A. "The Dark and Bloody Ground of Reconstruction Historiography." *Journal of Southern History* 25 (1959): 427–47.

Welter, Rush, ed. *American Writings on Popular Education: The Nineteenth Century.* Indianapolis: Bobbs-Merrill Co., Inc., 1971.

Wesley, Edgar B. *NEA: The First Hundred Years.* New York: Harper and Brothers, 1957.

White, E. E. "National Bureau of Education." *American Journal of Education* 16 (1866): 177–86.

White, Elipha. "Introductory Discourse." American Institute of Instruction, *Lectures and Proceedings* 8 (1837): 3–21.

White, S. H. "A National Bureau of Education." *American Journal of Education* 15 (1865): 180–84.

Wickersham, James P. "Education as an Element in Reconstruction." *American Journal of Education* 16 (1866): 283–97.

———. *A History of Education in Pennsylvania, Private and Public, Elementary and Higher, from the Time the Swedes Settled on the Delaware to the Present Day.* Lancaster, Pennsylvania: Inquirer Publishing Co., 1886.

Winship, A. E. "In Remembrance of William T. Harris." *Journal of Education* 82 (1915): 593–96.

Wood, Forrest G. *Black Scare.* Los Angeles: University of California Press, 1970.

Wright, Isaac M. "History of the United States Bureau of Education." Ph.D. dissertation, New York University, 1916.

MANUSCRIPT COLLECTIONS

Boston, Massachusetts. Massachusetts Historical Society. George F. Hoar Papers.

Chapel Hill, North Carolina. Southern Historical Collection. The University of North Carolina. Nathaniel H. R. Dawson MSS.

Hartford, Connecticut. Watkinson Library. Trinity College. Henry Barnard Collection.

Knoxville, Tennessee. University of Tennessee Library. Special Collections. John Eaton Papers.

New York, New York. Fales Library. New York University. Henry Barnard Manuscript Collection.

Washington, D.C. Manuscripts Division. Library of Congress. James A. Garfield Papers.

Washington, D.C. Manuscripts Division. Library of Congress. Andrew Johnson Papers.

Washington, D.C. Manuscript Division. Library of Congress. Elihu B. Washburne Papers.

Washington, D.C. Records of the Department of the Interior, Appointments Division. National Archives. Applications and Papers Pertaining to the Commissioner of Education.

Washington, D.C. U.S. Department of the Interior Letter Book, Miscellaneous Division. National Archives. Letters from the Secretary of the Interior.

Washington, D.C. National Archives. Outgoing Correspondence of the Commissioner of Education.

PUBLIC DOCUMENTS

U.S., Annals of Congress. Vols. 36–42.

U.S., Bureau of Education. *Report of the Commissioner of Education Made to the Secretary of the Interior for the Year 1870 with Accompanying Papers.* Washington, D.C.: Government Printing Office, 1870.

U.S., Bureau of Education. *Special Report of the Commissioner of Education on the Condition and Improvement of Public Schools in the District of Columbia.* Washington, D.C.: Government Printing Office, 1871.

U.S., Congress. *Biographical Directory of the American Congress: 1774–1949.* Washington, D.C.: U.S. Government Printing Office, 1950.

U.S., *Congressional Globe.* Vols. 6–46.

U.S., Department of Education. *Report of the Commissioner of Education with Circulars and Documents Accompanying the Same:* Submitted to the Senate and House of Representatives 2 June, 1868. Washington, D.C.: Government Printing Office, 1868.

U.S., Department of the Interior, Bureau of Education. *Report of the Commissioner of Education for the Year 1884–1885*. Washington, D.C.: Government Printing Office, 1886.

U.S., Department of the Interior, Bureau of Education. *Report of the Commissioner of Education for the Year 1886–1887*. Washington, D.C.: Government Printing Office, 1888.

U.S., Department of the Interior. *Report of the Secretary of the Interior*. U.S. House of Representatives. Executive Documents, Vol. 2. 40th Cong., 3d Sess., 1868.

U.S., Congress, House, Committee on Education and Labor, *Higher Education Act of 1971*. Report No. 92–554. 92d Cong. 1st Sess., 1971.

U.S., Congress, House, Committee on Education and Labor. *Report: Department of Education*. Report No. 25. 40th Cong., 3d Sess., 1869.

U.S., Congress, House, Committee on Education and Labor. Select Subcommittee on Education. *Hearings: To Establish a National Institute of Education*. 92d Cong., 1st Sess., 1971.

U.S., Congress, House, Committee on Education and Labor, Special Subcommittee on Education. *Study of the United States Office of Education*. House Doc. No. 193. 90th Cong., 1st Sess., 1967.

U.S., Register of Debates in Congress. Vols. 1–14.

U.S., Register of the Officers and Agents, Civil, Military and Naval in the Service of the United States on the Thirtieth of September, 1871. Washington, D.C.: Government Printing Office, 1872.

Index

Adams, Herbert Baxter, 169
Adams, J. S., 69
Allen, James E., Jr., 179, 192
American Association for the Advancement of Education, 41, 49, 66, 72
American Institute of Instruction, 31, 40, 41, 49, 59, 125, 145
American Journal of Education, 94, 98–101, 160. *See also* Barnard, Henry
American Lyceum, 40, 43, 44, 47, 63, 99, 108
Andrews, Mary D. (John Eaton's aunt), 152
Angerer, Augustus, 131, 137, 139
Archer, Stevenson, 143
Archer, William Segar, 40
Arnell, Samuel, 151

Bache, Alexander D., 48, 54, 77
Bailey, Stephen K., 188, 197, 198
Banks, Nathaniel, 66, 77, 81, 86
Bardeen, C. W., 105
Barnard, F. A. P., 169
Barnard, Henry: views on Prussian education, 33, 34; on school reform, 41, 48, 60, 61, 106–7, 119; plans for a central school agency, 49–54, 64–65, 72, 103, 107–10, 176–77; campaigns for bureau of education, 66–68, 74–75, 80; wants to be commissioner, 91, 94–95; appointed commis-

sioner, 97; early career, 102; reports to Congress, 112–16, 118–20, 131; conflicts with staff, 122–23, 137–40; illnesses, 96, 102, 103, 125; criticism of, 96, 101, 104–5, 113, 116–17, 129, 139–40, 146–48, 155; and the *American Journal of Education,* 50, 99, 111–12; defense against criticism, 125, 130–31, 135–36; defended by House Committee on Education and Labor, 141–42; on Emerson E. White, 92; on John Eaton, 165; political views, 105–6
Barnard, Josephine Denoyers (wife of Henry), 102
Bateman, Newton, 69
Bates, Samuel, 67
Bayard, Thomas, 161, 162
Blaine, James G., 85, 89, 135
Blair, Henry W., 165
Bode, Carl, 41
Boutwell, George, 80, 124
Brademus, John, 194
Brooks, Charles: on Prussian education, 33; reform activities, 37; plan for a national system of education, 38; advocates a federal education agency, 47, 62, 65–66, 77; disappointed with bureau of education bill, 74; mentioned, 60, 101, 108, 128
Brown, Elmer Ellsworth, 180

235

Donald R. Warren *is currently chairman, Policy Studies Department, College of Education, University of Illinois at Chicago Circle. He obtained his degrees from the University of Texas (A.B. 1957); Harvard University (S.T.B. 1960); and the University of Chicago (Ph.D. 1968). He is recipient of a Rockefeller Fellowship. He has written articles for the* Illinois Journal of Education, Education and Urban Society, School Review, Intellect, Phi Delta Kappan, *and* New York Teacher.

The manuscript was edited by Alice Nigoghosian. The book was designed by Julie Paul. The typeface for the text is Linotype Caledonia designed by W. A. Dwiggins about 1938; and the display face is Garamond Bold.

The text is printed on Nashoba antique paper and the book is bound in Holliston's Kingston Natural finish cloth over binders boards. Manufactured in the United States of America.